Also by Dr. Vincent Di Maio

Gunshot Wounds

Forensic Pathology (with Dr. Dominick Di Maio)

Handbook of Forensic Pathology (with Dr. Suzanna E. Dana)

Excited Delirium Syndrome (with Theresa Di Maio)

Also by Ron Franscell

The Darkest Night

Delivered from Evil

The Crime Buff's Guide Series

Nightmare at Noon (with Gregg Olsen)

Evil at the Front Door (with Rebecca Morris)

The Sourtoe Cocktail Club

Angel Fire

The Deadline

The Obituary

MORGUE

MORGUE

A LIFE IN DEATH

Dr. Vincent Di Maio
and Ron Franscell

FOREWORD BY
DR. JAN GARAVAGLIA

Discovery Channel's *Dr. G: Medical Examiner*

St. Martin's Press
New York

www.stmartins.com

The Library of Congress Cataloging-in-Publication Data is available upon request.

ISBN 978-1-250-06714-2 (hardcover)
ISBN 978-1-4668-7506-7 (e-book)

Our books may be purchased in bulk for promotional, educational, or business use. Please contact your local bookseller or the Macmillan Corporate and Premium Sales Department at 1-800-221-7945, extension 5442, or by e-mail at MacmillanSpecial Markets@macmillan.com.

First Edition: May 2016

10 9 8 7 6 5 4 3 2 1

To Dominick J. Di Maio, MD, and Violet Di Maio
My father and mother

Death is not an individual but a social event. When, with a barely noticeable sigh, the last gasp of air is exhaled, the blood stops pulsating through arteries and veins, and neurons cease activating the brain, the life of a human organism has ended. Death is not official, however, until the community takes notice.

—STEFAN TIMMERMANS
Postmortem: How Medical Examiners
Explain Suspicious Deaths

Every man's life ends the same way. It is only the details of how he lived and how he died that distinguish one man from another.

—ERNEST HEMINGWAY

Contents

It's All About the Puzzle

By Dr. Jan Garavaglia

People are fascinated by forensic pathology. Yes, some are primarily interested in the forensic details, but it is the stories of how and why the dead people ended up in the morgue that intrigue most.

TV shows, movies, and novels with fictional portrayals of forensic pathologists are phenomenally popular, not because they are accurate about the art and science of forensic pathology, but because they piece together a puzzle. But every day, real-life forensic pathologists pull back the curtain to shine the light of truth on what really happened, and explore the true, hidden dramas of the human condition, too.

Many think the forensic pathologist's time is spent on murder and crime, but in fact murders take up less than 20 percent of a medical examiner's caseload. We care just as much about the mystery of a decomposing unidentified corpse found in a pond as we do about why an infant died suddenly in his mother's arms. Our autopsies and scene investigations might have public health or safety implications, such as identifying an emerging epidemic of drugs or disease. We might determine a woman died prematurely from a genetic abnormality, which could have profound implications for future generations of a family. We scientifically identify the burned, injured, and decomposed beyond recognition, if for no other reason than giving dignity to the dead.

Then comes murder. We determine whether a death was caused by the actions of another human, which has huge implications if you are a suspect. Even when the cause of death is obvious, the body is meticulously examined for trace evidence, subtle injuries, angles and trajectory of wounds, even natural disease . . . anything that might shed light on what happened.

Alas, in spite of the crucial need for more forensic pathologists, it remains the medical specialty with the fewest new doctors. That's partly the perceived negatives of the job. On a daily basis, we deal with gruesome injuries, decomposing flesh, hideous smells, horrific violence, feces and gastric contents that must be meticulously examined (or at least handled). Then we must confront grieving families and (occasionally) obnoxious lawyers.

Despite these unpleasantries, those of us in the field consider it a calling. We love the challenge of piecing together the puzzles to find the truth. We can't imagine doing anything else.

That describes Dr. Vincent Di Maio, my mentor and friend. I worked under him for ten years in San Antonio and never tired of his keen insight, his wealth of knowledge, and his seemingly limitless collection of great stories. Now in this fascinating and well-written book, readers and forensic buffs, too, are privileged to hear one of the most respected forensic pathologists in America share some of his most intriguing and provocative forensic cases of a long career.

And you will see that it isn't just about the forensics. It's about the puzzles, too.

—Dr. Jan Garavaglia

Dr. Jan Garavaglia—better known as Discovery Channel's "Dr. G"— is the chief medical examiner for Orlando, Florida, and its surrounding counties. A graduate of the St. Louis University School of Medicine, she completed her fellowship in forensic pathology at the Dade County Medical Examiner's Office in Miami, and later worked for Dr. Vincent Di Maio at the Bexar County Medical Examiner's Office in San Antonio, Texas.

Her hit cable TV show, Dr. G: Medical Examiner, *is broadcast around the world and has made her one of the most recognizable faces of forensic medicine. She has appeared on CNN,* The Oprah Winfrey Show, The Rachael Ray Show, The Doctors, *and the* Dr. Oz Show. *She has also testified in some highly charged criminal cases, such as the Casey Anthony murder trial in 2011, and written a book,* How Not to Die *(2008, Crown).*

MORGUE

ONE

A Death In Black and White

I don't know what's in a human heart.

I have seen more than my share of hearts, held them in my hands. Some were young and strong; some were worn-out, shabby, choked. Many had leaked away an entire life through neat little holes caused by bullets or knives. Some had been stopped by poison or fright. A few had exploded into a thousand tiny bits or were shredded in some grotesque trauma. All of them were dead.

But I never truly knew what was inside these hearts, and never will. By the time I see them, whatever dreams, hopes, fears, ghosts or gods, shame, regrets, anger, and love they might have contained are long gone. The life—the soul—has all seeped out.

What's left is just evidence. That's where I usually come in.

SANFORD, FLORIDA. SUNDAY, FEBRUARY 26, 2012.

Tracy Martin dialed his teenage son's cell number and it went straight to voice mail.

It was late, well past ten, on a dark, wet Sunday night. Tracy and his girlfriend Brandy Green had been out most of the weekend, leaving seventeen-year-old Trayvon and Brandy's fourteen-year-old son Chad alone at her townhouse in the Retreat at Twin Lakes, a gated neighborhood in the relatively sedate Orlando suburb of Sanford, Florida. Tracy and Brandy had been dating for two years, and it wasn't unusual for Tracy and Trayvon to drive up from Miami, four hours each way, for an overnight or a weekend.

It wasn't just the romance. Tracy desperately wanted Trayvon to wise up, to get away from thug life in Miami, and those long trips were his chance to talk some sense into the kid.

Trayvon didn't seem to be listening. In some ways, he was a typical teenager, obsessed with girls, video games, sports, and the pounding of rap music in his earbuds. He loved Chuck E. Cheese and watching TV sitcoms. Someday, he thought he'd like to fly or fix airplanes. Family was important, too, even though some of their relatives were black sheep. He often hand-fed his quadriplegic uncle, baked cookies with his young cousins, and had begun wearing a button memorializing another cousin who'd died mysteriously after a drug arrest in 2008.

But Trayvon was no Boy Scout. At nearly six feet tall, he could be intimidating, and he knew it. He flirted with thug life, smoking pot and playing a badass on Facebook. In the past year, his Miami high school had suspended him three times, for tardiness, tagging, and having a bag of pot in his backpack. Tracy, a truck driver who'd been divorced from Trayvon's mother since 1999, began to hector the boy about his friends, his behavior, and his grades.

He dialed Trayvon's number again, and again it went straight to voice mail. Brandy's son Chad told them Trayvon had left around six p.m. to walk to a convenience store less than a mile away. They thought they might catch the NBA All-Star game on TV at seven thirty. Before he left, he'd asked Chad if there was anything he wanted. "Skittles," Chad said as he went back to his video games. Trayvon tugged on his hoodie and left. He never came back.

Maybe the kid had gone to the movies with a cousin nearby, the father thought, or maybe got sidetracked by a girl along the way. He did stuff like that.

Tracy called the cousin, but got no answer, so he shrugged it off and went to bed. Trayvon was still finding his way and got easily distracted. He was always testing his limits, and sometimes he went too far. He'd just turned seventeen, for god's sake. He'd turn up.

The next morning, Tracy got up early and dialed Trayvon's number again. The phone was still switched off, still dumping him directly into voice mail. He called the cousin over and over again until he finally answered—but he hadn't seen Trayvon at all.

Tracy started to worry. Around eight thirty, he called the sheriff's dispatcher to report his son missing. He described Trayvon: seventeen, wearing a gray hooded sweatshirt, light red tennis shoes, and probably slacks. He told her that he and Trayvon were from Miami but staying at his girlfriend's house in Sanford. In a few minutes, another dispatcher called him back with more specific questions, and she told him that police officers were on the way to the townhouse. He felt some relief that he'd soon have some help finding Trayvon.

Three police cars pulled up outside. A somber detective introduced himself and asked Tracy for a recent picture of his son. Tracy flipped through the camera roll on his phone and found one.

The detective gritted his teeth. He told Tracy he had a photo to show him and he wanted to know if it was Trayvon. From a manila envelope, he pulled a full-color image of a young black man. He was dead.

It was Trayvon.

At that moment, Tracy's boy was lying in a tray in the morgue, ashen and cold, shot once in the chest.

That instant blurred for Tracy Martin. And his sudden shock would soon evolve into a long, painful moment of profound anxiety across America.

The rain fell sullen and persistent as Trayvon left the townhouse. It was one of those ambivalent February nights in Florida, not quite cold and not quite warm, hovering in the mid-fifties. He pulled up his hood and walked through the Retreat, past the front gate, to the 7-Eleven convenience store on Rinehart Road, almost a mile away.

Inside the store, Martin grabbed a tall can of AriZona Watermelon Fruit Juice Cocktail from the cooler and a small package of Skittles from some shelves near the cash register. He fumbled in the pockets of his tan slacks and put a couple of bucks and some coins on the counter to pay for the snacks, then left. A store surveillance camera watched him leave at 6:24 p.m.

On the way back to the townhouse, the rain picked up. Trayvon took shelter beneath an awning over the community mailboxes and called Chad at the townhouse to say he was on his way home. He also called his friend DeeDee, a girl he'd met back in Miami, and with whom he talked and texted endlessly. In fact, they'd already spent about six hours on the phone that day. This time they talked for about eighteen minutes, but he got serious toward the end of the call.

Some guy, "a creepy-ass cracka" in a funky silver truck, was watching him, Trayvon told DeeDee. He sounded scared. He thought about running out the back of the little mailbox area and losing the white guy in the maze of townhouses, but DeeDee told him to run back home as fast as he could.

No, he wouldn't run, he said. The townhouse wasn't far. He yanked up his hoodie and started walking right past the truck, glancing at the guy as he kept walking.

But while they continued to talk on the phone, Trayvon started to run. DeeDee could hear his heavy breathing and the wind rushing across the tiny microphone of his earbuds.

After less than a minute of running, he told DeeDee he'd lost the guy, and he slowed to a walk again. DeeDee thought she heard fear in his voice, and she was scared for him, too. She told him to keep running.

But the white guy appeared again, persistent. DeeDee begged Trayvon to run, but he was still breathing hard and couldn't. After a few seconds, he told her the white guy was closer now.

Suddenly Trayvon wasn't talking to DeeDee anymore. She heard his voice talking to somebody else nearby.

"Why you following me for?"

Another voice, not far. "What are you doing around here?"

"Trayvon! Trayvon!" DeeDee yelled into the phone.

She heard a thump and a rustling of grass. She heard somebody yell, "Get off! Get off!" She called out again and again to her boyfriend, but the phone went dead.

Frantic, she called Trayvon's phone back, but nobody answered.

A little after seven p.m., George Zimmerman left his townhouse in the Retreat in his silver 2008 Honda Ridgeline pickup for his weekly grocery shopping at Target. Sunday nights weren't usually crowded, and tonight the rain would keep even more shoppers away. Perfect.

Between some houses, though, he saw a teenager in a dark gray hoodie, just standing in the shadows out of the rain. He didn't recognize the kid, who was just milling around. Zimmerman had an uncomfortable feeling about him. A month before, George had seen a kid at that same spot trying to break into a house, but he got away.

So his suspicion wasn't without reason. The Retreat at Twin Lakes had been rattled when the housing bubble burst. Home values plummeted and underwater residents bailed. Investors snapped up a lot of foreclosed townhouses and started renting them out. The neighborhood changed. Strangers came and went. Low-end people from the wrong side of the gates drifted through. Gangsta boys in low-slung, baggy pants and cockeyed ball caps started hanging around. Then the burglaries and home invasions started. Overnight, those gates didn't seem as secure.

After three break-ins in August 2011, Zimmerman proposed a neighborhood watch. The idea appealed to the anxious members of the homeowners association, so he invited a Sanford police official to explain how it'd work: Unarmed volunteers would keep an eye on the neighborhood and call the cops if they saw anything suspicious.

Vigilance without violence. Sounded easy enough. The board quickly appointed the pudgy, serious, twenty-eight-year-old George Zimmerman, who'd lived in the Retreat for three years, to coordinate the program.

This son of a former Virginia magistrate and his Peruvian wife was perfect for the job nobody else really wanted to do. A part-time college student who dreamed of being a judge someday, and a financial-fraud auditor at a private company in nearby Maitland, he took his unpaid job seriously. His own temper had flared in the past, getting the former altar boy in modest trouble, but his neighbors now knew him as a friendly, helpful, earnest guy.

He considered himself a kind of protector. Even before he became the watch "captain," he'd helped capture a shoplifter who filched some electronics from a local supermarket, and now duly "deputized," he was constantly calling the police dispatchers to report stray dogs, speeders, potholes, graffiti, family fights, and suspicious loiterers. He was even known to knock on doors to let residents know their garage doors were open. To some he was a godsend; to others, a badge-heavy doofus.

So on this gray, damp night, this unfamiliar black kid in a hoodie naturally caught his eye. Zimmerman parked his truck and called the cops on his cellphone.

"Sanford Police Department," the dispatcher answered.

"Hey, we've had some break-ins in my neighborhood," Zimmerman replied, "and there's a real suspicious guy, uh, [near] Retreat View Circle, um, the best address I can give you is 111 Retreat View Circle. This guy looks like he's up to no good, or he's on drugs or something. It's raining and he's just walking around, looking about."

"Okay, and this guy, is he white, black, or Hispanic?"

"He looks black."

"Did you see what he was wearing?"

"Yeah," Zimmerman said. "A dark hoodie, like a gray hoodie, and either jeans or sweatpants and white tennis shoes . . . he was just staring . . ."

"Okay, he's just walking around the area," the dispatcher said. It wasn't really question.

"Looking at all the houses," Zimmerman seemed to finish her sentence. "Now he's just staring at me."

About then the teenager started walking toward Zimmerman's truck, and Zimmerman kept up his play-by-play with the dispatcher.

"How old would you say he looks?" she asked.

Zimmerman squinted into the dim, drizzling darkness.

"He's got a button on his shirt. Late teens."

"Late teens, okay."

Zimmerman was getting a little nervous. "Something's wrong with him. Yup, he's coming to check me out. He's got something in his hands. I don't know what his deal is."

"Just let me know if he does anything, okay?"

"How long until you get an officer over here?"

"Yeah, we've got someone on the way," she reassured him. "Just let me know if this guy does anything else."

Adrenaline was flowing in Zimmerman's veins. "These assholes, they always get away," he said.

He had started to give directions to his location when the kid broke into a run.

"Shit, he's running," the watchman said.

"Which way is he running?"

"Down toward the other entrance to the neighborhood . . . the back entrance." Zimmerman cursed under his breath as he shoved his truck into gear and tried to pursue the kid.

"Are you following him?" the dispatcher asked.

"Yeah."

"Okay, we don't need you to do that."

Zimmerman copied, but his chase was already over. The kid had vanished between two buildings. Zimmerman got out of his truck to look for a street sign so he could tell the dispatcher his location, and he scanned the shadows for the dark-clad figure. But the kid was gone.

Seven thirteen. The watchman's call to police had lasted exactly four minutes and thirteen seconds.

In the next three minutes, Trayvon Martin and George Zimmerman would collide in a life-or-death struggle.

And one would die.

What happened next is murky. Accounts differ.

After he lost sight of the hooded teen, Zimmerman said he was walking back to his truck when the kid seemed to materialize out of the dank air. He was pissed, and angry words were spoken.

"Yo, you got a problem?" the hooded teen yelled.

"No, I don't have a problem," Zimmerman answered.

"You got a problem now," the kid growled as he punched Zimmerman in the face, breaking his nose.

Stunned by the blow, Zimmerman stumbled and fell on his back. Trayvon leaped on top of him. Zimmerman couldn't push him off, and soon the kid was repeatedly slamming Zimmerman's head against the concrete sidewalk that ran between the rows of townhouses.

Zimmerman screamed long and loud for help.

Trayvon clamped one hand over Zimmerman's nose and the other over his mouth, yelling at him to "shut the fuck up." In the commotion, Zimmerman's shirt and jacket were yanked up, revealing his Kel-Tec 9mm handgun, holstered on his right hip.

Trayvon saw it.

"You're going to die tonight, motherfucker," he said.

Zimmerman screamed again for help.

Nobody helped, but several startled witnesses called 911 to report the ruckus. In the background of their calls, dispatchers could hear desperate human howls.

"Does he look hurt to you?" the dispatcher asked one of the callers.

"I can't see him," the woman answered. "I don't want to go out there. I don't know what's going on, so . . ."

"So you think he's yelling 'Help'?"

"Yes," the frightened woman answered.

"All right," the dispatcher said calmly. "What is your . . ."

A single shot rang out.

The screaming stopped at seven sixteen.

A minute later, the first cop rolled up on the scene.

A young black man lay facedown in the wet grass, his arms under him, his hood pulled back. No pulse.

A red-eyed Zimmerman stood nearby, bloodied but responsive. His jeans and jacket were wet and grass-stained in back. He admitted he'd shot the boy. He raised his hands and surrendered his handgun to the officer, who handcuffed him and seated him in a squad car.

Later, he told investigators that in the struggle, the teenager had reached for his exposed handgun, but Zimmerman had been faster. He grabbed his 9mm and pulled the trigger. The kid slumped into the grass, face forward, startled.

"You got me," he said. His last words.

The stunned Zimmerman told police he'd quickly gotten up and moved the boy's arms out to his side, to make sure he had no weapons. He couldn't see any wounds, nor the boy's face.

Other cops soon arrived, followed by paramedics, who all tried unsuccessfully to revive this nameless kid, although they had no idea at the time who he was. Still no heartbeat. They pronounced him dead at precisely seven thirty.

One officer lifted Trayvon's hoodie and felt the heft of a large, cold can—the unopened AriZona watermelon juice drink—in its front pouch. He also found a package of Skittles, a lighter, a cellphone, forty bucks and some change, but no wallet or ID.

So the unidentified teen's body was sealed in a blue body bag and given a number before it was carted off to the morgue. Sadly, he was just a hundred yards from his house.

The paramedics examined Zimmerman and noted abrasions to his forehead, some blood and tenderness at his nose, and two bloody gashes on the back of his head. His nose was swollen and red, probably broken.

Zimmerman's wounds were cleaned up back at the station, he spoke freely in a voluntary interview, and later he walked detectives through his movements that night.

Days passed. The Sanford police followed up and were genuinely sad for the kid's family because, despite his teenage missteps, he seemed to be generally pointed in the right direction, but they couldn't prove Zimmerman committed any crime. In fact, all the evidence suggested his account was truthful.

The ordinary stuff in a dead kid's pockets didn't seem especially pertinent to their shooting investigation at the time, but the importance of any single thing is not always apparent at first glance.

The morning after the shooting, Volusia County's associate medical examiner Dr. Shiping Bao unzipped the blue body bag on his table in the Daytona Beach morgue and began his autopsy of Trayvon Martin.

Bao, who was fifty years old, was born and raised in China, where he got his medical degree and a graduate degree in radiation medicine. He became a naturalized American and eventually did a four-year residency in pathology at the University of Alabama in Birmingham. After three years at the Tarrant County Medical Examiner's Office in Fort Worth, he came to Florida for more money. He'd been on the job less than seven months.

Before him now was the corpse of a handsome, well-developed black teenager, neither scrawny nor stocky. Apart from the bloodless bullet hole in his chest and the sooty ring of stippled skin around it, Trayvon Martin looked fit, trim, and healthy.

Ah, but that hole.

The single 9mm bullet that killed him entered his chest square-on, just to the left of his breastbone. It pierced his heart sac, punctured the lower right chamber of the heart, and passed through the lower lobe of his right lung, fragmenting into three pieces along the way. Around the hole itself was a halo of soot, a powder tattoo measuring two by two inches.

His wounded heart had continued to pump, and each contraction gushed blood into his chest cavity, filling it with 2.3 liters of blood—more than two quarts, or about one-third of a normal person's total blood volume.

Bao didn't write it down, but he said later that he believed Martin had remained conscious for as long as ten minutes after he was shot, and was likely in great pain.

One thing is almost certain: Conscious or not, Trayvon Martin probably lived very briefly after being shot.

Most gunshot wounds to the heart are not instantaneously fatal. In fact, no matter what you see on TV or in the movies, only gunshot wounds of the brain are likely to be instantaneously fatal . . . and even then, not always. Unconsciousness depends on three factors: the organ injured, the extent of the injury, and the psychology/physiology of the wounded person. Some people immediately lose consciousness from a minor wound; some are shot through the heart and keep going. One can stay conscious at least five to fifteen seconds from a heart shot.

But we know for sure that when paramedics arrived on the scene ten minutes later, he was dead.

Other than the fatal wound, Bao's autopsy found only a small, fresh abrasion on Martin's left ring finger below the knuckle. He didn't cut into the knuckles of either hand to look for internal bruising around the knuckles that might have proven whether the boy had punched anyone. It might not have proven conclusively that he was the aggressor, but it might have proven he was in a fight.

Martin's blood and urine also contained low levels of THC—the active ingredient in marijuana—but nobody knows exactly when he used the drugs or if he was high the night he was killed.

This struck Bao as a routine shooting case. He wrapped up his examination in ninety minutes.

"The wound," Bao wrote in his final autopsy report, "is consistent with a wound of entrance of intermediate range."

Those two words—*intermediate range*—quickly reverberated in the echo chamber of American media, which didn't really know what they meant but seized on the phrase as somehow important. If the muzzle of George Zimmerman's Kel-Tec wasn't against Trayvon Martin's chest when he fired, how far away was it? Was this "intermediate range" shot fired into the kid's chest from an inch away? Five inches? Three feet? Different forensic experts (and a slew of inexpert commentators) couldn't seem to agree on the precise meaning of the term.

Worse, the angry drumbeat against Zimmerman was becoming deafening, and this single phrase—intermediate range—only turned up the volume. One side saw "intermediate range" as proof of a summary execution; the other side saw it as a validation of self-defense.

They were both wrong.

When a gun's trigger is pulled, the firing pin strikes the bullet's primer, creating a tiny jet of flame that ignites the powder in a cartridge. That sudden ignition creates a burst of hot gas that propels the bullet down the barrel of the gun. It all bursts out—the bullet, hot gases, soot, vaporized metals of the primer, and unburned gunpowder—in a spectacular and deadly plume.

How far this cloud of superheated debris travels varies by gun, barrel length, and the type of gunpowder. Gunshot residue can be found on the clothing and the body of a human victim. It might leave a film of soot, or tattoo the skin around the wound with unburned or partly burned particles of gunpowder that puncture the top layer of the skin, or produce nothing at all. The pattern of this damage—or lack of it—can tell us how far away the gun's muzzle was when it was fired.

That tattooing (sometimes also called stippling) is the hallmark of an intermediate range gunshot. Shots within a foot or less might leave soot residue. Without stippling, without soot, and without any other residue on the skin or clothing, a gunshot will be classified as distant. A contact wound, in which the muzzle is touching the skin when fired, leaves a completely different wound.

In Trayvon Martin's case, this tattooing or stippling encircled his wound in a two-inch pattern. The examiner noted soot, too. The pattern suggested to me that the Kel-Tec's muzzle had been two to four inches from the boy's skin—*intermediate range*—when George Zimmerman pulled the trigger.

But while the media-sphere haggled over what the stippling proved, few people noticed a tiny fact in another report hidden deep inside the mountain of documents investigators and prosecutors had dumped on the public before trial.

On this obscure little detail, the whole case pivoted.

. . .

Amy Siewert was a firearm and gunshot expert in the Florida Department of Law Enforcement's (FDLE) crime lab. With a bachelor's degree in chemistry from Massachusetts's Worcester Polytechnic Institute, she'd worked in the FDLE's forensic toxicology section before transferring to the firearms section, where she'd been an analyst for three years.

Her job was to examine George Zimmerman's Kel-Tec 9mm handgun and the teenager's light gray Nike sweatshirt and the dark gray hoodie he wore over it. Her main job was to connect all the dots that proved this was the gun that fired the bullet that penetrated the clothing and pierced the heart of a seventeen-year-old boy the world knew as Trayvon Martin. She'd also examine the garments microscopically and chemically for telltale gunshot residue that might suggest how the shooting happened.

The first thing Siewert noticed was an L-shaped hole in Martin's hoodie, about two by one inches. It lined up perfectly with the boy's wound. She noted soot around it, both inside and out. Frayed fibers around the hole were also burned. Chemically, she discovered vaporized lead. And a large, six-inch orange stain surrounded it all—Trayvon Martin's blood.

Martin had worn a second sweatshirt underneath the hoodie. It, too, was sooty and singed from the muzzle blast. Its bloodstained two-inch bullet hole bore a star shape.

But what Siewert couldn't find in two separate tests was a pattern of gunshot residue around and away from the holes.

The stellate hole, soot, vaporized lead, and no discernible pattern from the powder led Siewert to only one possible conclusion: The muzzle of George Zimmerman's pistol was touching Trayvon Martin's hoodie when he pulled the trigger. Not just close, but actually against the fabric.

But few people, much less the national media, realized the significance of Siewert's brief report. *Intermediate range* fit the narrative so much better. If they noticed Siewert's findings at all, they didn't grasp the forensic distinction between contact and intermediate range, or ask the vital question: How could a gun's muzzle be touching a sweatshirt but still be as much as four inches away from the skin of the person who wore it?

It was chalked up to a simple, minor contradiction. The media quickly moved on to the more emotional events swirling around Trayvon Martin's death.

The question nobody was asking would provide the answer nobody was expecting.

That single shot in the night set a tragedy of mythic proportion in motion, quietly at first but slowly building toward a deafening din.

For more than a week, the shooting of Trayvon Martin wasn't even much of a story. Local TV stations ran short items about it, the *Orlando Sentinel* published two news briefs, and the twice-a-week *Sanford Herald* ran just 213 words. But then on March 7, Reuters News Service circulated a 469-word wire story, based mainly on an interview with a lawyer for Trayvon's family, that made it sound more like a white vigilante had purposely hunted down an unarmed, innocent black child and shot him in cold blood, a murder being covered up by local cops. The wires carried an old childhood photo of Trayvon, provided by his parents, leaving the impression that the victim had been a happy, harmless, baby-faced middle schooler.

It was the first blood in the water, and the national media smelled it.

Reporters swarmed to Sanford, both covering and cultivating the burgeoning conflict. When black leaders began to cry racism, the stakes grew instantly more intense; ratings and readership soared. Tapes of Zimmerman's call to dispatchers were edited by one news network to make it appear he used a racial slur before the shooting; Martin's parents endorsed a petition on Change.org calling for Zimmerman's arrest and it got 1.3 million "signatures"; Reverend Al Sharpton and the rest of the racial-grievance industrial complex showed up to stir the pot; members of the New Black Panther Party offered a $10,000 reward for Zimmerman's "capture"; and the newest parlor game became "Guess what slur George mumbled in his 911 tape" when no such slur was apparent.

A lot of bloggers and TV talking heads became armchair crime scene specialists, offering forensic theories that came more from Hollywood whimsy than medical school.

President Barack Obama elevated the case to a presidential issue when he said, "Trayvon Martin could've been me thirty-five years ago," and "If I had a son he would look like Trayvon," as he called for nationwide "soul-searching." Instead of tamping down the rage, the president fueled it.

Angry rallies converted bags of Skittles into flags of protest. Hoodies and cans of tea became symbols of American racism.

"He may have been suspended from school at the time, and had traces of cannabis in his blood," wrote London's *Guardian* newspaper, "but when you look behind the appearance of a menacing black teenager, those Skittles say, you find the child inside."

Celebrities, politicians, and throngs of ordinary people demanded justice for Trayvon, but the only suitable justice they would accept seemed to be the arrest, conviction, and swift execution of that vile racist George Zimmerman.

On April 11, 2012—more than six tense weeks after Trayvon Martin was shot dead and a local district attorney found no evidence to file criminal charges—a special prosecutor ordered the nearly broke George Zimmerman arrested and charged with second-degree murder. A new defense team volunteered: Mark O'Mara and Don West, both well-known legal veterans and both top-notch defenders. The old friends made a good team: O'Mara was a masterful litigator, dignified and unflappable; West was a fighter who didn't apologize to anyone for feeling that the case against Zimmerman looked like mob justice.

And both had long experience in self-defense and Stand Your Ground cases. In fact, the deceptively affable Pennsylvanian West quit his job as a federal public defender in death-penalty cases to take Zimmerman's case.

He wasn't born yesterday. Regarded as one of the nation's top criminal defense lawyers, he'd worked some tough cases with even tougher clients. He knew defendants sometimes lied. He knew the evidence wasn't always perfect. He'd seen how the genuine facts in a shooting could be twisted beyond recognition by media.

But after spending time with Zimmerman, he barely recognized the public's monstrous caricature of him.

And soon both O'Mara and West recognized that the fanatical public clamor and local politics threatened to capsize some serious legal questions.

Many court watchers expected Zimmerman to claim immunity under Florida's so-called Stand Your Ground law, which said a victim under attack wasn't required to retreat and could legally use lethal force in self-defense.

But for many Trayvon supporters recalling the image of that smiling child, the possibility that George Zimmerman had feared for his life seemed absurd. To them, Stand Your Ground was a "Get Out of Jail Free" card. Outside of the courtroom, this case was more about race than self-defense, and blacks vocally decried a law they believed gave white people carte blanche to kill black folks. They demanded the immediate repeal of Stand Your Ground, and many politicians stood ready to accommodate.

Ironically, at the time of the Martin shooting, Florida's Stand Your Ground law had benefited blacks disproportionately. Since poor blacks who live in high-crime neighborhoods were the most likely victims of crime, the law made it easier for them to protect themselves when the police couldn't arrive fast enough. Blacks make up only about 16 percent of Florida's population, but 31 percent of the defendants invoking Stand Your Ground were black, and they were acquitted significantly more often than whites who used the very same defense.

The tumult didn't matter. O'Mara and West decided against a Stand Your Ground defense simply because they believed Zimmerman had a solid traditional self-defense case: He was on his back and couldn't retreat from Trayvon Martin's vicious pummeling. The law was irrelevant.

Even if Zimmerman had screwed up, they believed he had no evil intent. Would a killer call the police before he murdered someone?

And it was also possible that both Trayvon Martin and George Zimmerman feared for their lives, and that both chose to use force to defend themselves. If the jury believed that, under Florida law, Zimmerman was innocent.

But the prosecution had a different theory. Zimmerman had lied about everything except shooting Trayvon Martin. Zimmerman had stalked the unarmed teenager and forced a violent confrontation. He shouldn't have been armed at all. Zimmerman's wounds were minor, and he had no reason to think he might die. The cries for help overheard on the 911 tapes came from Trayvon Martin, not George Zimmerman. The neighborhood watchman shot the kid in cold blood as he lay in the wet grass.

The scene was set for an epic courtroom battle.

As each week passed, the protests grew, and a horrible event was simplified for mass consumption: A good-natured black child had simply gone to the store for some candy and a drink, only to be bushwhacked by a racist white man.

Some were already calling Trayvon Martin a modern-day Emmett Till. Hundreds of death threats drove George Zimmerman into hiding, while reporters described him as a "white Hispanic," seeming to accentuate the racist subtext in the tragedy. It didn't take long for the real Trayvon Martin and George Zimmerman to be lost in the Category 5 rhetorical storm that raged about race, guns, profiling, civil rights, and vigilantism.

O'Mara and West focused on the legal questions, but they weren't cloistered from the commotion on the street. They knew their future jurors were listening.

Zimmerman's defense team divvied up the daunting task brilliantly. Battling restive public opinion and prosecutorial sandbagging while trying to stay afloat, the smooth-talking O'Mara handled the intense media attention while West dived into the forensic issues.

Even if the media, the race-baiters, and the general public had already leapt to their own conclusions, justice moved more deliberately. Legal issues remained unsettled. The whole tragedy—the entire question of George Zimmerman's guilt or innocence—boiled down to a single legal question: *Who was the aggressor at the moment the trigger was pulled?*

This was a real case with real forensic issues, but for O'Mara and West, it was a nightmare. The case was complicated enough without a frustrating discovery process. Prosecutors were slow with or unresponsive to the defense's requests for evidence. A simple color photo of George Zimmerman's face after the crime took the prosecution months to deliver. Key exhibits like the complete Florida Department of Law Enforcement case file were withheld. The state claimed no evidence was recovered from Martin's phone, but a whistleblower claimed otherwise.

With almost no money for the defense, West began the arduous process of finding legal experts who could interpret the evidence, looking for any clue that could help explain what happened. He needed experts on gunshots, forensic pathology, toxicology, voice analysis, and computer animation.

A toxicologist friend mentioned my name as the go-to guy on gunshot wounds. West already knew my name and reputation. He even had a copy of my book on gunshot wounds. So he eventually reached out to me in September 2012, ten months before Zimmerman's trial was to start. They might not be able to pay me, he said, but it was an important case that raised important questions for America.

I had retired six years before as Chief Medical Examiner in Bexar County, Texas, where I had built one of the nation's most respected forensic medical facilities. I had performed more than 9,000 autopsies, examined over 25,000 deaths, and continued to consult in unexplained or questionable death cases all over the world. Now George Zimmerman's defense wanted me to connect the forensic dots in the last three minutes of Trayvon Martin's life.

I knew the furor that had engulfed America. I knew that race politics had confused the issue. I knew there were facts that had been misunderstood or overlooked. But I also knew the truth about what happened was hidden somewhere within the evidence.

I agreed.

To simplify it, my job as a medical examiner is to determine how and why a person died. In legal terms, the *cause* and *manner* of death. The cause is the disease or injury that killed him—maybe a heart attack, a gunshot wound, AIDS, or a car crash. The manner is one of four general ways a human can die—natural causes, accident, suicide, or homicide—plus a vexing fifth: undetermined.

Our determinations impact the living more than the dead. The dead are past caring, but the living can go to jail. Lives can be saved from viruses and germs. Innocence can be determined. Questions can be answered, suspicions authenticated. So medical examiners bear a heavy burden to reach an unbiased, fact-based, scientific conclusion, no matter what a dead person's family, friends, enemies, or neighbors wish it to be. Truth is always better than what we merely wish to be true.

Countless times I've delivered grim news to the relatives of suicides, and they've protested. Families often don't want to believe that a loved one felt so unloved that he killed himself. They want it to be a gun-cleaning accident or a missed step on a high bridge. They want a medical examiner to declare it an accident so they can carry on, officially guilt-free.

I've even seen relatives breathe a sigh of relief when I tell them a son or daughter was murdered, as if suicide would have been a worse way to go. It's not about the dead, but the living.

Sometimes what I told them they didn't want to hear, and sometimes what I told them they wanted to hear. But it didn't really matter either way, because I was telling them the truth.

I don't take sides. *What I know* is vital; *how I feel* is irrelevant. The forensic pathologist's mission is the truth. I'm supposed to be impartial and tell the truth. Facts have no moral quality, only what we project upon them.

Mysteries are, by definition, unanswered questions. If we could understand them, not only would they cease to be mysteries, but we'd probably consider them unworthy of being understood. Humans are funny that way.

This world itself isn't reasonable. We yearn for clarity in all things but too often embrace the murky: conspiracy theories, supernatural explanations, and mythology, among them.

I'm not a deep thinker. I don't seek profound meaning in the behavior of humans, or the stars, or the alchemy of little coincidences. We are occasionally astonished by these things simply because our world stubbornly refuses to reveal meanings, if they exist at all.

Forensic science is not magic or alchemy, even though complex technology and intricate research can take curdled blood, bullet fragments, bone shards, and flakes of skin and turn them into justice. I look for those tiny bits of truth that death leaves behind. Forensic science can see what ordinary humans often cannot, but science isn't enough. We need credible, honorable people to explain it all. Good men and women must interpret science for true justice to happen.

How long can a man with an exploded heart speak (or hope, dream, or imagine)? Can we precisely determine the moment a human's primitive instincts tell him he might die? Does every human interaction truly leave a trace?

I grew up with such questions floating in the air, and my career has been marinated in them, as this book will show. But the answers don't always satisfy.

And when they don't, my phone rings.

So it was with George Zimmerman.

Fact is, the community of medical examiners is very small—only about five hundred board-certified forensic pathologists live in the United States. Before West called, I already knew some details about the wound and that the bullet hole in the hoodie was a contact shot. I knew about the dueling conclusions of contact wound versus an intermediate range wound, but I knew why these observations were not incompatible. I shared my thoughts with West, who seemed surprised to hear them. He knew if I was right—and I was—that his whole factual case could pivot on it.

So my task was to document Martin's injuries, trace the path of the bullet and its physical damage, and examine Zimmerman's injuries to show whether they were all consistent with Zimmerman's account of the struggle. I wasn't hired to contrive an opinion to help the defense but to offer my expert opinion about whether any of it supported the shooter's account. I wasn't a hired gun coming to town to do the defense's dirty work. I hate that medical examiners sometimes appear to say what they've been paid to say—and undoubtedly, some might—but I don't work for the defense, the prosecution, the killer, the family of the victim, or the cops. I didn't get this far by selling my opinion to the highest bidder.

But the rest of the world had already taken sides. Without the benefit of facts, a lot of people saw this tragedy through the prism of their own biases and reached unyielding conclusions. This wasn't the first or the last time this had happened in my career, but it was among the most stark.

Don West sent me a thumb drive containing all the forensic material I'd need: Martin's autopsy report, crime scene photos, a video reenactment of the shooting that Zimmerman did with detectives the next day, toxicology, gunshot tests and residue, witnesses' 911 calls and statements, biological, trace, and DNA evidence, Zimmerman's medical records and his cellphone data.

This was a complicated case only in cultural terms.

Forensically, it wasn't complicated at all. It was tragically simple.

The second-degree murder trial of George Zimmerman began on Monday, June 24, 2013, almost sixteen months after the fatal shot was fired.

The prosecution's opening remarks began with calculated shock.

"Good morning. 'Fucking punks, these assholes all get away,'" state's attorney John Guy blurted out to the six-woman jury. "These were the words in this grown man's mouth as he followed this boy that he didn't know. Those were his words, not mine."

Over the next half hour, Guy repeated the profanities several times as he outlined the prosecution's case against Zimmerman.

"We are confident that at the end of this trial you will know in your head, in your heart, in your stomach that George Zimmerman did not shoot Trayvon Martin because he had to," Guy said. "He shot him for the worst of all reasons, because he wanted to."

Don West opened for the defense with a lame knock-knock joke that fell flat, but he quickly got to the meat of the case.

"I think the evidence will show that this is a sad case, that there are no monsters," West said. "George Zimmerman is not guilty of murder. He shot Trayvon Martin in self-defense after being viciously attacked."

Zimmerman watched from the defense table and Trayvon Martin's parents sat in the gallery as West suggested Martin's deadly weapon was a concrete sidewalk, "no different than if he picked up a brick or smashed [Zimmerman's] head against a wall."

"Little did George Zimmerman know at the time in less than ten minutes from him first seeing Trayvon Martin that he would be sucker-punched in the face, have his head pounded on concrete, and wind up shooting and tragically killing Trayvon Martin," West said.

The first shots fired, the trench warfare began.

Prosecutors played other 911 tapes where Zimmerman reported strange black men in the neighborhood . . . phone buddy DeeDee described her phone calls with Martin up to the point of the confrontation and denied the term "cracker" is racist . . . the lead detective said there were no major inconsistencies in Zimmerman's various accounts of the shooting, although he'd probably not suffered the dozens of blows he'd told police at the scene . . . a medical examiner who reviewed the case said Zimmerman's injuries "were not life-threatening" and "very insignificant," not even bad enough to require stitches (and had no answer when asked by O'Mara if George Zimmerman's very next injury might have killed him) . . . several eyewitnesses told conflicting stories about who was on top during the struggle . . . Martin's parents both said the voice crying for help on the 911 tape was Trayvon's . . . and five Zimmerman friends claimed the voice on the 911 tape was clearly George's.

The central question—*who was the aggressor when the shot was fired?*—remained unanswered ten days into the trial.

I took the stand on the eleventh day, just a day before the defense expected to wrap up its case. It was perhaps a blessing that Trayvon Martin's mother had left the courtroom because a victim's mother should seldom be forced to hear what I must usually say in a trial.

My testimony was no surprise to the prosecutors. They knew in detail what I was going to say because they had deposed me just two or three weeks before. In fact, a few hours before I testified, the prosecutors again questioned me on what I was about to say. In light of this, I thought that they would bring in a rebuttal witness to disagree with my opinions. They didn't.

I testified that George Zimmerman suffered multiple blunt-force injuries to his face and head: two swollen knots on his head, a couple of gashes and abrasions consistent with the head-banging assault he described, a likely broken nose that was pushed back into place, and bruises on his forehead where he was likely punched—all consistent with Zimmerman's story. It was possible for Zimmerman to have severe head injuries, even life-threatening ones, without any visible external wounds, I said.

Questioning continued. Zimmerman had recalled Martin lying facedown with his arms splayed out after the fatal shot, but by the time cops and paramedics arrived, the teenager's arms were beneath him. To prosecutors, this was evidence that Zimmerman was lying. West asked me if it was possible that the mortally wounded Martin had rolled over on his own.

"Even if I right now reached across, put my hand through your chest, grabbed your heart and ripped it out," I told West, perhaps a little too colorfully, "you could stand there and talk to me for ten to fifteen seconds or walk over to me because the thing that's controlling your movement and ability to speak is the brain, and that has a reserve oxygen supply of ten to fifteen seconds.

"In this case you have a through-and-through hole of the right ventricle, and then you have at least one hole if not two into the right lung," I continued. "So you are losing blood, and every time the heart contracts, it pumps blood out the two holes in the ventricle and at least one hole in the lung. He is going to be dead between one and three minutes after being shot."

West turned to Martin's bullet wound. Was there anything in Trayvon Martin's wounds that might tell us the positions of the two men when the fatal shot was fired? Could I tell who was on top and who was on his back?

I could.

"If you lean over somebody, you would notice that the clothing tends to fall away from the chest," I said. "If instead you're lying on your back and somebody shoots you, the clothing is going to be against your chest. So the fact that we know the clothing was two to four inches away is consistent with somebody leaning over the person doing the shooting and that the clothing is two to four inches away from the person [who is shot]."

There had been no contradiction between the medical examiner's intermediate range wound and the gunshot expert's contact shot. The Kel-Tec's muzzle touched Trayvon Martin's hoodie, which hung two to four inches away from his chest as he leaned over George Zimmerman. Gravity had pulled the can of fruit drink and the candy in the hoodie's front pouch—weighing almost two pounds—down even farther.

The forensic evidence, I said, proved Martin had been leaning forward, not lying down, when he was shot. That was consistent with Zimmerman's account that the boy was kneeling or standing over him, savagely beating him, when Zimmerman pulled the trigger.

If Martin had been on his back, his hoodie would have been against his skin, with no space between. If George Zimmerman had been tugging at his hoodie, the bullet holes wouldn't have lined up so perfectly.

The courtroom was deathly quiet. The jury was riveted. The prosecution's cross-examination tiptoed around my conclusion, which seemed to shut the door on their theory that Zimmerman, not Martin, had been on top in that fight.

I was excused from the stand, and Don West's daughter took me directly to the airport to catch a plane home to San Antonio. On the long flight, I thought about the two lives that intersected on a dark, rainy February night. No matter who was on top, it was a tragedy. Lives were changed, and not just for the two combatants.

None of us was there. There are no pictures or videos of the fatal moment. We cannot know what truly happened, and we certainly cannot know what was in those two men's hearts. But the scientific evidence told a story that many people didn't want to hear and refuse to believe even now.

That's how it is with truth. It isn't always welcome.

A few days later, there was nothing more to say. The case went to the all-female jury. While they deliberated, dozens of demonstrators gathered outside the courthouse, hollering slogans, waving signs, and arguing with one another about the case. Two weeks of testimony hadn't muted them at all.

After more than sixteen hours, the jury reached its verdict: George Zimmerman was not guilty of any crime in the shooting of Trayvon Martin.

He walked away from the courthouse a free man, but likely to spend the rest of his life looking over his shoulder.

An acquittal isn't always absolution.

Even now, it's difficult for many people to hear this, but the question of Trayvon Martin's death was not a miscarriage of justice, but rather a painfully perfect example of justice itself. Our system worked as it was intended. Questions were asked, scenarios explored, theories argued. It is simply the nature of any homicide—justifiable or not—that there will be winners and losers when the question must be settled.

Forensic evidence is the bedrock of justice. It doesn't change its story or misremember what it saw. It doesn't cower when a mob gathers on the courthouse steps. It doesn't run away or go silent out of fear. It tells us honestly and candidly what we need to know, even when we want it to say something else. We must only have the wisdom to be able to see it and to interpret it honestly.

So it was with Trayvon Martin.

Like so many words that have been twisted beyond recognition by politicians, pundits, and other modern-day logrollers, "justice" does not equal satisfaction or punishment. It should be a fair investigation of the facts and a reasonable, impartial conclusion, but for some people it is revenge. Trayvon Martin got justice, but his loved ones will never be truly satisfied. So it is, too, with the loved ones of Michael Brown in Ferguson, Missouri, or Freddie Gray in Baltimore chanting, "No Justice, No Peace," and promising to agitate until their killers are punished. What if vengeance isn't warranted?

Not for the first time, and certainly not for the last, people leapt to their conclusions before the facts were known. They saw the entire unfolding tragedy through the defective prisms of their own biases and an increasingly dogmatic media.

We weren't there. None of us saw a neighborhood-watch volunteer shoot an unarmed black teenager to death in the drizzling shadows of a Florida night in 2012. And despite the glare of media frenzy that followed, the facts grew murkier as a nation chose sides by what it imagined, not what it knew. We debated feverishly what nobody saw.

Every lynch mob begins with an assumption and a quick conclusion. We should certainly know by now, after so many crimes, that starting with an assumption and closing the case too quickly is deadly.

While many people made George Zimmerman's case about black and white, it was anything but black and white.

The real problem wasn't injustice, but an unfortunate series of ordinary human faults that led to a fatal overreaction by both men. Trayvon

Martin didn't need to die. A white guy misjudged the behavior of a black teenager, who misjudged the behavior of the white guy. They profiled each other. They saw each other as a threat. And both were wrong.

In the end, I can't see into their hearts. This homicide question was settled, but the bigger questions about humanity are going to take a little longer.

The "Why" Incision

My earliest memory is of death.

And from that day forward, death was never more intimate with me. I have kept death at a respectful distance. It became a job that I did in a brightly lighted room, not a wound that required darkness to heal. For someone whose very living comes from other people dying, who understands death better than most men understand their wives, and who knows he must eventually experience it himself, I seldom let it touch me.

And the few times it did, nobody knew.

One of the pleasures of childhood is that you feel something more than you understand it. There are great gaps in my conscious memories, events I can't recall entirely but that come back in emotional fragments. So there are many things in my childhood I can't explain, stuff that just stuck without much contemplation.

Here's one thing that stuck: I always wanted to be a doctor. Even in grammar school, when the other boys dreamed of being firefighters, cowboys, or detectives, I wanted only to be a doctor. I never had a discussion with myself or anyone else about it, never considered anything else. My parents never suggested I become a doctor, but I think they assumed I would, too. Not a single day passed when I thought I'd do anything else. It was a feeling, not a conscious decision. I just assumed I would be a doctor. Before I even knew what a future was, I knew what I'd be doing in it. And that was that.

Maybe it was in my DNA. My father was a doctor, my maternal grandfather was a doctor, and since the 1600s, all the men on my mother's side—with one exception—were doctors. (The lone black sheep was a magistrate.)

Both of my parents were first-generation Americans, the children of Italian immigrants who came here from Naples early in the twentieth century for better lives. My grandparents weren't fleeing poverty or hopelessness; they were educated, cultured people who nevertheless saw the opportunity and possibility that America offered. They brought the same traditions of hard work, adaptability, and risk for reward. And maybe above all, they were driven by a willingness to be uncomfortable.

My father's father, Vincenzo Di Maio, arrived in 1911 aboard the French-flagged steamer SS *Venezia* from Naples. He had fifty dollars in his pocket—the minimum—and the Ellis Island clerk noted a scar on his forehead. He was an Italian opera tenor who had enjoyed a modestly successful musical career onstage, in recordings, and maybe even one early movie (now lost) before he opened a music shop in Italian Harlem, where he sold pianos, phonographs, old-time music rolls, and records, and repaired any musical machines that came in the door. Vincenzo's wife, the former Marianna Ciccarelli, was a midwife who was popular among the young immigrant *gestantes*. She died of tuberculosis the year I was born, only fifty-three, so I never knew her.

Domenico Di Maio—Dominick, to everybody—was born in 1913 in Vincenzo and Marianna's Hester Street apartment on the Lower East Side. Marianna was a strong Italian mother and played the dominant role in my father's life. Her English was never good, so she drafted her eight-year-old son—my father—to deal with bankers she didn't trust. My father adored her.

My mother's father, Pasquale de Caprariis, came to America already a doctor in 1901, but he didn't come for his career. He left Italy for love. Not long after he landed at Ellis Island, he married a twenty-six-year-old Italian nurse named Carmela Mostacciuolo. His mother had wanted him to marry an upper-class woman, but Pasquale defied her. Disinherited, he came to America with Carmela, married her, opened a medical office in Manhattan, and started seeing patients in his home in Brooklyn, too.

Among his patients was the wife of Francesco Ioele, aka Frankie Yale, Brooklyn's most feared mob boss during Prohibition. Yale, who gave young Alphonse Capone and Albert Anastasia their first jobs, frequently complained to my grandfather that modern kids had grown too disrespectful and violent. (This is especially funny when you consider that Frankie Yale's most trusted enforcer was a guy named Willie "Two-Knife" Altieri because his trademark was killing his victims with two knives.) After Yale was assassinated in 1928 (possibly on Capone's orders), thousands of onlookers—maybe including my grandfather—watched a blocks-long cortege carry his $15,000 silver casket to one of the most lavish gangland funerals in crime history.

During the Depression, my grandfather was sometimes paid in eggs, vegetables, and chickens by sick Brooklynites who had no money. As a child, listening to stories about him, I always knew that when I became a doctor I, too, could survive on the meat and produce that my patients would bring to my house.

And Dr. Pasquale de Caprariis's Brooklyn house is where Italia Alfonsina Violetta de Caprariis was delivered by her father in 1912, a year and a day before her future husband was born.

Dominick Di Maio and Violet de Caprariis met as freshmen at Long Island University in 1930. They dated for a few years before getting engaged, a betrothal that stretched out for seven years in the Depression. They usually joined Sunday dinners after church at Vincenzo and Marianna's house, chaperoned by my mother's older sister.

After college, still in the smothering grip of the Great Depression, my father went to medical school at Marquette University in Milwaukee, where he became a clinical pathologist in 1940.

And my mother did something even more extraordinary: She attended law school at St. John's University. The quiet truth was that she loved history and wanted to attend graduate school at Columbia to become a college professor, but the federal government would pay for her graduate school only if she studied law. In 1939, she was one of only four women in her graduating class.

When Dominick and Violet married in June 1940, my mother never truly practiced law again. In those days, young Italian wives were expected to bear children and be the glue that kept a family together— even if she had a law degree. But my mother wasn't especially passionate about law anyway. It had just been a way to get her education. She'd draw up occasional legal papers for family and neighbors, but after she married, she never really earned much money from law. That hadn't been her goal. She preferred reading history books, which she did voraciously for the rest of her life.

Almost eleven months later, I was born in my doctor-grandfather's Brooklyn home, my father and grandfather attending. I was delivered by a lawyer into the waiting hands of a doctor. A good omen.

During the war, as I learned to toddle, my father served as a Navy doctor in US Maritime Service stations all over the New York City metropolitan area. One unexpected benefit: Within days after the war ended, I developed a terrible middle-ear infection. I was among the first American civilians to receive a new antibiotic called penicillin— which up to that point went only to soldiers. It cured me.

After the war, my father turned his prolific energies to his career and raising a family in Brooklyn.

Here's another thing that just stuck: My earliest memory is of seeing my grandmother Carmela, my mother's mother, lying dead on the dining room table. In the soft pastel colors of an old vision, I recall entering a room through a many-paned door. The table was in the center of the room, and she lay there during her wake, still. I walked up to the table and just knew she was dead, although I can't fathom how I knew what death was. I remember nothing else, not a funeral, not anyone else's sadness.

And I remember nothing before that day. I was only about five years old, and I didn't understand death or wakes or funerals or forever. I knew only that I'd never seen my grandmother on top of the table, and never so still. I don't remember being sad. It is just a snapshot that lodged in my young memory, and its only meaning is what I give it today, some seventy years later.

But I might have known even then not to cry.

The Brooklyn of my childhood is not the Brooklyn of modern culture, real or imagined. Race friction hadn't yet taken center stage, the Dodgers were a touchstone, and crime wasn't rampant. The borough was a mix of middle- and working-class families. Doctors and lawyers were neighbors of shopkeepers, dockworkers, and bus drivers. Our next-door neighbor on Fourth Street drove a truck.

But neighbors weren't our main network. Family was much closer, much bigger, and more reliable. I had an aunt and uncle on the same block, and all but one of my relatives lived in Brooklyn—I had an uncle in Long Island. We gathered on most holidays. For us, "family" was a real living thing you could touch, and it could touch you. Dominick and Violet Di Maio's kids were raised to honor our family, to not embarrass, disappoint, hurt, or dishonor it.

Like most Italians in that place and time, we were strict Roman Catholics. We all attended church together every Sunday, although my mother attended Mass at St. Rose of Lima Roman Catholic Church two or three times a week. She was devout enough to give one daughter the name of her patron saint, St. Thérèse Martin. On my mother's bedside table was a small ceramic statue of the Blessed Mother, but on her bureau was a much large figure of St. Thérèse Martin, a gift from my father, who every October 3—St. Thérèse's day in the Catholic Church until recently—gave Violet a red rose.

I was expected to keep the sacraments and go to confession, but religion wasn't a driving or conspicuous force in our house. I grew up believing in destiny and fate, in a kind of ultimate justice, and in life beyond. For me, death is proof that we have souls. I see humans as an ear of corn, with an outer, disposable husk and an inner core of kernels—the seeds of life itself. When I see a dead body, it is just a husk. The soul is gone.

I don't autopsy people. I autopsy bodies. A person is something alive and vibrant and different. Bodies are just what they leave behind.

People are naturally curious about my job (and about anyone who works with the dead). Somebody once asked me about the body of a woman who in life had been beautiful. Had she been beautiful, too, in death?

"No," I replied. "I have never seen a beautiful body, just a lifeless thing that looks like a person but isn't. The beautiful part is gone."

We lived in a three-story house built on our tree-lined street in 1930. The yard wasn't really big enough for children to play in—or for much of anything else—but we had the street, which was a more fascinating playground anyway.

Outside, children led different lives from their parents. I grew up in those primitive days when children were sent out in the morning to play, came home for lunch, and sent back out into the world until supper. And after dinner, on summer nights, you were usually free until the streetlights blinked on. Like other kids, I played stickball in the street, pitched cards, rode my bike, and got into the usual little-boy mischief.

But I was a reserved kid, more inclined toward reading than sports. I would often walk ten blocks to the public library, check out a stack of books, and then bring them home, where I'd lie in a hammock on our massive porch and voraciously consume every word. That was another of my mother's habits that stuck. Nothing distracted me from my journeys to Thermopylae, Belleau Wood, Waterloo, and a thousand other places my books took me.

I was a good student, but I didn't love school, so I made the best of it. Mostly. My first day of school reflected how I'd feel about classrooms for the rest of my days: The teacher introduced herself and turned her back to write on the blackboard. I saw my chance. I walked out of the classroom and ran all the way home. My mother marched me right back, and maybe out of respect for my mother, I spent the next nineteen years of my life in some type of classroom.

When the time came, my parents sent me to a private, all-boys Catholic high school, St. John's Prep in Bedford-Stuyvesant. In our parochial little 1950s world called Brooklyn, it was so far away it might as well have been in a different state, but in reality, it was only about five miles as the crow flies. I walked five blocks and took two trains and a bus to school and back every day. I couldn't have played sports, even if I'd wanted to, and I didn't work after school because I simply didn't have time between all the buses and trains. All my classmates lived outside my neighborhood, and none of my friends on the block went to St. John's, so high school was a solitary time for me.

Because I didn't really ever get to know any of the other boys at school—my introverted nature and hair that started turning prematurely gray at thirteen played big roles in that—I spent a lot of time in the school's vast library, reading. My favorite topic was history . . . until I discovered the section about guns. I didn't own a gun, and other than small-caliber plinking at cans on occasional upstate outings with my dad, I hadn't really spent much time around them. But I was fascinated by these machines—how they worked, how they were made, and what they could do.

My first gun, a Remington Model 513S bolt-action .22 rifle, was a gift from one of my father's colleagues, a big-game hunter who sent it when he heard of my budding interest in guns. I still have it.

I didn't know back then how important guns would be to the rest of my life.

At home, our lives weren't necessarily what you might expect from a household headed by a doctor and a lawyer. In time, my three younger sisters came along, and our house buzzed with constant activity. My mother commanded the child-rearing like General Patton, while my father ran off to fight different wars.

My frugal father always turned over his paychecks to my equally frugal mother, who managed all the finances. We were a solidly upper-middle-class family, but we didn't look like it to the rest of the world. My mother deplored ostentation. Quiet, austere, and very intelligent, she even dressed plainly. She didn't like jewelry, but on special occasions she'd wear pearls. She didn't think she was pretty, and she never wore makeup, her wedding ring, or a watch. She kept her hair cropped short.

Our house was filled with books, though. My mother read endlessly, especially history books, and she believed it was the key to her children's success, too. If she had to choose between buying a book or indulging in a new dress, it was no contest. Always the book.

Something else I remember about her: I never saw her cry in public, even when her parents and siblings died. She believed crying in public was undignified and showed weakness, and she chastised all of us when we cried.

It's funny, sometimes, the things that stick.

Dominick Di Maio lived in perpetual motion. He always came home for dinner, but often went back out afterward and on weekends. He worked part-time jobs in all of the small private hospitals all over Brooklyn and Queens, running from one to another, seven days a week and twelve hours a day. None had pathologists on staff, so he'd drop in, examine their day's lab reports, render his diagnoses, then move on to the next. At one point, he worked five different jobs simultaneously. Around the same time, he also took a part-time job, just $4,500 a year, doing autopsies for the New York medical examiner.

In his work, he was a dogged investigator with a sharp mind. Although he was undeniably a full-blooded New York Italian, he seldom exhibited the stereotypical flamboyant passion. The few times he ever truly exploded in full-throated anger tended to be when his sense of justice had been betrayed, and that was most often when an innocent child was dead.

Privately, he had an outgoing personality, but he never dominated the room. He didn't make many friends because he was always working, but more important, he didn't make many enemies, either. He didn't rattle easily, couldn't be bullied, and remembered slights. He collected stamps. He loved to relax by swimming, so he'd often go the beach and swim way out. The son of an Italian opera singer who also wrote music, my father could play piano by ear, mostly jazz and Big Band stuff. He once loved fishing and boating, but he gave them up when they started to impinge on his work.

My father was also a taskmaster who took a special interest in his kids' studies. He expected me to shine in the classroom, but he expected no less of his three daughters. He believed they were equals in every way and could achieve just as much. And they did: They all became doctors, too.

But work was never truly separate. In our house, death and life coexisted. Death was just something we lived with.

He'd developed an interest in forensic pathology even before it was a recognized specialty. Cases of child abuse particularly unnerved him, long before child abuse became a cause célèbre in the modern media.

And when he started his medical career in 1940, forensic medicine had far fewer tools than today. They had fingerprinting, blood typing, dental comparison, X-rays, and comparatively primitive toxicology. The best tools were a scalpel, a microscope, and a doctor's own eyes.

Dad started working part-time for the Chief Medical Examiner of New York in 1950, and was hired full-time in 1957 to be the deputy ME for Brooklyn, the most populous of the boroughs and therefore the morgue's busiest division.

My father dragged me and my three younger sisters to hospitals and morgues at a young age. He didn't want us to be afraid of death. It was partly because he just assumed that we'd all be doctors someday, but also because his own relationship with death was casual. He wanted us to respect the tragedy of dying, but be drawn to its mystery, too. He considered his grim work a lifesaving pursuit, an early warning system against epidemics, killers, and the simple human tendency to snap to judgment without the benefit of facts.

He needn't have worried about us. We kids often stole clandestine glances at Dad's gruesome crime scene and morgue photos, which he kept in files in his closet. We ransacked his bookshelves for surreptitious glimpses of corpses and fatal wounds. More than once, we were told to stay in the car when he was called to inspect a fresh body, and we strained mightily to see it.

To me, it was just life. It was a sad side of reality, but it was reality.

I recall a picnic on Staten Island when I was ten. At the time, my father was the deputy medical examiner for the largely rural borough south of Manhattan, and in those days his morgue was surrounded by open fields and undeveloped land. On weekends, the whole family often took the ferry to Staten Island—the Verrazano-Narrows Bridge hadn't yet been built—so my energetic father could squeeze in just a little more work. Afterward, we'd park in some shady spot behind his morgue, open the car windows, and listen to the radio while we ate lunch and played in what seemed to me, a Brooklyn kid, to be a vast wilderness.

On this particular day, we parked behind the morgue and piled out for another glorious outing. My father opened the trunk to retrieve the picnic basket and sitting right beside it, like some ordinary piece of luggage, was an open box containing a human skeleton.

He thought nothing of it. But more important, the little boy standing next to him—me—thought nothing of it either.

By the time he became New York City's fourth-ever Chief Medical Examiner in 1974, my father had a special phone under his bed for emergency calls. Cops would show up at the front door at all hours to take him to the latest killing floor.

Every night, he walked through the deepest, darkest hallways of the morgue to roust intruders who frequently sneaked in for macabre thrills. He even rooted out a secret call-girl and gambling ring that was operating out of the ME's office at night. And even though he managed the world's biggest and most political morgue, he still performed more than occasional autopsies alongside his 129 medical examiners, morgue assistants, investigators, drivers, and secretaries. All for just $43,000 a year, which was low even in those days, especially for the top forensic detective in a city that never sleeps and never stops dying. (As Deputy Chief Medical Examiner in Dallas at the time, I earned significantly more than my father.)

New York was broke, and the ME's office was slowly decaying. It was underfunded, understaffed, and inbred. My father was undeterred. Death didn't take a holiday.

Still going a mile a minute, he taught classes in medicolegal investigation at Brooklyn Law School, has staff privileges at several local hospitals, and lectured at St. John's University.

Through it all, his compassion and his coolness under fire remained intact. Not many people knew that whenever he got a new overcoat or pair of shoes, he didn't throw out the old ones. He took them down to "The Basement" and gave them to the low-paid dieners, the morgue attendants and autopsy assistants—diener being a term derived from the German word *Leichendiener*, which means "corpse servant"—who did the dirtiest work for the least reward.

My father didn't play political games well. In fact, he hardly played at all. He didn't back down from a fight, but he didn't pick them. And he didn't run to the *New York Times* with every high-profile death.

And there was death. Always death. Plenty of it. My father played a role in some of the biggest death cases in New York City history. Ironically, many of his cases would echo in my own career decades later.

In 1975, he reopened an investigation into the bizarre suicide of CIA scientist Frank Olson, who experimented with various biological weaponry for the government. In 1953, CIA agents secretly dosed Olson with LSD, and nine days later he plunged to his death from the thirteenth-floor window of his Manhattan hotel. The CIA told police Olson had suffered a nervous breakdown, and in a delusional, paranoid fog, he committed suicide. Based on the police investigation, my father, then only an assistant ME, declared it a suicide. Case closed.

Not quite. When my father learned twenty-two years later about the CIA's illicit drug experiments, he was angry. The Olson family sued the federal government, and my father took a fresh look at the case, which opened the door to an eventual exhumation in 1994. While no definitive conclusions could be reached forty years after Olson's death, many forensic experts believe Frank Olson was murdered by shadowy American agents who were never brought to justice.

During the four decades my father worked in the ME's office, bizarre and violent death was commonplace. The serial killer known as the Son of Sam paralyzed the city. He examined various remains thought to be Jimmy Hoffa (they never were). Mob hits happened with frustrating regularity. Malcolm X was assassinated at the Audubon Ballroom. Famed designer-to-the-stars Michael Greer was murdered in his Park Avenue apartment during an anonymous homosexual encounter, a 1976 case that remains unsolved to this day. Then as now, celebrities like gossip columnist Dorothy Kilgallen, poet Dylan Thomas, and troubled actor Montgomery Clift made headlines when they turned up dead in their hotel rooms, brownstones, or Upper East Side apartments. My father worked on many of them.

And he solved some mysteries, too. Take the strange 1954 death of Emanuel Bloch, famed defense attorney for atomic spies Julius and Ethel Rosenberg, found dead in his Manhattan bathtub at age fifty-two, just a few months after the Rosenbergs were executed. Bloch, the guardian of the late couple's two young sons, had made his bones defending unpopular figures. So it wasn't the first or the last of my father's death cases in which the media and public didn't wait for evidence before bubbling over with breathless cold war rumor-mongering. While the media cooked up anticommunist conspiracy theories, my father determined that Bloch had died of ordinary cardiac arrest. The headlines stopped quicker than Mr. Bloch's heart.

In the summer of 1975, the bodies of twin brothers Cyril and Stewart Marcus—both prominent gynecologists, bachelors, and peculiar geniuses who shared a thriving Manhattan practice—were founded dead on the floor of their luxury East Side apartment. They'd been dead for a week. Their inseparable, parallel lives ended just as they had started forty-five years before: together.

With no sign of foul play, detectives guessed it was a double suicide. Some blamed a simultaneous drug overdose, and the media had its own fanciful theories.

But my father revealed the real answer. The Marcus twins were barbiturate addicts, a secret kept by their closest associates. When their twin dependency threatened to leak out, they decided to go "cold turkey," just quitting one of the world's most powerful behavior-altering drugs.

Problem is, barbiturate withdrawal is a killer. It's worse than heroin withdrawal. An addict suffers convulsion and delirium, and his heart literally collapses. That's how the Marcus twins died. Their story alerted America to the problem of drug-addicted doctors and inspired David Cronenberg's 1988 movie, *Dead Ringers*.

Then something happened that for most of us would be unimaginable, but not for my father. It wasn't caused by a mysterious virus, a natural catastrophe, terrorists, or an especially prolific serial killer, but it thrust my father into the center of unspeakable carnage.

On a stormy June 24, 1975, an Eastern Airlines 727 crashed on its approach to John F. Kennedy International Airport in Queens. A mile from the runway, Flight 66 from New Orleans rose unexpectedly on a mammoth updraft, then slammed violently down in a microburst, sheering off its left wing on a row of light poles and falling to pieces in a spectacular disintegration.

One hundred thirteen people died in the fiery crash (although eleven people miraculously survived). It was America's third worst airline disaster at the time.

The charred and dismembered dead lay scattered everywhere. Within moments, a special phone rang in my father's Manhattan office, and he rushed to the scene to supervise the collection and examination of the remains. A slow parade of morgue wagons, packed with pine boxes full of human pieces and parts, filled the ME's office and a temporary tent-morgue on the crash site to overflowing. Working through the night and into the next day, my father and his team identified the dead, notified the next of kin, and prepared all 113 victims to be transported to their final resting places around the world.

And why wouldn't it have been unimaginable for my father? It wasn't his first mass-casualty disaster. It wasn't even his third or fourth. He'd been on the scene of the 1960 midair collision of two passenger jets over New York that killed 134 people, including six on the ground. He'd also worked with the remains of 95 people killed in the 1959 crash of a Boeing 707 that nose-dived into Jamaica Bay. And the 1950 Kew Gardens train crash that killed 78 commuters. And Eastern Airlines Flight 663, which killed 84 people when it crashed into the sea off Long Island in 1965.

If he hadn't seen all the ways a human can die, there were very few left for him to see.

One of my father's most notable cases, however, came after he retired as Chief Medical Examiner in 1978, and ironically didn't involve a death at all.

Three days before Christmas in 1984, a nebbishy electronics dealer named Bernhard Goetz, who was white, was surrounded by four black teenagers on a Manhattan subway. They wanted money from Goetz, who'd started carrying a concealed five-shot Smith & Wesson .38 after he was violently mugged in the subway a few years before.

Fearing he was about to be robbed by the youths, Goetz stood up, whipped out his handgun, and started shooting. He emptied his gun and wounded all of them. Nineteen-year-old Darrell Cabey took a single shot in his left side, and the bullet severed his spinal cord, paralyzing him as he slumped into a subway seat.

Crime in New York was at an all-time high and race relations were near an all-time low when the media dubbed Goetz the "Subway Vigilante." Goetz gave the world its seminal "stand your ground" case. One question obsessed the public: Had Goetz fired in self-defense, or was it a deliberate racist act?

It was the same question that echoed in the eerily similar shootings of Trayvon Martin in Florida and Michael Brown in Ferguson, Missouri, decades later. And just like those later cases, the nation erupted angrily about Goetz, split mostly down racial lines. Both sides made up their minds before the facts were collected.

At Goetz's trial for attempted murder, prosecutors argued that Cabey was sitting when he was shot and thus hadn't been a threat. The defense hired my father to examine Cabey's wounds and the crime scene, and he delivered a controversial opinion: Cabey had been standing when he was shot. The trajectory of the bullet was lateral and flat, not downward, my father said. Cabey couldn't have received the wound while sitting unless the six-foot-one Goetz had knelt beside him—which he didn't.

The jury of seven men and five women, including two African-Americans, was convinced. It acquitted Goetz of murder and assault charges, but convicted him of illegal possession of a weapon. He served just over eight months in prison. Cabey later sued and won a $43 million civil judgment against the bankrupt Goetz (who ran unsuccessfully for New York City mayor in 2005).

To New Yorkers, Goetz had committed another serious crime: He owned a gun. Only cops and criminals owned guns in New York City, and the city fathers deemed everyone else too dumb to be trusted with firearms.

In 1978, my father retired at age sixty-five, but his expertise was still sorely needed, and he still had enormous energy. He continued to consult on many death cases around the nation, and he joined me in writing a 1992 textbook called *Forensic Pathology*, which has become one of the science's preeminent references and remains in print today.

On September 11, 2001, Dominick Di Maio was a spry eighty-eight-year-old retiree living on Henry Street in Brooklyn Heights, just across the East River from Manhattan. On ordinary days, he could see the Twin Towers of the World Trade Center soaring over the Financial District, a little more than a mile away. He was a proud lifelong New Yorker, and he'd watched them go up.

On that day, he watched them come down.

In more than thirty years as a medical examiner, he'd never witnessed a murder, much less a mass murder, but here it was happening before his eyes.

He already knew what horrible carnage they'd find. He already knew what horrors man could visit upon his fellow men. He already knew there'd be no mystery about how all those people died.

But he never spoke a word of it to me.

That was my father. He never wanted to let death know it had touched him, and he never cried.

That stuck, too.

I grew up as strong-willed as he was. After I started medical school and started blazing my own path, we often clashed professionally. Not acrimoniously nor angrily, but vigorously. Our discussions could be epic and maybe a little loud, but I never stopped believing in my father. He set a standard I still aspire to. I still live with his expectations of me.

We carry our childhoods forward, even if we don't remember them perfectly or even as they truly were. We collect the stuff that sticks and haul it across the bridge of our teenage years into adulthood. When I check my baggage, I find my father's energy, his sense of justice, his fascination with mystery, his tendency to work away from the limelight, his ability to corral his emotions. I also find my mother's austerity, her pragmatism, her love of books and history.

And her stoicism.

When I entered St. John's College in Queens, New York, in the fall of 1958, I had none of the typical teenager's angst about where I was going. I'd known my purpose from the start. I was going to be a doctor.

I didn't find college that hard or stressful. I began as a chemistry major, then switched to biology, but the hardest part of my undergrad years was the traffic between my house and the campus.

Most people don't know that some medical schools will admit students after their third undergraduate year if they've successfully finished their necessary premed classes. So during my junior year at St. John's, I applied to two New York medical schools. One turned me away, saying it only took college graduates; the other, State University of New York's Downstate Medical Center in Brooklyn, less than three miles from where I grew up, left its door slightly open. It was all the encouragement I needed.

So, at nineteen years old, I passed the Medical College Admission Test (MCAT), sent in my application, and even went to SUNY for a nervous interview with some administrator in the medical school.

During a blizzard in February 1961, I went out to buy a newspaper for my mother. When I returned, cold and wet, I handed her the paper, and she handed me a letter from SUNY.

I had been accepted to medical school without a college diploma. I was to start that fall.

The first day of med school, the faculty gathered all the new students in a lecture hall for a pep talk. "Don't sweat about graduating," they said soothingly as they delivered sobering stats on graduation rates. The more they assured us, the more we worried. Imagine somebody telling you, "It's completely safe to fly in an airplane; only one in ten of you will die in a fiery crash." That's when I knew this wouldn't be a walk in the park, but failure wasn't an option. I couldn't be anything but a doctor.

Truth be told, I detested medical school. It was four years of Marine boot camp, but not as pleasant.

The first two years involved continuous sleep deprivation. Every day we did about twenty-six hours worth of study—not a misprint—on six hours of sleep. The next two years involved the same sleep deprivation and study but added hands-on procedures. We suddenly found ourselves doing things we never thought we could (or would) do.

Gushes of real-life amniotic fluid ruined my shoes. I went home at night with flecks of blood and vomit on my clothes. I discovered that patients often lie. I saw that it was actually pretty hard to kill somebody. And I learned to sleep standing up, braced against the walls during rounds or with my eyes wide open while a professor lectured.

To this day, when I must wait, whether in an airport or in a court-room hallway, I try to sleep.

But we also learned to stay calm, no matter the situation. I always thought doctors would be good in combat for their coolness under fire.

Everyone who was accepted to SUNY was certainly smart enough to get an MD. Lack of intellect didn't wash them out. The ones who left just didn't have the fortitude, the persistence, or the determination to survive the professors' withering cross fire. It took me a couple of years to realize what they were doing. They were brainwashing us, teaching us to think like doctors. Not lawyers, not accountants, not stockbrokers. Doctors think differently. We were beginning to adopt a certain emotional distance, learning not to get so close to patients that we couldn't do our work or so far from them that we couldn't hear what they had to say about their pain and fear.

Not every lesson was in a textbook. We learned to think logically, to not always accept what we were told, and to question what seems obvious. Non-physicians often jump from A to D, but a good doctor goes from A to B to C to D. One must attempt to accumulate all the facts.

My classmates were fascinating, too. There was Barbara Delano, who loved to argue politics with me in those heady days of the mid-1960s, as America tilted toward the worst days of Vietnam, racial strife, and campus revolt in a tectonic shift of our cultural plates. Once she accused me of holding thirteenth-century political notions. "No," I corrected her brusquely, "they're definitely tenth-century." (She later chaired Downstate's School of Public Health.)

And there was Chester Chin, who was so thin that the campus nurses tried to fatten him up with daily chocolate shakes. It didn't work, and he came to detest medical school (and probably chocolate shakes). After graduation, he became an orthopedic surgeon and refused to ever return, even for reunions.

But the first of us to become famous—infamous, really—was Stephen H. Kessler. A brilliant but troubled guy, he'd graduated from Harvard and entered medical school at Downstate with me. Before long, he started behaving erratically. One day he was caught tossing scalpels like darts at the cadavers in the anatomy lab. The dean forced him to take a leave of absence after his first year, and he checked into a mental hospital.

Kessler eventually returned to medical school but was kicked out again when he was caught giving LSD to patients.

Rumors circulated that Kessler was due to return for a third try when startling news broke in April 1966: Kessler had viciously slashed his fifty-seven-year-old mother-in-law to death in her Brooklyn apartment. (Coincidentally, my father did her autopsy and counted 105 separate wounds.) Kessler claimed he'd been tripping on LSD at the time, so the media dubbed him the "LSD Killer." It turned out he was high on lab alcohol and pills and suffered from paranoid schizophrenia, so he was eventually found not guilty by reason of insanity. He disappeared into the asylum at Bellevue and was never heard from again.

During those frantic med-school days, I often visited my father in the Brooklyn morgue. I'd seen dead bodies before, but these weren't the slides in my father's closet, or pictures in a medical textbook, or even the cleaned-up cadavers we poked and prodded in anatomy class. These were freshly dead, real people, pale or blue, with real bullet wounds, knife gashes, or no visible injuries at all.

I was fascinated mostly by the mobsters who seemed to come through my father's morgue doors with regularity in the late 1960s. The New York mob wars came and went, but the hits never stopped. The Mafia dead were always well-dressed, with alligator shoes, silk underwear, manicured hands. I'd never seen a man wearing clear fingernail polish until I examined those dead wiseguys on my father's slab.

As the end of medical school approached, I had to choose my specialty. What were the choices? There was an adage to consider: "Internists know everything but do nothing; surgeons know nothing but do everything; psychiatrists know nothing and do nothing; and pathologists know everything and do everything, but it is too late."

There was more. I had learned in medical school that (like my father) I had no bedside manner and that I couldn't master the complex knots a surgeon must know. I realized I'd be better with patients who didn't require reassurance and operations that didn't require lifesaving knots. Pathology was perfect. Pathologists were doctors' doctors.

After my one-year pathology internship at Duke University Hospital in Durham, North Carolina—where I finally decided to pursue forensic pathology—I started my three-year residency at the Kings County Medical Center in Brooklyn. During that time, I started performing autopsies for the Chief Medical Examiner's Office in Brooklyn under my father's watchful eye. By the time I finished my residency, I had already done more than a hundred autopsies before I worked a single day as a certified forensic pathologist.

My residency changed my life in another, more significant way when one of my supervisors introduced me to her secretary, Theresa Richberg, who at the moment was bent over her typewriter, her long blond hair obscuring her face. When she looked up, I was thunderstruck. She was beautiful. I guessed her to be in her mid-twenties, and when she spoke, I heard an articulate woman who seemed to be as smart as she was pretty. And among the first things she told me in that confident voice, scented with just a tantalizing whiff of Brooklyn, was that she was engaged to be married. She flashed a diamond ring to prove it.

I was deflated but not defeated. Over the next few days, I made a point of speaking to Theresa any time I passed her office. In our water-cooler chats, I learned that she sewed her own clothes, which looked to me to be the height of New York fashion. She laughed at my dry humor, which not everybody did. She was bright, strong-willed, opinionated, and sometimes argumentative—my kind of woman.

And when I told her I was just twenty-six, her jaw dropped. She'd thought I was just another bespectacled, distinguished, gray-haired old gent in his forties, nothing like the cocky, crude Italian boys on her block. I had class, she said.

A few weeks after we met, she came to work without her ring. She told me she'd broken off her engagement. (In fact, the ring was in her purse and she hadn't yet revealed to her fiancé that he'd been booted.) The next day I asked her out.

She also dropped another bombshell: She was just eighteen, albeit a very intelligent and sophisticated eighteen. Apparently neither of us looked our ages.

On one of our first dates, I picked up Theresa to go to the movies. She spied a big jar in the backseat. It was the stripped skin of a human hand floating in formaldehyde.

Another time, we had arranged to meet at the Brooklyn morgue before our date, but Theresa refused to go inside. So I told her to wait at the back door for me. While she stood there, a morgue wagon pulled up. Two attendants pulled a dead body from the back and placed it on a gurney—then placed the dead man's head on his chest.

After that, I wouldn't have blamed her if she fled screaming and never saw me again, but within a few weeks, she officially broke off her engagement to the other fellow.

A year after we started dating, Theresa and I were married at the venerable St. Blaise Catholic Church in Brooklyn's East Flatbush neighborhood. It rained right up to Theresa's arrival, then stopped, supposedly an omen of good luck. All our Italian relatives were there, there was lots of food, and the reception looked like a scene from the movie *Goodfellas*.

Back then, we were just a happy couple on the brink of our careers, but I had married a Renaissance woman. In many ways, her future was even brighter than mine: She would eventually leave her secretarial job and go to college, where she'd get a bachelor's degree in fine arts, become an in-store designer for Neiman Marcus, work as an interior designer, and sell her custom-made jewelry to Saks Fifth Avenue. She raised two children who grew up to become a doctor and a prosecutor. Incredibly, in years to come, she'd return to college for a bachelor's degree in nursing, work as a psychiatric nurse, be trained as a forensic nurse, and coauthor a book, *Excited Delirium Syndrome*, about a complex cocktail of mental and physical conditions that have proven suddenly fatal in many police arrests. Her work shed new light on the syndrome and led, in part, to its adoption as an accepted diagnosis by the American College of Emergency Physicians and the National Institute of Justice.

And, oh, she's an excellent cook, too.

Sadly, we divorced briefly in later years. I married another woman who, in a fit of anger, fired four shots at me. I very nearly became a customer at the morgue. She missed, thankfully. It's a very interesting experience, being shot at (and missed). I highly recommend it as a way to clarify your mind. You don't hear the gun going off. I saw it, but I couldn't hear it.

Anyway, we quickly divorced, and I immediately reconnected with Theresa, with whom I'd never really fallen out of love. We remarried after an almost ten-year estrangement, and I am blessed to have her again at my side.

I learned a lot during that middle period of my life. Most significant, maybe, is that when a woman pulls a gun on you, never say, "You wouldn't dare shoot."

But back in those early days, before those troubles, Theresa and I were just happy to have each other. I was locked in the rigors of becoming a doctor and she was finding herself, but we had each other, and we made a good team.

We still do.

Doctors have been solving crimes for a long time, even if medicine had no name for them until the mid-twentieth century.

Two thousand years ago, in 44 BC, Julius Caesar was stabbed to death by Roman senators in history's highest profile murder. A doctor named Antistius was summoned to examine the emperor's corpse. He reported that Caesar had been stabbed twenty-three times in the face, belly, groin, and arms, but only one wound—an upward thrust under his left shoulder blade that probably pierced his heart—had been fatal. The attack was so frenzied that many of the would-be assassins were cut, too. Antistius believed that if Caesar had not died from a sliced heart, he would have bled out in a few minutes as he lay unattended on the Senate floor at the foot of Pompey's statue.

It was history's first recorded autopsy.

A thousand years later in medieval England, the king appointed local cronies without any medical training to represent his financial interest in all criminal cases (as well as hear confessions, investigate shipwrecks, pardon criminals, and confiscate royal fishes). Also among these clerks' duties was to inspect the corpses in all unnatural deaths and record their observations in an "inquest." The appointee's duty to "keep the pleas of the crown"—in Latin, *custos placitorum coronae*—naturally led to his title as "crowner" or "coroner."

Leonardo da Vinci and Michelangelo dissected corpses to improve their art, but they also became fascinated by the irregularities they saw. Pope Clement VI ordered that corpses of plague victims be opened to see what was inside.

By the 1600s, the Age of Enlightenment, scientific advances and a fresh social conscience breathed new life into death and crime investigations. And in the late 1800s, fingerprinting revolutionized forensics.

In 1890, Baltimore gave two doctors the title of medical examiner and assigned them to perform all autopsies ordered by the county coroner. Many big American cities followed suit and eventually gave the responsibility for all death investigations to physicians, although our system of elected coroners, who often have no medical training at all, remains firmly entrenched in America today.

The first true medical examiner system was established in New York City in 1918 when the city abandoned its coroner system.

So we have two types of medicolegal systems in America: the coroner and the medical examiner. The coroner system, which dates back to tenth-century England, still prevails in about 40 percent of America's 3,144 counties, with 2,366 offices. In those places, the coroner is virtually always elected and almost never a physician. Even when the elected coroner is a doctor, he (or she) is not usually a forensic pathologist.

The job requirements? Oh, have a local address, not be a felon, be at least eighteen years old. That's about it. But that's no problem. Once elected, the car-salesman-turned-coroner magically acquires the necessary medical and forensic knowledge he needs to solve extraordinarily complicated deaths. And that leaves time for the most important job any politician has: getting reelected.

Elected coroners are often small-town morticians or cemetery workers whose daily contact with death makes it easy for voters to assume (incorrectly) that they are perfectly suited to the grim tasks of autopsies, blood work, body handling, and the occasional exhumation. Later in this book, I will tell a story about a backwater undertaker who boasted that his primary qualification to be the coroner was that he was the only guy in town who had a car big enough to properly haul a dead body.

Most coroner systems produce poor, inconsistent work; most medical examiners good, consistent work. In a 2009 book entitled *Strengthening Forensic Science in the United States: A Path Forward*, the National Research Council advocated eliminating the coroner system entirely, an idea that had been bandied about since 1924.

To date, nothing has been done. What was good for the tenth century is apparently still good for the twenty-first. And even in America today, when we have far more forensic tools than my father had when he became a doctor in 1940, the chances of a smart killer getting away with murder are higher in an elected coroner's jurisdiction than any jurisdiction with a medical examiner.

Despite the imperfection and inadequacy of the old coroner system, autopsies had solved thousands of American crimes by 1959, when forensic pathology was first recognized as a distinct discipline by the American Board of Pathology. In a huge moment when forensic pathology was finally legitimized, my father—then the Chief Deputy Medical Examiner for New York City—was among the first eighteen certified forensic pathologists in America.

That first class of medical detectives comprised some of forensic medicine's lions.

Dr. Milton Helpern, my father's boss in New York City from 1954 to 1973, was only the third medical examiner since the city scrapped its coroner system in 1918. He once said, "There are no perfect crimes. There are only untrained and blundering investigators, slipshod medical examiners." His name still graces the award given to the highest honor for any medical examiner, the Milton Helpern Laureate Award, which I received in 2006.

Dr. Russell Fisher was the Chief Medical Examiner for Maryland and built America's best forensic team and facility in Baltimore. Such was his reputation that in 1968, just before I worked for him in my first job out of medical school, he led the so-called Clark Panel in concluding that the autopsy on the slain John F. Kennedy—the autopsy of the century—was so badly done that it "left doubt where there should only have been absolute certainty."

Dr. Angelo Lapi had been Denver's first medical examiner and then moved to the Kansas City morgue. Blessed with a photographic memory, he was part of an elite team that listened to survivors of Nazi death camps and POW stalags describe wanton slaughter, dug up the decayed bodies, and collected evidence against their killers for the Nuremberg war crimes trials.

As the chief pathologist for the Cleveland coroner, Dr. Lester Adelson was a key witness against Dr. Sam Sheppard, an osteopath accused of murdering his pregnant wife. Convicted in his first trial and acquitted ten years later in his second, Sheppard's case was a media phenomenon that inspired countless articles, books, The Fugitive TV show, and several movies. After a thirty-seven-year career and more than eight thousand murder autopsies, Adelson retired to teach and write The Pathology of Homicide, one of the standard texts for forensic pathologists.

All these men had stories to tell. They'd seen death in all its violent colors. They were the best and brightest in a new discipline.

But forensic pathology wasn't then and isn't now perfect, either.

My father's and my career encompass the entire modern era of forensics, from a time when fingerprints and basic blood typing were the most "high-tech" forensic tools available, to today's DNA profiling and massive computer databases. But I believe with all my heart that if we could magically drop a 1940s medical examiner into a modern morgue with an afternoon's training on the new science, he'd function quite nicely. Why? Because a good forensic pathologist's best tools are still his eyes, his brain, and his scalpel. Without those, all the science in the universe doesn't help.

Today, there are only about 500 working, board-certified forensic pathologists in the United States—about the same number as twenty years ago. Problem is, we need as many as 1,500 to keep up with the steadily increasing parade of unexplained deaths.

Why, at the height of the profession's popularity, thanks to TV shows such as *CSI* and *NCIS*, is there a shortage of forensic pathologists?

Because it ain't as glamorous as TV makes it. One in five new forensic pathologists drops out right after training, and over a ten-year period, we lose 10 percent more of these new doctor-detectives.

The reasons are simple. For one, the job is complicated. To become a forensic pathologist requires four years of college, four years of medical school, and as many as five years of extra training after medical school. One must train first as an anatomical pathologist, at a minimum, before becoming a forensic pathologist.

But hospital pathologists earn twice the money in a job that's far less messy. A young doctor with $200,000 in student loans is easily seduced by a bigger paycheck (and needn't explain a lower salary to a befuddled spouse). To make matters worse, some forensic pathologists accept government salaries that are lousy even for underpaid FPs.

And the ultimate reality is that the job isn't nearly as glamorous as TV makes it.

They never mention how you can wake up to smell the stench of a decomposing body on your clothes or in your hair the next morning.

They don't show the maggots falling on you. They certainly never show autopsies that fail to find a cause of death.

TV isn't interested in the scientific truth, only a world it can imagine might possibly be true . . . maybe. But that's understandable because viewers aren't interested in scientific truth, either. Nobody really wants to see in prime time the pulverized innards of a baby who's been beaten to death, or a head that's been halved like a squash by a shotgun.

So it goes. You go home and you just forget about it. You can't live expecting everyone to be a sociopath or psychopath—they aren't. Only 1 or 2 percent of us are. You get mad, maybe, that people do such things. You just shake your head and go on with your life. Another mystery will roll through the morgue door any minute.

When the time came to do my one-year fellowship—a final year of training after residency—my father discouraged me from doing it in New York City. Once the paradigm of forensic excellence when my father started there in the 1940s, the New York City Chief Medical Examiner's Office had decayed. Even in the great Milton Helpern's last years as the chief, the biggest medical examiner's office in the world lacked state-of-the-art equipment, morale was funereal, it had become hard to fire some entrenched workers, and corruption had seeped in around the edges.

Baltimore, my father said, was the best. Dr. Russell Fisher had recruited the nation's best team of medical examiners and was in the process of building the most cutting-edge forensic facility ever conceived.

With a little nudge from my father, Dr. Fisher hired me, and on July 1, 1969, at age twenty-eight, I started my fellowship at the Office of the Chief Medical Examiner of Maryland with high hopes.

But Dr. Fisher's ultramodern morgue wasn't quite ready when I arrived. Instead, I started on one of the hottest days of a sultry summer in the nineteenth-century building on Fleet Street, near the harbor, that had housed the ME's office since James Garfield was assassinated.

In the old days, when ordinary people were more familiar with death, unidentified bodies would be propped up in the morgue's street-side window in hopes a passerby might recognize them.

The low-slung, old brick morgue was virtually attached to the city's sewage treatment plant, possibly by city fathers who wanted all of the municipality's malodorous mechanisms in one spot. Worse, it had no air conditioning, and the autopsy room grew unbearably hot in summer, so autopsists would open the old sash windows and hope the screens were intact so hungry corpse flies wouldn't stream in to feast on and lay their maggot eggs in our "guests."

In Baltimore, I began to see how other people grew blasé about death.

The Baltimore morgue had only two main areas, the autopsy room and the administrative offices up front. Before dawn every morning, the dieners would array the day's corpses on the tables in the small, unventilated autopsy room, ready for the medical examiners to splay them out under unforgiving, hot lamps that left patches of dark in the corners. Before the rest of the city was eating breakfast, the place already looked like a well-organized abattoir.

By midmorning, the secretaries and clerks would arrive for work, and the easiest way to the public offices from the parking lot was directly through the dank, fetid autopsy room.

Most of these administrative workers were young girls right out of high school—maybe seventeen or eighteen. Dressed in their summer skirts and fancy blouses, they would thread their way among the body-filled autopsy tables, primly carrying their sack lunches, chatting and giggling as if the corpses were not there.

Even then, I accepted my own nonchalance around dead people as a professional quality, but it seemed odd to me when "normal" people were detached around corpses.

Baltimore was a violent city then, as much as it is now. The parade of corpses never stopped, even when we moved a couple of months later into Dr. Fisher's palatial new morgue on Penn Street, where the air was cooled and cleansed, our cutting was hidden away, the lights illuminated every detail, and the office girls no longer sashayed among the dead.

I'd been on the job less than three months and was still just twenty-eight years old when one of the most fascinating and most important cases of my life landed on my table in the frail form of a dead baby.

‹ T H R E E ›

An Empty Nursery

A baby dies without dreams or memories.

That's why the death of a child is so tragic. We wish for them to know what we know about life, about us. They haven't yet wondered why there are stars, sung a song, or truly laughed. We yearn for them to have a chance to be happier than we ever were. We invest these new, tiny lives with hope.

Then that baby—that hope—dies, and we lose a little hope.

I'm often asked if it is harder to examine a dead child, but to be honest, it would be harder to look away.

BALTIMORE, MARYLAND. SUNDAY, SEPTEMBER 21, 1969.

Toward the end of a crisp fall weekend, the phone in our little suburban Baltimore apartment rang. On the other end was Walter Hofman, who was also a fellow at the Office of the Chief Medical Examiner of Maryland.

"Vince, I need a favor," he said. "Yom Kippur starts tonight and I'm taking off tomorrow. Would you cover my cases? There's not much. The only one I know for sure is a baby boy coming in from Hopkins."

Hofman didn't know much more about the case, except the child had multiple admissions but nobody really knew what killed him. I'd just have to look at the hospital's paperwork.

"Sure," I said. "Shouldn't be any problem at all."

The child was born February 9, 1969, to an unwed thirteen-year-old Maryland girl. Her pregnancy had been uneventful, but her child was born breech, meaning he'd come out feet or buttocks first, posing some risks as his head and umbilical cord squeezed through the birth canal together. Luckily, the birth was otherwise routine, and a healthy baby boy, six pounds and nine ounces, took his first breath on a Sunday in the midst of a killer nor'easter.

Nameless and unwanted, the small but healthy newborn fell directly from the delivery table into the cold hands of the government. A temporary foster family saw him through his first five months, during which he had no illnesses of any kind. His foster mother reported him to be a happy baby who was seldom irritable. In less than five months, his weight doubled, and he showed no signs of any defect whatsoever.

That spring, a perfect family appeared. Army sergeant Harry Woods, his wife Martha, and their two-year-old adopted daughter Judy had recently been transferred to Maryland's Aberdeen Proving Ground, where the US military tested chemical weapons and other equipment.

Harry was a mess-hall cook and Martha a stay-at-home mom. They'd each grown up in big families in Columbus, Ohio's blue-collar Bottoms neighborhood, where they met in 1958 after both had failed first marriages. They married in 1962 just before Harry shipped out to Korea while Martha stayed behind. Over the next few years, Harry went to Vietnam and Germany while Martha moved in and out of homes in Columbus, Ohio; Fort Gordon, Georgia; and Fort Carson, Colorado—where they adopted the infant they named Judy Lynn in

1967—before being transferred to the Army's Aberdeen Proving Ground.

Martha, now forty, had lost three natural-born children and suffered almost a dozen miscarriages. She desperately wanted another child, preferably a boy she could name after her youngest brother, Paul, who'd lost an infant child of his own eleven years before. The child could be physically or mentally disabled, she told the lady from the adoption office, but given her past heartbreaks, she'd rather not have a child who was physically unhealthy. She needed a new chance to prove what a good mother she was.

No red flags. A typical itinerant military family. An eager mother. A steadily employed father. A healthy older sibling. Harry and Martha were approved.

So in early July, a county adoption officer unexpectedly phoned. She told the Woodses a little boy was available. They could see him and, if they wanted, take him home. Ecstatic, they hurriedly shoved a crib into Judy's room in their Army-issue two-bedroom bungalow, bought some baby clothes, and welcomed their new son—Paul David Woods—on July 3.

Martha had what she wanted: a new chance.

A month later, on August 4, a paramedic carried Paul into the emergency room at Kirk Army Hospital, a worried Martha close behind.

Martha told the ER doctor that a little after lunchtime, Paul had been playing with Judy on a blanket spread across the living room floor when his head arched backward unnaturally and he keeled over. He stopped breathing and turned blue around his mouth, nose, and eyes. Martha scooped him up and began mouth-to-mouth resuscitation as she frantically dialed for an ambulance.

By the time the ambulance reached the base hospital, just a mile away, little Paul had recovered. The doctor described him as alert, active, and not in distress. The doctor ordered an X-ray to be sure the baby hadn't aspirated a toy, but his airways were clear. Maybe the child had suffered some kind of mild seizure, or maybe the mother had overreacted, but nothing appeared wrong. Twenty minutes after they'd arrived, the doctor sent them home.

A few hours later, Paul was rushed back to the Kirk emergency room, conscious but pale, limp, and cyanotic—the medical term for the bluish skin discoloration caused by a lack of oxygen in the blood. Martha told a new doctor that she'd returned from the hospital and laid Paul in his crib for a nap. After a while, she heard gasping, choking noises and found the baby had stopped breathing again.

This time Paul was admitted. The doctors still had no idea what might have caused his spells. For three days, they ran tests—chest and skull X-rays, an electrocardiogram, complete blood work, urinalysis, even a spinal tap—but all showed the baby to be completely normal. And during those three days, he showed no signs of breathing trouble. Perhaps more to soothe an anxious mother's nerves, the doctor blamed it all on an upper respiratory infection, although he saw no real signs of it. So the hospital released Paul a little before noon on August 7.

He wasn't away long.

The next afternoon, August 8, Martha told doctors Paul was playing in a bouncy chair while she talked to a neighbor through an open window when Paul suddenly gagged and went stiff. Again he stopped breathing, and again he turned blue. Again Martha called the ambulance. And again Paul was alert and active when he got to the hospital.

Puzzled doctors admitted Paul for a new round of tests—all of which showed nothing wrong, and Paul had no further breathing spells in the hospital. The attending physician attributed the episode to "breath-holding." Paul left the hospital four days later, August 12, happy and hearty.

But in less than twenty-four hours, he was back. This time, Martha reported he'd stiffened in a kind of seizure, convulsed, then stopped breathing completely while she held him in her arms. Harry had been just a few feet away when Paul started turning blue. At the hospital, doctors injected him with an anticonvulsive drug called paraldehyde, and within a few hours, Paul was again alert and active. A neurological examination and another spinal showed no problems whatsoever.

His doctors at the little post hospital were flummoxed, so the next day, they transferred Paul to Walter Reed Medical Center, the US Army's flagship hospital in Washington, DC, where they'd have more resources to solve this mystery.

But after five days of brain scans, electroencephalograms, more skull and chest X-rays, and a battery of other sophisticated tests, Walter Reed's doctors were stumped, too. They decided Paul suffered from "a convulsive disorder of undetermined etiology" and sent him home on August 19 with a prescription for phenobarbital.

Paul Woods had spent most of his sixth months on earth in hospitals that couldn't understand why he was there.

And he wasn't done.

The next afternoon, August 20, Paul was rushed to Kirk Army Hospital. He was in cardiac and pulmonary arrest—his breathing and heart had stopped. Working furiously, ER doctors injected adrenaline directly into his lifeless heart, shoved a tube down his little throat, and restored his breathing, but he was comatose and didn't respond to any painful stimuli. He was quickly transferred to Baltimore's Johns Hopkins Hospital, one of the world's best hospitals. His chart bore a simple narrative: "Worthy of interest is the fact that the baby never presented any difficulty while in the hospital, but always at home and less than twenty-four hours after discharge."

Martha told the Johns Hopkins doctors that she had laid Paul in his crib after lunch. As she got Judy ready for her nap, she noticed Paul wasn't breathing. His lips and face were blue. She blew little breaths into his mouth, but he was unresponsive. She ran outside and screamed for somebody to help. A neighbor rushed them to the hospital.

Doctors closely questioned Harry and Martha, who swore Paul had suffered no physical trauma, nor had he ingested any poison. But the parents raised a different possibility, almost as an afterthought and certainly never mentioned before: something toxic in the air. "Nerve gases" were being tested at the proving ground, they said, and the bay beside their home had been closed because "all the fish were dying from some chemicals that were spilled."

Suddenly doctors had a lead. They sent samples of Paul's urine and blood to a lab that identified "something abnormal," a foreign substance the lab said might (or might not) be an organophosphate known as diazinon—an insecticide. While they treated Paul for possible diazinon poisoning, they also learned the Army routinely sprayed two other insecticides on the post, although the dates didn't correspond to any of Paul's breathing spells, and subsequent tests of Paul's blood were inconclusive.

Then a shock. On September 9, twenty days after Paul fell into a coma, his adoptive sister Judy was admitted to Johns Hopkins. Dr. Douglas Kerr, a pediatric resident and a new father himself, worked the ER that afternoon and found Judy to be a lively child. No outward sign of any difficulty.

But Martha told Kerr that two-and-a-half-year-old Judy had collapsed, stopped breathing, and turned blue for a couple of minutes. After she started breathing again, she remained limp and sleepy, so Martha brought her in to be checked.

Martha struck Kerr as intelligent, caring, and knowledgeable, even as Harry appeared submissive and slightly dim-witted. She did most of the talking but was cooperative and courteous as he asked about Judy's surprisingly extensive medical history, which included at least five similar breathing episodes where she was rushed to the hospital after turning blue since she came to the Woodses as a five-day-old infant.

But Kerr sensed a reluctance in Martha on the subject of her own medical history—three natural-born children who died as infants of various defects, a stillborn baby, ten miscarriages, and sundry other ailments. He felt the middle-aged Martha might just be uncomfortable talking about such personal things.

Kerr was startled to learn that Judy's little brother lay comatose in Johns Hopkins's ICU, a few floors below. When he heard of the insecticide theory, he grew even more curious. Judy and Paul slept in the same room. If their air had been poisoned, wasn't it reasonable to think they'd both suffer the same symptoms?

The more he learned about the ongoing tests being ordered by Paul's doctors, the more Kerr suspected a darker story. Experts had found no insecticide in the Woodses' home; doctors found none in Judy's blood. A team of entomologists even collected insect carcasses in the area and found no unusual toxins. The house's ductwork wasn't leaking carbon monoxide or any other gas. Environmental explanations were thinning out.

The mystery obsessed Kerr. He learned more about Martha's first three dead children. He visited Judy every day. He pored over Martha's tragic and improbable reproductive history. He ordered more tests and asked more questions. If he had free time, he thought about Judy. He couldn't sleep. Some of the older doctors scoffed at Kerr's youthful passion; they'd stopped wasting time on crib deaths. But until he figured out what was causing these children to stop breathing, it wasn't safe to let Judy go home. He held the poor little girl close in a kind of protective custody.

Kerr's gut ached.

The young pediatrician contacted Child Protective Services with a chilling theory. Judy's and Paul's medical histories, and Martha's own words, hinted at something more horrible than insecticide spraying.

Finally, in an uncomfortable meeting, he revealed his suspicions to Harry and Martha. He told them things they didn't want to hear. They disputed it all. They got angry and pushed back. "Let the grass grow tall, and we'll cut it down," Harry snarled, and Kerr feared it was a threat.

Ten days after Judy was admitted, child welfare workers secretly checked her out of Johns Hopkins and took her away. When Martha went to Judy's room and Judy was gone, she wilted into a depressive blackout. She knew she'd never see Judy again.

Harry and Martha were forbidden from seeing Paul, too.

The little boy had continued to waste away. Only a machine kept him alive. His tiny limbs were jerking with involuntary spasms, his breathing grew so labored that doctors cut a hole in his throat to make it easier, and his body broiled with fever as his brain decayed.

Two days later, on Sunday, September 21, 1969, seven months and twelve days after he was born, and a month after he was admitted in a coma, Paul David Woods died, alone.

And the young Dr. Douglas Kerr had no idea that the dark story that haunted him would grow even darker.

When I arrived at the chief medical examiner's office in downtown Baltimore on Monday morning, Paul was waiting for me. The morgue wagon had delivered him the night before, and now he lay there under the brilliant fluorescent lights on my table.

I'd seen dead babies. I'd already done over a hundred forensic autopsies before I started my fellowship in Baltimore. I didn't get sad or angry. My faith and my training protected me. What I have on the tray is not a person but a body. Just a husk. The person, the soul, is gone.

In this case, I knew a Johns Hopkins pediatrician suspected abuse. I knew the mother had other children who died under questionable circumstances. I knew the insecticide theory. I knew this little boy had been to the hospital many times with unexplained breathing spells. And I knew a sister had experienced similar spells. It was time to let this child speak for himself.

I examined Paul, inside and out, for a few hours. He was twenty-seven inches long and weighed fifteen pounds. There were no external signs of physical abuse, although his last hospitalization had left its own painful marks. His eyes were clear. His nose and throat were unblocked. I saw a well-developed, well-nourished, seven-month-old boy whose first teeth hadn't yet come in.

I removed Paul's organs, one by one, examining them closely before making microscopic slides of their tissues. I was especially interested in his brain and lungs, which would reveal more of his story, but I looked at every part of him in a way that none of us ever sees (or wants to see) another human. For the most part, he had no infections, no poisons, and his heart was good.

I found nothing that would explain Paul's many breathing spells. Nothing. He had no apparent allergies. He was older than most crib deaths, which peak at three to four months. The presentation and sequence of his symptoms didn't match any disease process I knew. His death puzzled me, especially since so many doctors had found absolutely nothing wrong with him. It is impossible for anyone, much less an infant, to hold his breath long enough to die.

But he was dead. My job was to determine why.

His brain had been dead about a month, starved of oxygen. His brain injuries dated to the time of his last admission—the moment of his last breathing episode. He'd been dead even before he arrived at Johns Hopkins, but his revived heart continued to beat and his resuscitated lungs continued to breathe for a month. As the days passed, certain brain-controlled functions ceased. His lungs clogged with fluid, and blood backed up in his other organs until he died thirty-one days later.

Cause of death: Paul James Woods died of bronchopneumonia related to brain death.

In light of the other infant deaths in Martha Woods's history, and knowing that Paul's symptoms were consistent with deliberate temporary asphyxiation that left no marks or clues, my conclusion about the manner of Paul's death was rare at the time. And it was supported by my boss, Dr. Russell Fisher, one of the most respected medical examiners of his day.

"It is our recommendation," the report said, "that homicide be given serious consideration in this case."

I believed Paul Woods had been murdered, possibly by someone in his family, but I had no idea at that moment how this little boy's death would unravel an infernal crime bigger than all of us.

A few days later, Paul Woods was buried in the Babyland section on the western edge of the Harford Memorial Gardens near Aberdeen.

Harry, Martha, and one of Martha's sisters watched the tiny casket lowered into the ground. Nobody else came. The state paid for his heart-shaped bronze marker bearing only his names and dates. What else was there?

Very soon, Judy Woods was adopted by a loving Mormon family, and her breathing spells stopped entirely.

But the suspicions didn't subside, although nobody really knew just how big this case might be. Because Paul's possible murder had happened on a military post, the FBI got the case, but in its earliest days, it was tragically simple: Somebody killed a baby.

It didn't stay simple. His killer had made a huge mistake. Paul died of an interruption of the oxygen flow to his brain. He was smothered. The lack of oxygen to the brain caused brain death at the time he was assaulted. The assault was committed on a government reservation to a civilian (Paul). This meant that the case fell under the jurisdiction of the FBI, which had the time and deep pockets needed for a comprehensive investigation.

The more FBI agents dug, the deeper, darker, and sicker the story became. They dredged up decades of musty records from small-town courthouses, sifted through family memories, interviewed far-flung friends and neighbors, and chased leads that bounced back and forth across the country. A chilling image came into focus. What began as a *question* of abuse quickly became a *likelihood* of murder.

And all the evidence pointed to the woman who only wanted everyone to know she was a good mother: Martha Woods.

Martha was born at home on April 20, 1929, the tenth of thirteen children born to William and Lillie May Stewart, a truck driver and his especially fertile housewife. Born on the eve of the Great Depression, Martha mostly grew up in an extended family of seventeen people crammed into a two-bedroom, $15-a-month rental with very little of anything. A middle-school dropout, she'd worked a few menial jobs, in diners, laundries, and shoe factories, but never long.

Just before Thanksgiving 1945, at only sixteen, Martha Stewart got pregnant by a neighborhood boy. She had damn little to be thankful for. Just when she should have been attending high school dances and going steady, she was an unwed teenage mother-to-be without any income.

A month before her due date, Martha went into labor. A baby boy was born prematurely, weighing just over four pounds. She named him Charles Lewis Stewart, after two of her older brothers, one of whom drowned in Germany's Moselle River during the last days of World War II. But she just called him Mikey.

Mikey stayed in a hospital incubator for eleven days, but when he was finally released, he still struggled. Mikey slept with Martha in the upstairs bedroom she shared with her sister, a nephew, and several smaller children. He barely ate anything, Martha said, and when he did, he vomited it up. At one point, Martha's mother was feeding Mikey with an eyedropper, but it didn't do much good.

Then one day, quite suddenly, Mikey just stopped breathing and turned blue while Martha held him. Her parents rushed mother and child to Columbus's Children's Hospital. Doctors determined he was severely malnourished. Mikey was admitted, and over the next seven days, he brightened up and gained a surprising half a pound. He was sent home with some vitamins and some new formula.

Two days later, on August 23, Mikey died. Just like that. He'd been lying on the living room couch when he abruptly stopped breathing and turned blue. The police ambulance raced to the house, but it was too late. The coroner came and took Mikey's corpse away in his little black medical satchel.

Mikey wasn't autopsied, but his death certificate blamed an enlarged thymus (a typical diagnosis for dead babies in the 1940s) and "status lymphaticus" (a high-sounding term for crib death that's equivalent to a medical shrug, meaning absolutely nothing).

Only one month and four days old when he died, Mikey was buried not far from his war-hero uncle and namesake in the Wesley Chapel Cemetery on the outskirts of Columbus.

It wouldn't be long before another child's grave was dug beside him.

Four months later, at Christmas 1946, four children in that claus-trophobic little house had taken sick. One of them was Martha's plump three-year-old nephew Johnny Wise, son of her sister Betty, who was also a single, teenaged mother. Johnny had been playing in the snow on Christmas Day, and the next day the normally jolly toddler com-plained of a headache and sore throat.

That night Martha tucked Johnny in her own bed upstairs while Betty showered. A few minutes later, Betty screamed and ran down-stairs with Johnny's limp body. He had stopped breathing and was turning blue. The ambulance arrived too late to save him, but the house was quarantined for three days when health authorities feared an outbreak of diphtheria, a highly contagious upper respiratory infec-tion that was becoming rarer in the 1940s. On the fourth day, the quarantine was lifted and the family buried Johnny beside his late cousin Mikey in the frozen ground of Wesley Chapel Cemetery.

An autopsy was done, but the child's neck organs were not removed and examined—all necessary to diagnose diphtheria. Instead, the death was certified as diphtheria based solely on the other illnesses in the house, not on anything the autopsist saw.

In early 1947, seventeen-year-old Martha was arrested for forgery and sent to reform school for a year. When she got out in 1948, she flitted through a few waitressing gigs until a girlfriend introduced her to a twenty-two-year-old laborer named Stanley Huston. Within a few months, she was pregnant again, so she married Stanley in a hasty ceremony in January 1949 and lived in a series of apartments and bun-galows. Unfortunately, amid the chaos, Martha had the first of ten miscarriages, by her own count.

But she soon conceived again. Mary Elizabeth Huston was born prematurely on June 28, 1950, and stayed in the hospital for three weeks before Martha was allowed to take her to their new home, a five-hundred-square-foot rented bungalow. A week later, the month-old Mary suddenly stopped breathing and turned blue. Martha rushed her to the hospital, where doctors found nothing wrong and released her after two days of observation.

Eight days later, Mary was back in the hospital. Inexplicably, while Martha cradled her, she had stopped breathing and turned blue. Martha revived her with mouth-to-mouth, but doctors could find no cause for the breathing episode. They tapped her spine, shaved her head, and put needles in her scalp, but they found nothing. For three days, they watched the baby, who showed no signs of illness. In the end, they blamed it on an unknown respiratory infection and sent the baby back home.

On the morning of August 25—less than two weeks after her hospital stay—Mary again stopped breathing and turned blue in Martha's arms. Again Martha resuscitated her and took her to the hospital. Again doctors found the baby to be alert and vigorous and released her.

That same afternoon, Martha bathed Mary and fed her before laying her in her crib for a nap. Within a few minutes, Mary had stopped breathing and was turning blue. By the time she arrived at the emergency room, the baby was dead. She had lived only one month and twenty-seven days, most of them in a hospital bed.

Mary Elizabeth Huston was buried in a largely vacant family plot in the Beanhill Cemetery, a rural graveyard near her father's hometown in rural Vinton County, Ohio. No autopsy was done, but her death certificate said she choked on a mucus plug that was never found.

One more miscarriage and sixteen months later, Carol Ann Huston was born on January 22, 1952. The pregnancy had been a difficult one, and the baby was born by a cesarean section at only seven months. At birth, she was only about four pounds, so she stayed in the hospital about three weeks before going home to a new rented house in West Jefferson, a small town west of Columbus. Martha visited her almost every day.

For the first time in Martha's mothering, a baby thrived for a few straight months in her care. But it wouldn't last.

In May, Carol Ann caught a stubborn cold and developed a persistent cough. On the morning of May 12, before his hospital rounds, a local doctor came to the house and gave her a shot of penicillin.

An hour later, the baby was dead. Martha said Carol Ann had simply choked and turned blue. She died before the ambulance arrived.

Based on what Martha told him, the doctor signed the death certificate without an autopsy and declared the cause of death to be epiglottitis, a dangerous condition that happens when an infected epiglottis—a little cartilage "flap" that covers the windpipe—swells and blocks air flow to the lungs. He later admitted he hadn't actually observed such an infection but based his conclusion purely on what Martha told him.

Carol Ann had lived just three months and twenty-one days, the longest life span of Martha's three natural-born children. She was buried beside her late sister in the Beanhill Cemetery, where today they share a marker.

Martha fell into a depression bad enough that she tried to kill herself. On a morning in early December, after Stanley went to work, she pulled one of his guns from the closet. She chose an unusual one, an "over-under" double-barreled rifle that shot .22-caliber cartridges from one barrel and .410 shotgun shells from the other. The shooter toggled between them by pushing a little button.

She lay on the bed and held the barrel against her chest as she pulled the trigger. The gun roared, but miraculously she was still alive, with only a nasty graze across her left shoulder from a .22 bullet. She ran outside screaming until a neighbor drove her to the hospital, where doctors simply swabbed her powder-burned skin with antiseptic and bandaged her superficial wound with some tape. Martha told doctors she thought she was pushing the safety button when in fact she had switched the firing mechanism from shotgun to .22.

Martha scared Stanley. She was crazy. He drove her directly from the emergency room to the Columbus State Hospital, where he committed her involuntarily for almost two months.

Home alone in the spring of 1953 after the asylum released her,

Martha needed distraction. She took a job as a cottage attendant at the Columbus State School (which had only recently changed its name from the Institution for Feeble-Minded Youth). There she cared for mentally handicapped kids, aged six to nine, eight hours a day, five days a week. The perfect job for an experienced mom like Martha.

One day Martha was dandling a retarded child on her lap when she claimed he lapsed into an epileptic fit. He clamped his teeth on her fingers when she tried to prevent him from swallowing his tongue. He then just stopped breathing and turned blue. Her bosses praised Martha for saving his life.

Another time, one of her young charges was wheeled away on a gurney . . . unconscious, not breathing, blue around the mouth and nose. He was lucky Martha was there.

Life went on, day after day. It was a strange place for strange people, so nobody paid much attention to the strange things that happened to retarded kids.

In June 1954, Stanley was drafted into the US Army. By the time Stanley shipped out to Germany that fall, the marriage was on life support.

Twenty-five-year-old Martha bunked briefly at Stanley's parents' farmhouse in Vinton County. One day while she was there alone, Martha saw smoke billowing from the barn, so she rushed out to save all the animals inside just before the structure burned to the ground.

Although her in-laws praised Martha as a brave heroine, she soon moved back to her parents' Columbus house. When her divorce was final in August 1956, she rented a tiny row house that she shared with her unmarried teenage sister Margaret, who already had two young children of her own. Laura Jean was a toddler, and Paul Stanley was a newborn.

One day little Paul suddenly stopped breathing and turned blue. A hysterical Margaret called her boyfriend, a young auto mechanic named Harry Woods, who was about to join the US Army. Harry rushed them all to the hospital in his car, with Martha screaming the whole way to go faster.

In the emergency room, a nurse perched the barely breathing baby on a table beside a wall-mounted oxygen hose but couldn't find a mask small enough to fit the child. When she left the room to search for one, Martha grabbed a paper cup, jabbed a pair of scissors through its bottom, and inserted the oxygen line. After she pressed her improvised oxygen mask over Paul's nose and mouth, he quickly began breathing easier. Once again, the quick-thinking Martha had averted a catastrophe and saved a baby's life.

She also eventually stole her sister's boyfriend, Harry Woods. They started flirting later that year, just before Harry was sent to Korea for two years.

By May 1958, Martha was living alone in an efficiency apartment, where she slept on a sofa bed off the kitchen. At the time, Martha's only income was $108 a month from a worker's compensation claim after a career-ending head injury she suffered in a scuffle at the state school. She told doctors she was having terrible headaches and as many as twenty seizures or blackouts every day, and they concluded she must have epilepsy. (Those symptoms magically vanished completely when the State of Ohio paid off Martha with a lump sum of $2,800 in 1959.)

Ever the dutiful sister, she invited her unemployed little brother Paul Stewart, his wife, and their fourteen-month-old daughter Lillie Marie to live with her until Paul could find work. Four people shoehorned into a no-bedroom apartment would be tight, but Paul's family could sleep on Martha's couch and she'd bunk on a borrowed cot in the breakfast nook.

On May 18, they all went to bed early. Some time before midnight, Martha got up to go to the bathroom but heard a choking noise in the dark. It was the baby. Martha cried out.

Lillie Marie's startled parents awoke to see Martha in the shadows, holding their limp baby. Then she ran downstairs and down the street, two blocks to her parents' house, where they called an ambulance.

But it was too late. Lillie Marie Stewart hadn't breathed for several minutes, and her face was blue. She was dead when the medics arrived.

No autopsy was performed, but doctors attributed her sudden unexplained death to acute pneumonitis, the general term for a lung inflammation they never actually saw.

And she was buried at Wesley Chapel Cemetery beside her cousins Mikey and Johnny, who'd died so similarly. The family plot was filling fast with little graves.

All a heartbreaking coincidence, the family said.

Crib death must just run in our blood, the family said.

And poor, poor Martha had bravely tried to save them all, the family said.

After dating steadily for a few years, Martha and Harry were married in the pastor's study of her mother's Columbus church on April 14, 1962, a week before Martha's thirty-fourth birthday. They lived with Martha's parents briefly before Harry shipped out to Korea for a year, and then in early 1964, Harry returned Stateside to Fort Carson, Colorado. He and Martha rented a cozy one-room cottage between two of Harry's buddies in nearby Colorado Springs.

Martha made fast friends with the other young Army wives. So fast that she'd hardly unpacked her moving boxes when the wife of a military mechanic who lived in the cottage behind the Woodses asked Martha to babysit while she worked. Martha was delighted to help.

Marlan Rash was just a year old on January 10, an unseasonably warm winter day in Colorado. Martha was alone with him in the house when Marlan suddenly stopped breathing, passed out, and turned blue.

Martha administered mouth-to-mouth and rushed Marlan to the nearby Army hospital. He was conscious when they arrived, but lethargic. Doctors poked and prodded him for five days, testing his spinal fluid, blood, and urine, X-raying his skull and chest, examined his brain patterns . . . and found nothing wrong with the child. They chalked up his breathing spell to an epileptic seizure and sent him home.

It happened again a few months later, May 3. This time Martha said she found little Marlan lying in the yard, unconscious, feverish, convulsing, not breathing, blue. Again she gave mouth-to-mouth and rushed him to the hospital, and again the child was subjected to four days of testing that showed nothing. Once more, baffled doctors sent him home with a vague diagnosis of "acute pharyngitis and seizures."

Back home on May 7 after another exhausting hospital stay, Marlan's mother again left him in Martha's care and went to work. The baby bawled when she left, but Martha left him in his crib to cry himself to sleep. Only a few minutes later, she claimed to hear a gurgling noise and found Marlan rearing his head back, choking and turning blue in the face. She tried to breathe into his mouth, but it didn't work. Little Marlan Rash, just eighteen months old, died in her arms.

His autopsy said simply: "Death, sudden, cause unknown." When he was buried a few days later in Evergreen Cemetery, Martha dutifully attended to support his bereaved mother.

Harry shipped out to Vietnam in 1965 and Martha moved back to Columbus to care for her ailing widowed mother. In 1966, her mother died, Harry came home from the war, and they returned to Fort Carson, where they eventually ended up in the same cottage where Marlan Rash had died.

But now they had new neighbors, the Thomases, another of Harry's Army buddies, his wife, and two children. One day, while the ever-helpful Martha babysat the couple's eighteen-month-old son Eddie, the child choked in his crib and turned blue. Martha revived him in the front yard by dislodging what she called a large mucus plug from his throat, then drove him to the hospital. Afterward, she offered to show Eddie's mom the actual mucus plug in the grass, but couldn't find it. Dogs must have eaten it, Martha surmised.

Eddie survived, and Martha continued to babysit him and his

siblings for almost a year as Harry and Martha applied to adopt a child of their own. Their dream of starting their own family came true in July 1967 when a five-day-old baby came into their lives. She'd been born to an unwed teenager in Denver. They named her Judy Lynn.

Almost from the start, Judy was in and out of the Army hospital with colds, infections, and breathing spells. In December, five-month-old Judy was hospitalized for a week after passing out in her crib and turning blue. Then it happened again the next March. Twice.

During those first few months, other strange things happened to the new little family. The family home caught fire twice, but both times Martha saved Judy. And then a strange woman began calling almost every day after Harry left for work, demanding that Martha surrender Judy or die. Martha reported the frightening calls to military police and civilian cops, but they continued for months.

One day when Martha was home alone with Judy, a menacing dark man appeared at her living room window. He wanted Judy. When he threatened Martha, she picked up Harry's handgun and shot the man through the screen. He ran away wounded, Martha later told police, and got into a car driven by a woman.

The incident rattled Harry and Martha, so they asked the Army to transfer them out of Colorado, beyond the reach of these strange people who wanted to take Judy away. The Army obliged, plucking them out of Fort Carson and setting them down in new quarters at the Aberdeen Proving Ground, Maryland.

But it didn't work. Within days, the calls started anew. Then Martha reported the swarthy man she'd wounded in Colorado was back at her door in Aberdeen, demanding Judy. She chased him away again—possibly saving Judy's life again—and again reported the incident to military police.

This time Army detectives told Martha they'd put a "trap" on her phone to catch the culprits. The calls and scary visits stopped. Years later, the cops admitted they'd never actually tapped Martha's phone.

With the threat behind them, Harry and Martha sought to adopt another child. They applied to the county authorities, submitted to interviews, and openly discussed the loss of Martha's three little babies.

They left everything else out. Nothing about Johnny Wise. Or Lillie Marie Stewart. Or Marlan Rash. Or Eddie Thomas. Or those two retarded kids. Or Judy's spells. Or the fires. Or the mysterious callers.

And certainly nothing about how many children who'd come within arm's reach of Martha Woods and stopped breathing long enough to turn blue.

The math is grotesque but simple. Over twenty-three years, at least seven children died and at least five others suffered dangerous breathing spells in Martha's care. They all had different parents, lived in different places, had different histories, but their deaths were eerily similar. And one person was always there: Martha Woods.

The FBI had seen enough. In November 1970, more than a year after Paul Woods died, Martha Woods was indicted by a federal grand jury on eleven counts, including the first-degree murder of Paul and the attempted murder of Judy.

Martha pleaded innocent to everything.

The case was assigned to a young assistant US attorney named Charles Bernstein, barely a couple of years out of the University of Maryland law school. He was a plucky young guy who'd clerked for a judge during the day to pay for his night classes.

Until Bernstein called me, I'd forgotten about Paul Woods. I didn't know his case had gone any further, much less that his mother had become the prime suspect in his murder. My fellowship in Baltimore was done and I was now a major in the US Army. I was about to become the new chief of the Wound Ballistics Section of the Armed Forces Institute of Pathology, the office that studied fatal war wounds for all branches of the military—still a busy place in those waning years of Vietnam.

When I autopsied Paul, I believed there was about a 75 percent chance he'd been murdered. A good chance, but plenty of reasonable doubt for a jury to acquit any accused killer.

When I read Judy's complete medical history, my certainty rose to about 95 percent. Almost a sure thing, although still room for a legal doubt.

But when I saw the pile of dead babies strewn in Martha's wake over the past twenty-three years, and how they died, I knew *without a doubt* that Martha Woods had killed those children.

Federal murder cases were rare when Martha Woods's file landed on Bernstein's desk. To be honest, he thought she was crazy as a loon and was likely headed straight for a padded room at St. Elizabeth's mental hospital. But shrinks who examined Martha at Walter Reed during Paul's and Judy's hospitalization found no signs of insanity. In fact, they found Martha to be remarkably sane, forcing Dr. Kerr to find another reason to remove Judy from the home.

Nevertheless, Martha's sanity was a central issue at her trial. Her court-appointed lawyer offered an unusual defense: She didn't kill Paul (or any other children), but if she did, she was insane.

Bernstein's argument was no less unusual: He couldn't prove Paul's death, all by itself, was murder, nor could he prove any of the other six children's deaths, separately, were murders. Only when these unexplained deaths in three decades were considered together did the sinister pattern emerge. Only then was Martha Woods's true guilt apparent.

Problem is, dating back to British common law, courts had forbidden "prior bad acts" as proof of the defendant's guilt. The fact that other children died similarly in Martha's care—especially if she hadn't been charged in those deaths—couldn't be used as evidence that she murdered Paul.

Bernstein faced an uphill legal battle. He'd never prosecuted a murder. Martha's defense lawyer was a sharp-minded and sharp-tongued veteran named Robert Cahill. Bernstein's defendant was a soft-spoken, motherly little lady who didn't look like a killer. His key witnesses were a young pediatrician and a young medical examiner, both of whom had barely started their careers. And one of the American jurisprudence's most monolithic concepts stood between him and a guilty verdict.

Bernstein took the death penalty off the table, fearing it might be a last, insurmountable hurdle for wavering jurors. At worst, Martha faced life in prison.

The stakes were high. If Martha was acquitted or found not guilty by reason of insanity, she would walk away a free woman. At the time, federal law made no provision for hospitalizing delusional people who committed crimes. They were simply not held responsible for the damage they did.

But Martha swore she wasn't guilty and she wasn't crazy, either. She yearned for her day in court. She believed she could convince a jury of her innocence, just as she'd so often convinced friends and relatives she was a hero, not a killer.

On February 14, 1972—Valentine's Day—the trial began, with US District Judge Frank A. Kaufman telling the jury of four men and eight women that he expected the case to last only about three weeks. While he spoke, Martha fidgeted with the buttons on her simple cloth coat, her doting husband Harry beside her at the defense table. Every day for the rest of the trial, Harry worked his duty hours in the early morning and drove to Baltimore to sit with Martha in the dock.

Early on, the pretty Mormon mother who had adopted Judy Woods testified that Judy had suffered no further breathing spells since coming to her home, and was proving to be a normal, active child. (Outside the courtroom, she told Bernstein how the toddler Judy once tried to quiet a crying baby by pinching its nose and holding its mouth closed. Where would a little girl learn such a thing?)

A string of witnesses pieced together the grim death toll, from Mikey in 1946 to Paul in 1969, in a blizzard of alien medical terms. Even if the jurors didn't understand the words, they knew in their hearts that this was no unfortunate series of accidents. They had to ask themselves: How many babies have I seen choke and turn blue? How many babies have I watched die? How many of them was I holding in my arms?

The insecticide defense fell apart quickly, too, as experts, including me, said no evidence existed that Paul (or Judy) was poisoned.

The insanity defense, based largely on a defense contention that Martha suffered epileptic seizures during which terrible things might happen (not that they ever admitted these terrible things actually happened, mind you), was damaged by Martha herself: She didn't think she had epilepsy and vehemently denied she was insane.

Two psychiatrists, two psychologists, two neurologists, and a medical doctor agreed with her.

"One crucial theme is the tremendous importance she attaches to being a good mother, a role that appears to constitute much of her identity," said one psychiatrist who examined Martha. "For her, being a good mother seems to involve being overprotective of a totally dependent child . . . she described the hurt she felt when a child showed the earliest signs of autonomy, such as rolling over without aid."

Did Martha smother those babies when they showed the first signs of not needing her, or were they simply the easiest to kill? They certainly didn't fight back and they couldn't testify against her, and killing them was so simple it left no marks. But her motive remained elusive.

I testified for a week about Paul's autopsy, my growing certainty about Paul's case being a homicide, the other cases, and the medical improbability of one family's having multiple crib deaths. (The term "sudden infant death syndrome" was just coming into the lexicon and not widely used at the time.)

Martha's defense lawyer quarreled with my theory, citing the case of a Philadelphia family that had lost eight of its ten children from 1949 to 1968 to unexplained crib deaths (the other two died of known natural causes). The Noe family's extraordinary tragedy was even featured in a 1963 *Life* magazine article that dubbed matriarch Marie Noe "the most bereaved mother in America." At that moment, none of us knew the Noe family's dark secret.

The most riveting witness was Martha herself. She testified for a full week. With an extraordinary memory for dates, places, addresses, and names, she chronicled her life, loves, homes, jobs, ailments, paychecks, conversations, and deaths she'd observed, sometimes even correcting lawyers on both sides when they stumbled. She spoke so softly that the judge had to ask her several times to speak up. She remained cool on the stand, dabbing her eyes with a handkerchief most often when she talked about Paul or Judy.

When confronted with incriminating or conflicting testimony from relatives, friends, and even her husband, she asserted in her unruffled little voice that they simply weren't remembering correctly.

One day during a break, Martha stood outside the courtroom, cuddling a friend's baby in her arms. Bernstein was horrified by what he considered an overt stunt, but the judge couldn't very well order her—a woman presumed innocent for the moment—to avoid babies.

For more than thirty hours of testimony, Martha Woods was the epitome of sanity, even if Bernstein increasingly saw her as a brilliant sociopath.

A big question hung in the air: If she'd killed those kids, what was her motive? Millions of words had been spoken in this trial, but nobody knew.

The trial expected to last three weeks dragged out for five months. Along the way, four charges related to Judy's assault were dismissed, focusing the verdict entirely on the death of Paul Woods.

In his closing, defense attorney Cahill savaged Dr. Kerr and me as inept rookies (and if he could have gotten away with it, he might have said the same about prosecutor Bernstein). Bernstein's whole case, Cahill said, was a "house of cards" built on suppositions, assumptions, and bad science.

"I submit, ladies and gentlemen," Cahill said, "that Dr. Di Maio should add another specialty to his curriculum vitae, and that's meteorologist, because he renders opinions like a weatherman . . . a seventy to seventy-five percent chance [of murder]. . . ."

Prosecutor Bernstein hammered back, answering Cahill's attacks point by point. Then he apologized, in a way, for more than five months of sad, thick, tragic, uncomfortable, nauseating, sometimes contentious jabber.

"Somebody is not being heard from, ladies and gentlemen," he said. "It's these children who were killed, who were attacked before they learned to speak. . . . Who speaks for Paul Woods? There is no lawyer here for him. Who speaks for Judy? Who speaks for Charles Stewart? For Carol Ann? For Mary Elizabeth? For John Wise? For Lillie Marie? For Marlan Rash?

"The answer is, ladies and gentlemen, you do. They'd like to have some justice."

The jury took almost two days to reach its verdict: Martha Woods was guilty on all counts.

"I did not hurt the child," a sobbing Martha said at her sentencing a month later as the ever-loyal Harry embraced her. "If I did not want the child I would not have went and got him."

She also offered an odd deal to the judge: If he didn't send her to prison and gave Judy back to her, she'd let her brother raise the little girl and she'd never associate with children again.

"I don't want to be around a baby," she said, weeping. "All my life, all I wanted was a family. Now I don't want one. I don't want children. I don't want to be around them."

Judge Kaufman sentenced her to life in federal prison, plus another seventy-five years on the lesser counts. She wouldn't be eligible for parole until 2003.

Martha went directly to Alderson Federal Prison Camp, a minimum-security lockup for women that was nestled in the scenic Allegheny foothills of West Virginia. Built in 1928 to resemble a college campus, Alderson was nicknamed "Camp Cupcake" when a different Martha Stewart was incarcerated there in 2004.

Now in her forties, Martha Woods was older than most inmates and kept to herself. Over the years, she impressed her guards as being matronly, cooperative, eager to please, and a snitch. She was also quick to complain about various ailments, real and imagined, to get special perks.

Harry moved to West Virginia to be near her and retired from the military in 1980. He visited faithfully every week, and they'd sit together in the prison dining room talking for hours.

In 1975, would-be assassin Sara Jane Moore, who took a shot at President Gerald Ford and missed, came to Alderson. She was about the same age as Martha, and they were drawn to each other immediately. They remained close until Moore escaped briefly in 1979 and was transferred to another prison. She was freed in 2007.

"Being a baby killer in a prison full of women, she had a hard row to hoe," Moore recalled recently.

Martha's appeal was denied. In a 2–1 decision, the Fourth Circuit US Appeals Court upheld the argument that, in this extraordinary case, her "prior bad acts" were admissible.

Martha remained defiant. Sixteen years into her life sentence, she fired off an angry six-page letter to the court, claiming she was railroaded in a "grave miscarriage of justice" and asking to be freed immediately from prison. She condemned me and other "so-called expert witnesses," the government, her own lawyer, even the judge. She claimed, in the end, no hard evidence of murder was ever shown in any of the babies' deaths. Her request was denied.

In 1994, sixty-five-year-old Martha was transferred to Carswell Federal Medical Center, a prison hospital in Fort Worth, suffering from hardening of the arteries of the heart and chronic obstructive pulmonary disease (COPD). Doctors managed her symptoms, with frequent setbacks, over the next eight years.

Just before dawn on April 20, 2002, in the prison hospice, Martha Woods stopped breathing and died. She was seventy-three.

Her dying wish was to be buried in the Wesley Chapel Cemetery, in the same family plot where her parents, war-hero brother, son Mikey, nephew Johnny, and niece Lillie Marie lay. But the plot had no more empty graves—partly because Martha had helped fill them— so Harry took her body back to his home in West Virginia, where she was buried in a private graveyard on Madams Creek. And although Harry remarried after Martha's death, he was buried beside her in his full military dress uniform when he died in 2013.

He never stopped believing she was innocent.

The murder of a child by an adult, especially a parent, is one of the most difficult crimes for us to understand. Such murders are usually committed in the heat of passion or insanity. Much rarer, thankfully, is the deliberate and systematic murder of children over a long period of time for no apparent reason.

At the time of Paul Woods's smothering, there was no such diagnosis as Munchausen syndrome by proxy, a psychological disorder first defined in the late 1970s. Even today, skepticism persists. It is not listed as a specific behavior in the *Diagnostic and Statistical Manual of Mental Disorders* (*DSM*), although modern medical literature cites more than two thousand cases of Munchausen by proxy worldwide. But the St. Elizabeth's psychiatrist who examined Martha didn't need a fancy name: "I won't testify to this, but [Martha's] getting something out of this," she told Bernstein privately. "She likes the attention."

Nor did we have the term "serial killer"—not widely used until the 1980s—when Martha Woods was convicted. The public is naïve about a human's potential to kill. They expect murderers to be easily detectible fiends, but they aren't. Woods was a psychopath who had no trouble killing kids and never thought twice about it. Still, her name shows up on few lists of American serial killers even though she murdered more people than infamous American psychos such as "Son of Sam" David Berkowitz, Aileen Wuornos, Gary Heidnik, Ed Gein, and Westley Allan Dodd.

In 1974, Charles Bernstein and I wrote about Martha Woods's crimes in the *Journal of Forensic Sciences*. "A Case of Infanticide" became a watershed article that radically changed the way medical examiners and prosecutors looked at cases of multiple "crib deaths" in a family.

The case was important for two reasons, medical and legal. A peculiar kind of serial killer—a kind not typically recognized and prosecuted at the time—was unmasked by medical and forensic evidence.

But after Woods, prosecutors and pathologists had a new tool. The case changed how the law looks at "prior bad acts," especially in these cases where a series of seemingly ordinary events add up to a terribly extraordinary calamity. Martha Woods set an unwitting precedent, especially in infanticide cases: Similar deaths in the past may be used as evidence against an accused killer, even if the prior deaths aren't charged.

We gained a new maxim in forensic pathology, too. In 1989, I wrote in my book *Forensic Pathology*: "One unexplained infant death in a family is SIDS. Two is suspicious. Three is homicide."

Remember the Noe family that defense lawyer Cahill held up as an example of multiple crib deaths in a family? In 1998, seventy-year-old Marie Noe was arrested in her Philadelphia home and charged with deliberately smothering eight of her natural-born children between 1949 and 1968.

All were born healthy but died from unexplained causes at home. None lived longer than fourteen months. In each case, they were alone with their mother.

Marie confessed to killing four of her children but claimed she couldn't remember what happened to the others. Marie didn't pay the same price as Martha Woods: She got only twenty years of probation, five of which were spent under house arrest. (The extraordinarily light sentence came in a 1999 plea deal. Since no direct physical evidence linked Noe to the deaths, and the case rested solely on insufficient autopsies and her confession about decades-old events, prosecutors feared she'd walk. The deal might have served more as closure than justice.)

Then there was Marybeth Tinning. Her nine healthy children died suddenly between 1972 and 1985 before they turned five. All died at home in Schenectady, New York . . . all while alone with their mother. In 1987, Tinning was convicted of smothering her three-month-old infant daughter and sentenced to twenty years to life in prison. At this writing, she was still incarcerated but coming up every two years for parole.

At first I didn't grasp the scope of Martha Woods's case, but over time I got angry for three reasons. First, if the FBI hadn't been involved, no local police agency would have spent the time and money to unearth Martha Woods's sordid past. She would have continued killing kids.

Second, she could have been stopped sooner with adequate forensic investigation and autopsies, but the medicolegal systems in many parts of the country are junk, especially where coroners are elected by popular votes and might have no real forensic training.

And finally, I am angry that I still don't know her true death toll. There are huge gaps in her history. Years. We have no idea how many children she killed or injured. Just the dozen or so cases we found made me sick.

Were there other victims? Probably. The FBI's investigation of Martha's past was efficient, not deep. The bureau was overwhelmed in the early 1970s with antiwar and racial unrest, domestic terror, political chicanery, and fear of more assassinations. A frumpy housewife wasn't a high priority. To have found more of Martha's victims might have answered some other families' questions, but it might have taken another year or more. Did we want Martha Woods walking free during that time? Regrettably for any other possible victims, the government had to go with what it had.

Today, nobody who ever cradled Paul James Wood, who remembers him laughing or crying, who saw him smile, is still alive. In his very short life—only seven months—he landed in the care of nobody who valued him enough to tend his memory, much less his health. His birth mother gave him up to a woman who wanted only to kill him and a system that failed him.

A few of us knew him only in death, which is not a fair way to be remembered, even if his death brought Martha Woods's crimes to light. And we're forgetting that, too.

The Office of the Chief Medical Examiner of Maryland has filed Paul's autopsy file under a different name, and the cemetery where he was buried has lost all records of him. So Paul James Woods's entire memory is now contained in a heart-shaped bronze grave marker and four seldom-seen cardboard boxes in a cavernous federal warehouse, where the sketchy records of Martha Woods's murder trial are stored.

Maybe we were destined to someday forget him entirely, but it feels way too soon. If he had lived, he'd be a man in his mid-forties today, not much older than Martha Woods when she was convicted of smothering him. God knows what he might have become. I'll admit that I rarely think about him. I rarely ponder lives unlived, not because I am apathetic and cold, but because I would be overwhelmed.

Still, I wonder what became of Judy Woods. Does she know she was rescued from almost certain murder? I'm told she continued to contact Harry Woods from time to time until his death in 2013, and that he might have helped her out with money now and then. After Harry's funeral, she called the mortuary to ask if he'd left her anything in his will, but they didn't know.

No matter how Judy's life turned out, she was a lucky one.

Of all the doomed children who lived under Martha Woods's roof or were entrusted to her care, at least Judy got out alive.

‹ FOUR ›

Bombed Beyond Recognition

What would you die for?

Our world isn't made up of good guys and bad guys, like cops and rob-bers. We're just bewildered humans, prone to misunderstandings and fears, steeped in hatred, aroused by our self-interest, doing what we feel is best for ourselves and our own. The world is a messy place. And we're all part of it, sometimes doing the right things for the wrong reasons.

Or the wrong things for the right reasons.

So maybe the question should be: What would you kill for?

BEL AIR, MARYLAND. MONDAY, MARCH 9, 1970.

As the least senior guy in the barracks, barely a year out of the academy, Maryland state trooper Rick Lastner drew the short straw: He was the only state cop on ordinary patrol duty in the graveyard shift. Everybody else had a bigger assignment.

All was quiet, one of those cold March nights in Maryland, where darkness fell early and drained the color from Bel Air. Toward mid-night, only lampposts, porch lights, and the occasional passing car il-luminated the silent streets. Between the sliver of a moon and the relative quiet of a Monday night, this farming town was a black-and-white hush.

But the dark had eyes. A big trial started the next day. Notorious black militant H. Rap Brown, who'd seized control of the once-peaceful Student Nonviolent Coordinating Committee (SNCC) and declared "We're gonna burn America down," was to face a jury for inciting violent race riots that nearly gutted the nearby town of Cambridge, Maryland.

Rumors swirled through town that there was more violence ahead for Bel Air, where Brown's high-profile trial was moved. As it drew closer and raucous protesters whipped the town into a frenzy, the governor had deployed the National Guard, volunteers were hastily deputized, and local cops went on high alert, all fearing a firestorm. Bel Air was on edge.

Tonight, sitting in the side-street shadows, a sheriff's deputy watched a dirty white 1964 Dodge Dart slowly circle the redbrick antebellum courthouse a couple times, then vanish back into the night. He thought he saw two figures in the front seat, maybe men, but it was too dark to make out any details, including the license plate. Maybe nothing, he thought. Nobody followed.

Out on Route 1, trooper Lastner rolled through Bel Air toward Baltimore, which glowed faintly in the clear night sky a half hour south. It was too quiet, he thought. *Damn radio's probably gone out again.* The older radios' tubes burned out occasionally. He might be cut off from everybody else.

Lastner wasn't the kind of guy who lost his cool. He grew up in the inner city and joined the Marine Corps right out of high school. Before he was twenty, he'd been shipped to Vietnam. He served in the hottest zone, I Corps, which the grunts nicknamed Indian Country. Before he was wounded himself, he'd seen things nobody should see. Other kids his age were in college, but he was carrying the remains of his dead comrades in ponchos, watching them bleed out in the jungle. Now he was the oldest twenty-five-year-old he knew. His training kept him cool; his memories kept him wary.

To test his radio, Lastner knew to click the microphone and relay a test sequence back to dispatch. There was only one car on the road ahead of him, so he cruised around it. He glanced casually at it as he passed. A white Dodge Dart. A couple of guys, both in front. Not speeding or swerving. Except for the time of night, nothing else seemed amiss. No reason to be suspicious. It barely registered with him. He just wanted to get someplace to test his radio.

The trooper accelerated. When he was safely more than a block ahead, he picked up his radio microphone to test it.

As he keyed up his mic, the night erupted behind him in a massive orange fireball.

The Dodge Dart vaporized.

Stunned by the explosion, Lastner slammed on his brakes and whirled his cruiser around as the twisted front end of the disintegrated, driverless car rolled past him. He squinted back into the snarled wreckage. A smoking crater a foot deep in the middle of the highway marked the epicenter of the blast. Heaps of twisted metal lay scattered for a hundred yards in all directions. Wisps of foam and cotton batting from the Dart's demolished upholstery floated down like snow.

He leaped from his car and stepped on something soft. It was a steak-sized slab of human flesh. The air reeked with the coppery stench of a burning flare, but there were no fires and no sounds. Dead quiet.

Nothing that resembled a car remained, much less the two humans inside.

Lastner saw two mangled bodies on the asphalt—really just the bigger remnants of two bodies—steaming in the cold night. They'd been thrown almost a hundred feet in the detonation. One was just a torso with stumps where his limbs and head should be. The other was shredded but at least still looked vaguely human.

When he finally radioed that he had an explosion with two fatalities on Route 1, the dispatcher was at first incredulous, then chided him for broadcasting fatalities without the 10 code.

But they were unquestionably dead.

Soon sirens wailed in the distance. Lastner just stood in the midst of the dark, silent, fetid havoc and waited for the cavalry to arrive.

It was Vietnam all over again.

I heard the news on my car radio as I drove to work the next morning

I was just a few months short of finishing my one-year fellowship in the Office of the Chief Medical Examiner of Maryland. In July, I'd literally start my next tour of duty—as almost all doctors did at the time—as a major in the Army Medical Corps. My first assignment was to head the Medico-Legal Section of the Armed Forces Institute of Pathology in Washington, DC. The following year, I was assigned to the Wound Ballistics Section, where I'd finally get a chance to see, up close and on a massive scale, the ruinous effects guns and bullets have on the human body.

But at the moment, the two corpses on our tables—or more pre-cisely, the pieces of two corpses—were not killed by bullets or mis-siles. They died in an explosion, likely a bomb, less than twelve hours earlier. I didn't know too much more that next morning when I saw their shattered remains for the first time.

Deputy chief medical examiner Werner Spitz assigned my colleague Dr. Irvin Sopher and me to autopsy our two unidentified corpses. But our usual mission—who were they and how did they die?—was suddenly more urgent than ever.

Before all their unfortunate pieces had been collected from the scene, rumors were already circulating that one of them was H. Rap Brown himself, and that he'd been assassinated by a bomb thrown into the car or planted beneath it. Within an hour of the blast, still in the wee hours, the FBI was demanding answers, fast.

The American landscape was already on fire with antiwar and ra-cial unrest. In the fourteen months before the Bel Air explosion, more than 4,300 bombs had been set off by militant groups like the Black Panthers and the Weather Underground, and another 1,000 were dis-armed, failed, or went off prematurely. Thousands of bomb threats every day closed government buildings, oil companies' offices, big factories, draft offices, and skyscrapers across a skittish America.

If the militant Brown had been assassinated, federal agents feared his violent followers might unleash a hellish backlash. An already festering America might rupture into a race war. It'd make the riots in Watts and the nationwide anarchy after the King assassination look like prayer vigils.

Less than twenty-four hours after the Bel Air explosion, even as we worked to identify the victims, a dynamite bomb in a ladies' restroom blew a thirty-foot hole in the Dorchester County Courthouse, where H. Rap Brown's trial had originally been scheduled before it was moved to Bel Air. A white woman was seen hurrying away and was never caught.

The clock was ticking. And every minute seemed to be marked by a deafening roar.

Our task was a grim one, but we had to be right and we had to be fast. Nobody had to remind us about the consequences of failure.

Dr. Sopher had the easy job.

On his table lay a reasonably intact black man around thirty years old, his face still recognizable. A neatly trimmed mustache and goatee framed his mouth. Fully dressed in shredded slacks and shirt, he was stiff with rigor mortis.

He'd been found lying on the roadway beside a curb eighty feet from the blast crater, thrown to the driver's side of the car. He still smelled strongly of unburned gasoline, burned flesh, and smoldering hair.

He carried a wallet and driver's license, but investigators had found charred identification papers for several people in the debris. We couldn't be sure that the name on the driver's license was in fact the dead man lying before us, even though there was a resemblance to this picture.

When his ragged clothes were removed, Dr. Sopher noticed a single deliberate scar over his left nipple: a two-by-two-inch diamond around the letter K—similar to the logo of Kappa Alpha Psi, a traditionally black college fraternity. He'd been branded.

His injuries were confined to the right side of his body. The bones of his mutilated right leg had been shattered into little pieces, dislocated completely at the knee, the skin and muscles shredded. The skin of his lower left leg and what little remained on his right leg was burned and black with soot.

The bones of his right forearm and hand, like his right leg, were smashed to bits, held together only by his charred skin.

But his lower-body injuries ended in a bizarre line at mid-thigh, exactly twenty-seven inches from the soles of his feet. There was no damage—burns, cuts, or anything else—on his back and buttocks, and very little on his front torso. X-rays showed no shrapnel in him, and toxicology found no alcohol or drugs.

Dr. Sopher opened him up and found catastrophic damage to his hearts and lungs. They had hemorrhaged profusely in the blast. It was an injury seen commonly during the London blitz in World War II, when the concussion of exploding Nazi bombs killed people who might show no serious external injuries. Their vital organs had literally been smashed by the jolt of the blast.

So, too, had the bones on the right side of the victim's face. His brain looked as if he'd taken a mammoth punch.

Because of where the body was found (on the driver's side of the wreckage, near where the steering wheel had landed) and the injuries to the right side of his body, we determined this victim had been the driver and that the blast had come from low on the passenger side of the car. His relatively undamaged torso and upper thighs had been protected from the explosion by the seat of the car.

But maybe more troubling was not what we found inside the body, but in its pockets.

It was a kind of manifesto, half suicide note and half warning. It was crudely spelled and typewritten:

To Amerika: I'm playing heads-up murder. When the deal goes down I'm gon be standing on your chest screaming like Tarzan and the looser pays the cut. Dynamite is my response to your justice.

Guns and bullets are my answers to your killers and oppressors and victory is my sermon in your death. For my people I will chase you into a pit of hell with both barrels smoking and maybe the best man win and God Bless the loser. Power than peace.

Friends who'd rushed to the scene claimed they recognized the man, and later relatives identified him positively at the morgue. Fingerprints eventually confirmed it. He was Ralph E. Featherstone, a thirty-year-old male with a Washington address.

Who was Ralph Featherstone? State investigators quickly confirmed Featherstone founded and managed the Drum and Spear Bookstore in downtown Washington, which specialized in books by and about black people and was a focal point for an increasingly militant racial politics. When the firebrand H. Rap Brown took control of the SNCC, he made Featherstone one of his key lieutenants. Together, they forcibly transformed the SNCC from a nonviolent integration group to a full-fledged black power movement that promoted violence against racist white society.

Featherstone started as an unlikely militant. A graduate of the District of Columbia Teachers College, he'd taught "speech correction" in several local elementary schools. In 1964, he participated in the historic Mississippi Summer Project to register black voters and opened about forty "Freedom Schools," where he taught literacy classes, constitutional rights, and black history to some three thousand students. Friends recalled him as quiet, studious, and contemplative.

He'd been arrested in Selma, Alabama, during the 1965 freedom marches, and spent eight days sleeping on the concrete floor of the county jail, eating beans and cornbread for every meal, and getting angrier and angrier.

But inside Brown's newly radicalized SNCC, "Feather" (as he was nicknamed) also grew belligerent and bitter. He admired Ernesto "Che" Guevara and Karl Marx. He came to see all blacks as twentieth-century slaves who must revolt against their white masters and create an autonomous African-American state, with absolute power over every aspect of their lives. He became an unapologetic black separatist.

He didn't know it, but the FBI started watching Featherstone in 1967. As the SNCC got bolder, the feds got more interested in Feather. J. Edgar Hoover's file on him was already a couple of hundred pages in March 1970. They knew that he'd traveled to communist Czechoslovakia in 1968, then later flew to Havana to celebrate the anniversary of Castro's Cuban revolution.

Just a few weeks before he died, Featherstone had married a teacher who was also active in the movement. Still a newlywed bride, she was now also a widow. A month after the fatal blast, she would scatter his ashes in Lagos, Nigeria.

In life, Featherstone had been a hero to the black community in Washington. In death, he was a martyr. Within hours of the incident, before any details were known, the SNCC issued an angry press release that morning, calling the deaths "vicious murders." Black neighborhoods around Fourteenth Street started to seethe. *Feather was assassinated by the white man,* they murmured. They plotted revenge, but Featherstone's family urged restraint, a calm before any storm.

But a storm was definitely building.

We had identified one of the victims, Ralph Featherstone, but we still didn't know how and why a bomb might have exploded in or near his car.

If there was any good news amid this grimness, it was that our first victim wasn't H. Rap Brown. But our second victim, whose damage was far worse, was a much more difficult and dangerous forensic puzzle.

And we didn't have a good feeling. H. Rap Brown hadn't been seen since the night before and couldn't be found anywhere.

There wasn't much left of the body on my table.

The blast had amputated both legs below the knees. His right forearm and left hand were also missing. His upper right arm had a nasty fracture from which the humerus protruded at a peculiar angle. His thighs were split like fish up to his crotch, the arteries, skin, and muscle cut to ribbons by the blast. His genitals were gone.

His buttocks and pelvis had literally been blown apart, splitting his lower body in half.

A jagged wound stretched from the pubic area to his breastbone, exposing his pureed intestines and frayed chest muscles, but an odd three- to five-inch band of undamaged skin stretched across his belly. His neck, arms, and chest bore even more deep gashes, although the skin of his back was intact.

His jaw, neck, and pharynx were a bloody pulp. His face was flattened and collapsed; what was left of his skull was in a hundred pieces beneath the skin, like broken marbles in a torn paper bag. His eyeballs had burst in their sockets and dried into crusty shells.

Inside, this man's heart and lungs had suffered even worse hemorrhages from the blast. His brain was mush.

Most of the damage was to the front of this man's body.

Like Featherstone, this unfortunate victim had no alcohol or drugs in his system, but X-rays showed something more intriguing: A metallic object embedded in the back of his mouth proved to be a 1.5-volt mercury battery. The films also showed scattered metallic parts—a spring, several rivets, two half-inch-long wires, and many other unidentifiable metal fragments—in his chest and abdomen.

And in a final bit of forensic sleuthing, I found his penis and a flap of his palm in the man's jumbled intestines.

This victim was found about sixty-three feet from the remnants of the passenger side of the Dart, the opposite direction from driver Featherstone. Taking this location and the nature and distribution of his injuries into account, we deduced this was the passenger.

In the meantime, the FBI's experts had concluded the bomb had been about ten sticks of dynamite wired to a battery and a key-wound Westclox alarm clock. They identified the clock from tiny pieces found at the scene. The explosion had been so immense that it shook houses two miles away.

We were starting to see what happened.

The bomb couldn't have been in the glove compartment, under the instrument panel, or under the seat because that didn't fit the nature of the two men's injuries. It had to be somewhere near the passenger-side floorboards.

It couldn't have been planted under the car because the blast pattern, the damage to the chassis, and the angle of the wounds suggested it was inside the car.

It couldn't have been thrown into the car, crime scene specialists said, because all the windows had been rolled up and Trooper Lastner had seen no other vehicles anywhere on the road that night.

There was only one explanation: The bomb had been on the passenger-side floor, between the legs of our unidentified victim. His grievous injuries suggested he had been leaning over it, possibly with his hands on it, when it exploded.

How did we know? His injuries were symmetrical, proving the blast had been directly in front of him. That strange band of skin across his belly was protected because he had been bent forward, creating a fold of skin across his abdomen. His chin and neck had absorbed the bulk of the blast. And the force had blown his hand and genitals upward into his body.

When the bomb went off, Featherstone's right hand was on the wheel, and his right side bore the brunt of the explosion.

It all added up to one thing: Featherstone and his still-nameless passenger knew they were carrying a lethal package. They couldn't have missed it.

Now we knew the driver's name; we also knew that the bomb was inside the Dodge Dart. We strongly believed these two men were knowingly transporting the bomb when it detonated prematurely. Had they intended to blow up the Bel Air courthouse but were scared off by the enormous police presence there? We still don't know to this day, but it's a good theory.

Eager to forestall charges of a cover-up, the Maryland state police publicly revealed what we knew about Featherstone and the bomb's location, and the reaction was immediate.

"Almost before the wreckage was cool," responded US representative John Conyers, Jr., a black Michigan Democrat, in a letter signed by twenty of the biggest names in the civil rights movement, "the Maryland authorities were certain they had the answers. Ralph Featherstone, they said, was fooling around with high explosives. Those of us who knew him are sufficiently convinced of his level-headedness to be desirous of a better explanation of his death."

But a day later, we still didn't know who Victim No. 2 was.

The FBI was picking up chatter about new violence related to the Bel Air bombing. Brown's lawyer William Kunstler, a champion of leftist causes, publicly questioned whether the FBI or any other government agency could fairly investigate this tragedy. "I'm always suspicious of the official story," Kunstler told the *Washington Post*. Militants openly charged authorities with assassinating innocent Americans. A hungry media was already starting to ask, "Where's H. Rap Brown?"

Time was running out.

We worked through the night to identify the nameless man in our morgue.

His own mother wouldn't have recognized his obliterated face. Other than the obvious damage, he had no identifying scars, deformities, or tattoos. His hands were gone, so there were no fingerprints. We had some teeth, but without some idea of who he was, we'd have no dental records to compare. We had requested dental files for the missing H. Rap Brown but so far, none had been found.

Making matters worse, investigators sifting through the debris found two different identity cards with different names (C. B. Robinson and W. H. Payne), Navy discharge papers for a William Payne, a library card for somebody named Will X., and three photographs bearing three different names—but all showing adult black males consistent with our unknown corpse. (And none were H. Rap Brown.)

Was Brown fleeing prosecution with new identities? Or was our dead man one of several Featherstone friends the FBI couldn't find? We knew nothing.

While police meticulously scoured the blast site for more clues and started tracing the documents, Dr. Sopher set to a grim task: reconstructing the dead man's face with its own tissues, hoping to create an accurate enough copy that somebody might recognize him.

The documents yielded our first clue.

The military documents said William H. Payne had enlisted in Covington, Kentucky, and would now be in his mid-twenties, which was consistent with our dead man. The US Navy's Department of Medical Records rushed Payne's 1961 medical history to us and we quickly saw that his blood type (O+) matched the corpse.

But the dental records didn't match. The Navy's dental X-rays clearly showed five filled cavities in the young sailor's mouth. Our corpse had only one.

We scratched Payne off our list of possibilities.

Problem was, we were hitting dead ends in our search for C. B. Robinson, and without records that would include or exclude H. Rap Brown, we were dead in the water.

Dr. Sopher's facial reconstruction was our best bet. Using copper wire and a drill, he pulled the shattered bones of the corpse's face back into place and wrapped the flensed face around them. We took photos of the new face (shading the areas of the worst damage) and prepared to circulate the pictures in the news media, hoping somebody would step forward with an identity.

But the macabre reconstruction furnished an unexpected benefit: We suddenly noticed a strangely irregular front hairline and random bald patches in the man's coarse black close-cropped hair.

Comparing our dead man's hairline to recent photos of Brown, we saw significant differences. And when we compared the distinctive shape of the corpse's left ear to photos of Brown's left ear, they didn't match.

So H. Rap Brown didn't die in the Bel Air explosion. That relieved a lot of people, but Victim No. 2 was still somebody and it was our job to determine who.

The second morning after the bomb went off, we got a break. A searcher found two small patches of skin at the scene that looked like fingertips. Along with the ragged palm skin that I retrieved from the corpse's belly, FBI fingerprint analysts came to a disturbing conclusion.

The two bits of skin were actually a man's right thumb and left pinkie finger.

And they belonged to William H. Payne.

We were mystified. How could the same man's fingerprints and dental records be different? Could one or both be wrong? We needed more evidence before we could say that a man named William H. Payne had been blown to bits in Bel Air, possibly by a terror bomb he intended to plant in a very public place.

The personal papers from the wreckage held the key.

The two different identity cards held no obvious clues. The one for C. B. Robinson had a picture, W. H. Payne's didn't. The birthdates were similar, but not the same.

Will X.'s library card held no obvious clues either.

But on the back of one of the photos, someone had scrawled the name "Minnie" with an Alabama phone number.

Police detectives called and Minnie answered. She didn't know anybody named C. B. Robinson or W. H. Payne, but she admitted giving the photograph to her close friend Will X. several months earlier. She said Will always wore a gold earring in his pierced ear. Minnie didn't know where Will might be now, but she gave the cops a Detroit phone number where he might be reached.

The Detroit number was Will's employer, who confirmed that Will had been there earlier that same day. A few hours later, Will called the Medical Examiner's Office with a new piece of the puzzle. He knew W. H. Payne, who'd visited just a few weeks earlier. And the library card and Minnie's photo had been in his wallet, which he lost around the time Payne was visiting.

When asked to describe his friend Payne, Will said his only physical peculiarities were "a funny forehead hairline" and "patches of baldness." Not only had we observed the corpse's irregular hairline and alopecia, but the photo on C. B. Robinson's identity card showed a similar hairline . . . but Will X. knew nobody named C. B. Robinson and had never heard Payne mention anybody by that name.

Finally we had somebody who might be able to visually identify our corpse. We believed C. B. Robinson and William H. Payne were probably the same person, but until Will X. looked at the Robinson photo or the dead man's face, we wouldn't have solid proof.

In the days before email or even common fax machines, we had to be creative. We asked a newspaper reporter to help us wire a photo to a Detroit TV station, where, at a time prearranged with Will X., the photo would be broadcast. Will X. had instructions to look at it and call us as soon as possible.

Well, it all fell apart in a flurry of technical difficulties, but the photo was published the next morning in the Detroit newspapers, and Will X. positively identified C. B. Robinson's identity-card photo as his friend William Payne.

Later in that third day since the Bel Air explosion, Payne's family rushed to Baltimore from Kentucky. They, too, recognized the C. B. Robinson photo before looking at the reconstructed face for a further, conclusive identification. It was definitely their twenty-six-year-old son and brother, William H. Payne.

Payne and Featherstone were key members of the faction that led a coup on the SNCC leadership in 1966. Although not as prominent in the movement as Featherstone, Payne played a behind-the-scenes role as one of Brown's most trusted lieutenants, one of his strong-arm goons.

Payne's history paralleled Featherstone's. He grew up the fourth of eight children in a lower-middle-class family and attended the University of Kentucky and Xavier University in Cincinnati. When he dropped out of Xavier in his junior year, he spent two years in the Navy before rejoining the SNCC as a field worker in the Deep South.

Friends described him as having "a general antipathy for whites." At a recent Washington demonstration, Payne had interrupted the speakers and yelled, "Let's go home and get our guns—enough of this talking!"

His militancy earned him the nickname Che, after the violent revolutionary Che Guevara, but not everybody saw him that way.

"He wasn't any more militant than any of the rest of them," his mother told a young *Washington Post* reporter named Carl Bernstein— still a few years before his Watergate reporting—when Payne was publicly identified as the second bomber. "Most young colored boys and girls are militant now. They're just not swallowing what the old folks swallowed."

A few days before the blast, Payne had arrived in Washington from Atlanta for H. Rap Brown's trial. Friends told police he had arranged to meet with Featherstone and Brown in Bel Air that weekend.

Payne spent most of Monday, March 9, with Featherstone at the Drum and Spear Bookstore. Around two p.m., Featherstone borrowed a car from his neighbor, also a friend in the SNCC, but he didn't tell her where he was going and she didn't ask. A little after eight p.m., Featherstone closed the bookstore and left with Payne.

The last time anybody saw them alive was a few minutes later when Featherstone stopped briefly at his father's townhouse on Tenth Street NW.

Four hours later, they both lay in pieces on the asphalt outside Bel Air.

We concluded, officially, that Ralph E. Featherstone and William H. Payne (aka C. B. Robinson) died when a bomb they were transporting detonated prematurely at 11:42 p.m., March 9, 1970, on Route 1 just south of Bel Air, Maryland. The cause of death in both cases was massive trauma from a dynamite explosion. The manner of death was an accident, not a homicide.

The discrepancy between the Navy's dental records and the teeth in the corpse's mouth was never resolved. We assumed that the military records had been mixed up, not uncommon in those days, but we never solved that mystery.

And the FBI's bomb experts never pinpointed why the bomb went off. Did a nervous Payne accidentally set it off when a state trooper unexpectedly passed in the middle of the night? Had it been set to go off at the courthouse but never placed because of the police presence and never fully disarmed? Did a powerful electronic pulse from trooper Lastner's police radio trigger the detonator? We still don't know and never will.

A few days later, William H. Payne's family took his ruined body home. He was buried in a little cemetery on the outskirts of Covington, Kentucky, where every Memorial Day his grave is marked like every veteran's, decorated with the flag of a country he wanted to overthrow.

But where was H. Rap Brown, the elusive firebrand who'd set this tragedy in motion and kept America on the brink of chaos for several days? Had he slipped out of their grasp again?

Almost two months later, on May 5, 1970, the FBI added Brown to its Ten Most Wanted list. Post-office posters warned that he was likely armed and dangerous. "Where's Rap?" became a rallying cry among black radicals as cops everywhere in America looked for the incendiary rebel.

But Brown wasn't in the United States. He'd secretly fled to Tanzania, where many SNCC expatriates had gone.

Eighteen months later, a New York City cop shot an African-American man on a rooftop after a robbery at a West Side bar. The wounded man identified himself as Roy Williams.

But Roy Williams's fingerprints matched Hubert Gerold Brown, better known as H. Rap Brown. Charged with armed robbery and attempted murder of a policeman, Brown pleaded innocent. He was convicted after a ten-week trial and sent to New York's Attica Prison, where he converted to Islam and changed his name to Jamil Abdullah Al-Amin.

Released in 1976 from Attica, Al-Amin moved to Atlanta, where he opened a small grocery store. SNCC had dissolved, and the old militants had died, moved on to new issues, or just given up. And H. Rap Brown, aka Al-Amin, claimed to be a changed man, too. He literally followed in his hero Malcolm X's footsteps by making a pilgrimage to Mecca. He told a newspaper reporter that Allah doesn't change societies until the individuals change themselves. He wrote about revolution through prayer and character, quite different from his war-like earlier book, *Die, Nigger, Die!*

Soon he cofounded a mosque in Atlanta's West End, a mostly black enclave where he lived. Through programs of "spiritual regeneration," he was credited with creating neighborhood patrols, starting youth programs, rescuing drug abusers, and all but cleansing the neighborhood of prostitution. He'd apparently evolved from a ferocious extremist to a merely passionate spiritual leader.

But not everybody was quick to applaud. The FBI had kept an eye on Al-Amin, amassing a 40,000-page file on him. Local cops secretly suspected him of murder, gunrunning, and at least one assault.

On March 16, 2000, a Fulton County sheriff's deputy was killed and another wounded in a shootout in the West End while trying to serve Al-Amin a warrant for an unpaid speeding ticket. He fled briefly before he was arrested. In 2002, he was convicted of first-degree murder and twelve other counts, and sentenced to life in state prison without the possibility of parole.

Georgia handed over the troublesome high-profile killer to federal authorities. Today he is in his seventies, incarcerated in the ADX Florence Supermax federal prison on the plains of Colorado with terrorists, cartel kingpins, mob hit men, and serial killers such as al Qaeda's Richard Reid and Zacarias Moussaoui, Unabomber Ted Kaczynski, and Oklahoma City bomber Terry Nichols.

H. Rap Brown might have changed his spots, but deep down, he remained the sociopath who spawned a wave of domestic terror that has reverberated over more than forty years.

And I can't help but think that Ralph Featherstone and William Payne, among others, died for his sins.

FIVE

Digging Up Lee Harvey Oswald

*It's possible that we love our conspiracy theories because they almost al-
ways explain tragedy as an intentional act of people who are smarter
and more powerful than we are. It's perversely reassuring somehow.
Whether it's black helicopters, the Illuminati, Roswell, the moon landing,
the collapse of the World Trade Center, or the assassination of President
Kennedy, we simply don't want to believe we're wrong or unlucky, that
Fate sometimes works against us, or that lone, deluded, lunatic punks
can change the course of human history.*

DALLAS, TEXAS. SUNDAY, NOVEMBER 24, 1963.

Ninety minutes after the world watched Jack Ruby shoot Lee
Harvey Oswald, the suspected assassin lay dead on a bloody operating
table at Dallas's Parkland Hospital, mere steps from the room where
President Kennedy was pronounced dead two days before (and in the
same surgical room where Ruby himself would die a little more than
three years later).

Ruby's .38-caliber bullet had entered Oswald's lower chest just
below his left nipple and lodged in a noticeable lump under the skin

on the right side of his back. It pierced nearly every major organ and blood vessel in his abdominal cavity—stomach, spleen, liver, aorta, diaphragm, renal vein, a kidney, and the inferior vena cava, a major vein that carries deoxygenated blood from the lower extremities back to the heart. Oswald bled out very quickly through a dozen or more holes. Trauma surgeons poured fifteen pints of blood into him and manually squeezed his faltering heart to revive it, but it simply stopped for good at 1:07 p.m. local time.

Oswald arrived for his autopsy already a chopped-up mess. The suspected assassin had endured a brutal two days since the president was shot. His left eye was bruised and his lip split while resisting arrest. His guts had been mortally shredded by a bullet fired point-blank into his chest. Emergency surgeons had tried to save him through a gaping, foot-long slit in his belly and another long slice near the entrance wound.

Dallas County medical examiner Earl Rose started his autopsy less than two hours after Oswald was pronounced dead. He was already cool to the touch. Blood, no longer being pumped by his dead heart, was pooling naturally in the corpse's hollows. Aside from the wounds of the past two days, Rose's external examination found nothing remarkable: The average-sized, wavy-haired, slightly balding man on Rose's slab had slate-blue eyes, decent oral hygiene, a few old scars, no sign of alcohol or drug abuse, a shaved chest and pubic area, and was in otherwise good physical shape, if you didn't count being dead.

Rose sawed open Oswald's skull to find a completely normal brain. Apart from his tattered innards and a heart roughly handled by his would-be lifesavers, Oswald's other vital organs appeared normal. Even his bowels went miraculously untouched by the bullet. So Rose sealed all of his severed parts in a beige plastic bag the size of a grocery sack, and tucked it in Oswald's abdominal cavity before sending him off to be prepared for a hurried burial the next day.

The autopsy had taken less than an hour.

At Miller's Funeral Home in Fort Worth, undertaker Paul Groody couldn't waste any time. On a hunch that Oswald would someday be exhumed, he pumped a double dose of embalming fluid into the body and dressed him off the funeral home's private rack: white boxers patterned with little green diamonds, dark socks, light shirt, thin black tie, and a cheap, dark brown suit whose trousers were cinched around the waist not by a belt but by an elastic band. Keeping with a typical custom, the corpse wore no shoes. The family was charged $48 for the going-away outfit.

Oswald's hair was washed and combed, his visible bruises were concealed with makeup, and his eyes and lips sealed for eternity.

Then Groody placed two rings on Oswald's fingers. One was a gold wedding band and the other a smaller ring with a red gemstone.

The body, looking presentable again, was laid in a $300 pine casket with a curved lid. Several photos were taken, a grave was reserved, $25 worth of flowers ordered, and Groody's clerk typed up a $710 invoice, due within ten days.

The assassin's burial—deliberately scheduled the next day around the same moment as the president's nationally televised funeral and the somber services for Officer J. D. Tippit to discourage any public mourning—were attended only by Oswald's small, destitute, shell-shocked family, a handful of reporters, and a local pastor who didn't know Oswald but believed no man should be buried without a prayer. Since nobody else came, six reporters were drafted as spur-of-the-moment pallbearers to lug his cheap pine casket to a mangy little rise at Rose Hill.

The Reverend Louis Saunders's eulogy had been painfully brief, partly because two other ministers had refused at the last minute out of fear they themselves would be assassinated by a sniper. He recited passages from the Twenty-third Psalm and John 14, then added only:

"Mrs. Oswald tells me that her son, Lee Harvey, was a good boy and that she loved him. We are not here to judge, only to commit for burial Lee Harvey Oswald. And today, Lord, we commit his spirit to Your divine care."

His widow Marina, her eyes red and swollen from crying for three straight days, stepped up to the sealed coffin and whispered something nobody could hear before it was lowered into the damp hole. Everyone left and the grave was filled in for eternity.

But eternity is for poets. Conspiracy theorists aren't that patient.

Michael Eddowes wasn't a Fleet Street tabloid scribbler or a paranoid witch-hunter. Instead, he was a distinguished, educated gentleman who'd played tennis at Wimbledon and cricket in Britain's minor leagues. He graduated from the venerable Uppingham School but abandoned his dream of attending Oxford in order to help at his ailing father's London law firm, where he became a full-fledged lawyer himself. When he sold the firm in 1956, he opened a chain of popular upscale restaurants and dabbled in sports car design.

A Renaissance man of sorts, Eddowes was also fascinated with injustice. In 1955, he wrote a book, *The Man on Your Conscience,* which explored the case of a Welsh laborer named Timothy Evans, who'd been hanged in 1950 for murdering his wife and infant child. He proved how prosecutors had hidden evidence in the deeply flawed case. Eddowes claimed Evans could not have been the killer . . . and he was right. A serial killer who lived downstairs in the same building later confessed. Eddowes's reporting was credited with helping to abolish England's death penalty ten years later.

Eddowes was sixty years old when John F. Kennedy was assassinated in America in 1963. He eventually moved to Dallas to be closer to the story, and he was intrigued by the rumors he heard about Oswald's defection to the Soviet Union after he left the Marines in 1959.

In 1975, he self-published *Khrushchev Killed Kennedy,* in which he alleged that a "look-alike" Soviet agent had killed Kennedy, not Oswald. Eddowes believed the KGB's Department 13—its sabotage and assassination squad—had trained a body double named Alec to assume Oswald's identity. This agent (not Oswald, Eddowes says) met the young Marina Prusakova at a dance in Minsk, married her six weeks later, and returned to America in 1962 with his wife and infant daughter. He was such a dead ringer for Oswald, "Alec" was able to fool Oswald's own mother.

His mission: Blend in, wait for the right moment, kill the president, and die in the chaos that followed.

Evidence of the switch? Eddowes lists several specific "inconsistencies" between Oswald's Marine Corps medical records and his autopsy report.

Eddowes wasn't alone in his suspicions. As odd as it sounds, FBI director J. Edgar Hoover himself and other government officials feared in 1960 the Russians might try to replace the defector Oswald with a deadly impostor.

In 1976, Eddowes published another book, *Nov. 22: How They Killed Kennedy,* in England (later titled *The Oswald File* when it was released in the United States). His timing was perfect: The new House Select Committee on Assassinations had rekindled American interest in JFK's murder.

Eddowes doubled down. He proposed that Oswald's body be exhumed to prove that the man buried in Fort Worth's Rose Hill Cemetery was not Oswald but his doppelgänger Soviet substitute, Alec.

Eddowes's quest began with Dr. Feliks Gwozdz, then medical examiner for Tarrant County, Texas, where Oswald was buried. When Dr. Gwozdz refused to dig up Oswald, Eddowes filed a lawsuit to force the exhumation, but it was dismissed quickly.

While he appealed the ruling, Eddowes approached Dr. Linda Norton, then an assistant medical examiner in Dallas, suggesting that the Dallas County Medical Examiner's Office reassert its original jurisdiction over Oswald's body.

Norton was intrigued. After consulting with her boss, Dr. Charles Petty, Dallas County's Chief Medical Examiner, she ordered a copy of Oswald's medical and dental records from the Military Personnel Records Center. They'd ultimately be crucial for any identification because they were dated before Oswald's defection to the USSR and thus contained authentic identity data of the "real" Lee Harvey Oswald.

"I feel it would be in the best public interest to conduct the exhumation," Dr. Norton told the *Dallas Morning News.* "If there's a question and a reasonable question that science can resolve, then that's our business."

In October 1979, Dr. Petty formally requested that his Fort Worth forensic colleagues exhume Oswald and bring him to Dallas for an examination. They balked. The Tarrant County medical examiner wanted the approval of his district attorney and widow Marina Oswald before he dug up the assassin.

While the two MEs quarreled into 1980, opponents were gathering. Indignant newspapers editorialized. The forensic community grumbled. And G. Robert Blakey, the former chief counsel to the recently disbanded House Select Committee on Assassinations, slammed Eddowes's theory.

"I have read his book and it is trash," Blakey said. "This whole question is a non-question. The committee carefully looked into the so-called two Oswalds theory . . . there is nothing to it."

And Earl Rose, the Dallas ME who had done Oswald's original autopsy, told reporters he was certain that the "real" Oswald was buried in Rose Hill because he'd personally compared the fingerprints.

The whole mess seemed to dissipate when Tarrant County surrendered jurisdiction to the Dallas medical examiner in August 1980. But Dr. Petty shocked everyone when he shrugged it off, saying he saw no need to dig Oswald up.

Eddowes was undeterred. Promising to pay all expenses, he persuaded Marina Oswald—who suspected the grave was empty—to consent to a private autopsy by Dr. Petty. Marina was haunted by a 1964 visit with government agents who asked her to sign a stack of cemetery papers without explanation. With only a basic understanding of English, Marina came to believe that her late husband's remains had been disturbed somehow. She'd grown morbidly suspicious that he'd been secretly removed.

But a new hurdle popped up. News of the impending exhumation prompted Oswald's older brother Robert, a former Marine himself, to get a temporary restraining order.

The legal wrangling rattled the Dallas county commissioners. Fearing "adverse publicity," they forbade the use of any county facility for the autopsy.

Even before the legal path was cleared for Oswald's possible reemergence into the world, Dr. Norton was picked as the exhumation's chief forensic pathologist because of her familiarity with the case, and she assembled a small team, including two of the country's best forensic odontologists and me. She wanted to move quickly when the time came.

I had worked with Dr. Norton before. After my Army tour of duty ended in 1972, I joined the Dallas County Medical Examiner's Office under Dr. Petty. Pleasant and reserved, Dr. Petty had quietly built up another of the best ME offices in the country. I started as a junior assistant medical examiner, but within a few years, I was the deputy chief. I worked there through most of the Oswald controversy until February 1981, when I became the Chief Medical Examiner for Bexar County, Texas, in San Antonio. So Dr. Norton knew me and trusted my abilities.

The courtroom battle over Oswald's remains raged for a few months after I left Dallas, until August 1981, when a frustrated Marina sued her former brother-in-law Robert. A month later, a Texas court ruled Robert had no standing to thwart his brother's exhumation against Marina's wishes, and Robert withdrew his opposition.

At midnight on October 3, 1981, Robert's restraining order expired.

Before the sun rose on October 4, we stood at the killer's open grave. On that unseasonably muggy morning, we dug up Lee Harvey Oswald—or somebody—just to be sure America had buried the right man in 1963.

Ironically, almost nobody paid any attention when Oswald went into the ground, and now a crowd of reporters clustered outside the cemetery gates and a half-dozen news helicopters swarmed overhead like corpse flies as we lifted him out.

To be sure, there hadn't been much doubt at the time. Oswald's corpse had been fingerprinted in the mortuary, and authorities were

In the Bexar County Medical Examiner's morgue.
(*San Antonio Express-News*/ZumaPress.com)

Dominick and Violet with me as a
toddler during World War II.
(Di Maio collection)

With Theresa in 2014. (Di Maio collection)

With my beautiful bride at our first wedding,
1969. (Di Maio collection)

My first real job as a medical examiner was in this nineteenth-century building in Baltimore, an unventilated edifice where we hoped the window screens were strong enough keep the flies out. (Office of the Chief Medical Examiner of Maryland)

With my mentor, coauthor, and father Dr. Dominick Di Maio in the late 1960s. (Di Maio collection)

My father (left) with me and my sister Therese, around 1968, when we were both studying to be doctors. All three of my sisters eventually became physicians. (Di Maio collection)

My anger over unreported deaths at San Antonio's Bexar County Hospital made headlines and foreshadowed the shocking case of killer nurse Genene Jones.
(SAN ANTONIO EXPRESS-NEWS/ZUMAPRESS.COM)

Trayvon Martin's fatal wound was small and clean, but the single bullet did massive damage. The teen's skin bore the telltale stippling that told us the gun was fired from "intermediate range."
(OFFICE OF THE MEDICAL EXAMINER, SEMINOLE COUNTY, FLORIDA)

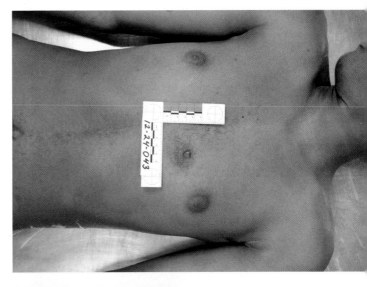

Using an enlarged image of George Zimmerman's face, I described his injuries to the jury deciding if he murdered the teenager Trayvon Martin. (POOL VIDEO STILL/ EIGHTEENTH JUDICIAL CIRCUIT, FLORIDA)

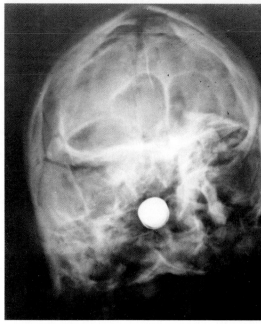

Infant Paul Woods's suspicious death unmasked serial baby killer Martha Woods, who'd murdered her own natural and adopted children, as well as nieces and nephews, over a twenty-year period. (RON FRANSCELL)

An X-ray of suspected terror bomber William Payne's skull revealed a mercury battery blasted into his brain. (OFFICE OF THE CHIEF MEDICAL EXAMINER OF MARYLAND)

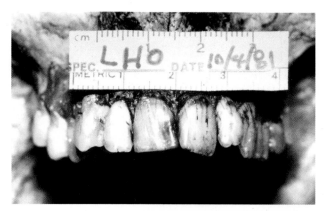

Unique dental traits helped identify the corpse in Lee Harvey Oswald's grave as the assassin himself, not a Soviet agent.

(DI MAIO COLLECTION)

Accused assassin Lee Harvey Oswald's booking photo on November 23, 1963, two days before his death.

(DALLAS POLICE DEPARTMENT)

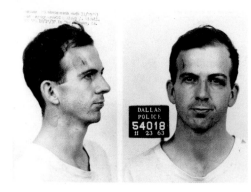

Former pediatric nurse and accused baby killer Genene Jones arrives at a Texas court in 1984. (*San Antonio Express-News*/ZumaPress.com)

Illegal immigrant Martin Frias was arrested for shooting his live-in girlfriend Ernestine Perea in the back in Wheatland, Wyoming, in 1984.

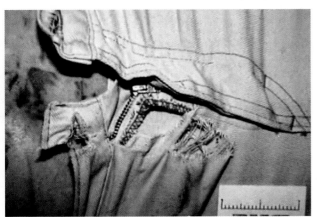

The torn button and zipper on shooting victim Ernestine Perea's jeans suggested a struggle, maybe even a rape attempt. (Platte County Wyoming Sheriff's Office.)

Actress Lana Clarkson was shot in the mouth and died in this chair at music producer Phil Spector's mansion. (Her head had rested on her blood-spattered right shoulder, but was turned to the left later by investigators.) (ALHAMBRA CALIFORNIA POLICE DEPARTMENT)

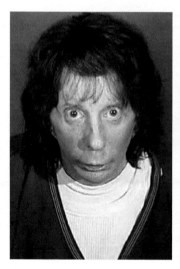

Legendary record producer Phil Spector was arrested for the murder of actress Lana Clarkson in February 2003.

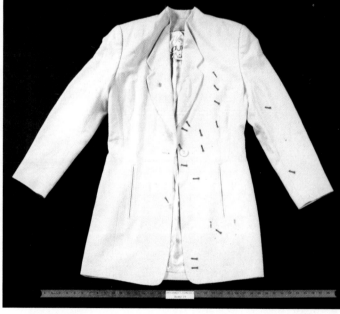

If Phil Spector had shot actress Lana Clarkson his white jacket would have been splattered with blood . . . but there was very little. The criminalist's tags show the spots where only very fine blood droplets were found. (ALHAMBRA CALIFORNIA POLICE DEPARTMENT)

Three troubled teenagers were arrested, tried, and convicted in the horrific torture slayings of three little boys near West Memphis, Arkansas, in 1993. But did they do it? (WEST MEMPHIS ARKANSAS POLICE DEPARTMENT)

The mutilated bodies of three young boys were found in a woodland near West Memphis, Arkansas, in 1993, and suspicion immediately fell on three teenagers.

Oscar-winning producer Peter Jackson, of *Hobbit* fame, also produced the documentary *West of Memphis*, on which I appeared. (DI MAIO COLLECTION)

Did the disturbed genius Vincent van Gogh commit suicide, as legend has it? Or did he die another way?

Auberge Ravoux still operates as an inn in Auvers, but the tiny room where van Gogh died is no longer used. (HENK-JAN DE JONG/ VELSERBROEK, NETHERLANDS)

Admirers regularly leave messages at Vincent van Gogh's grave in Auvers-sur-Oise, France, where he died in a strange suicide in 1890. (RICHARD TAYLOR/EDINBURGH, SCOTLAND)

convinced that the twenty-four-year-old ex-Marine who defected to the USSR from 1959 to 1962, the laborer who worked in the Texas School Book Depository, the shooter whose palm print had been found on the suspected murder rifle and boxes near the sniper's perch, the feisty fugitive who had been arrested at the Texas Theatre, and the suspect mortally wounded by Jack Ruby were all the same man: Lee Harvey Oswald.

And almost eighteen years later, I wasn't expecting any surprises either. Forensically, I'd always been ambivalent about JFK's assassination. It was an uncomplicated gunshot case that had gotten tangled up in a thousand different agendas. As with so many historic and newsworthy cases before and since, people quickly came to believe what they wanted to believe, damn the facts. I had been initially reluctant to join this exhumation team, knowing that our findings would just be fed into the conspiracy meat grinder. Any questions we might answer would only spawn new questions.

Second autopsies like this are often a waste of time. Too often, they're not prompted by new evidence, but by profit, curiosity, and urban legend. A second autopsy on President Kennedy might have definitively answered questions that went unanswered in his unskillful first, but digging up Oswald to satisfy a widow's discomfort with media speculation made little medical or legal sense.

And it wasn't rocket science. Any forensic pathologist—and maybe even a couple of backwoods coroners—could have done it. This promised to be a simple task I'd done thousands of times: identify a dead man. We had enough dental X-rays and other medical records from the US Marine Corps to help us prove, one way or another, if Lee Harvey Oswald was buried in Lee Harvey Oswald's grave.*

But history sucked me in. The simplicity of the challenge was trumped by the significance of this dead killer's role in human events.

---

* In 1981, DNA profiling was not yet available. Had we been able to use it, the task would have been simplified even further. But we were limited in this case to the tools of pre-DNA forensics: dental comparisons and other telltale medical evidence.

In the end, I couldn't resist taking one last look at a man who changed the course of history—no matter who he might be.

The actual exhumation took much longer than expected.

We had planned to simply lift the entire 2,700-pound, steel-reinforced vault out of the grave and open it elsewhere, but the vault—guaranteed to last forever, they said—had cracked, allowing water to seep in. The rotting casket inside had grown brittle and was splotched with stains and mildew. Its metal handles were badly corroded. Part of the lid over the cadaver's upper body had already caved in and we glimpsed, at the very least, that Lee Harvey Oswald's grave wasn't empty.

So much for best-laid plans and eternal warranties. On the fly, gravediggers cut a trench parallel to the defective vault, which would be removed so they could carefully slide the delicate, crumbling casket onto a makeshift wooden platform in the trench. In all, an operation that should have taken less than an hour went on for almost three hours.

And in the meantime, a large crowd of reporters and curious bystanders had gathered all around us. The situation was getting crowded and a little chaotic. I was nervous. We had to get the casket out of there as quickly as possible and start our work securely.

So as soon as we could do it without spilling a corpse onto the lawn in front of a hundred hungry news cameras, Oswald's crumbling casket was lifted out of the musty earth and slid into a waiting hearse. The exhumation team and official observers, including Marina Oswald, Michael Eddowes, a hired photographer, the original morticians, and four lawyers representing Marina, Eddowes, Oswald's brother Robert, and Rose Hill Cemetery, convoyed to the examination site in private cars.

The press had started murmuring that the second autopsy would be done at the Southwestern Institute of Forensic Sciences in Dallas. A logical conclusion, since Marina had publicly insisted that her late husband's body not leave the Dallas–Fort Worth area, and DIFS—home of the Dallas City and County medical examiner and my former workplace—was a top-notch morgue and uniquely outfitted for this kind of work.

But unknown to the public, the Dallas county commissioners had refused to host Oswald's second autopsy at the institute. We had to hunt for a new autopsy space in the metropolitan area, and we had few options.

Above all, we needed a highly secure facility. Marina dreaded the possibility that gruesome unauthorized morgue photos of her late husband would leak out, as they had after his 1963 autopsy. We had to be able to control who got in and what they could do.

Luckily, Baylor University Medical Center's autopsy suite in Dallas fit our bill. It had the layout and all the equipment we'd need. More important, it had only one door in. At one point, some two dozen people—most of them merely observers—would squeeze into the tiny lab.

So when our grim cortege exited Rose Hill Cemetery's gates, a hearse sped east toward Dallas. It was a decoy, and it worked. The media throng raced twenty miles ahead to the Southwestern Institute of Forensic Sciences to be there waiting when we arrived—while we diverted with a second, secret hearse to Baylor Hospital virtually unnoticed.

Inside, the cardboard-covered casket was rolled on a gurney through a warren of basement corridors and narrow hallways to our makeshift morgue. Orderlies wheeled it to the far end of the cramped lab, where we had already prepared for the autopsy. If all went as planned, it wouldn't take long to confirm whether we had dug up Lee Harvey Oswald or someone else.

All we needed was his head.

I've always hated the stink of decomposing bodies. This may be a professional flaw or just a natural human reaction, but I never got so accustomed to it that I didn't notice. Fortunately, a severely deviated septum dulled my sense of smell for most of my career. Some maladies are lucky.

The decaying lid of Oswald's casket, likely damaged when gravediggers removed the cracked vault, came completely loose in our hands as we opened it. The smell of moldy dirt, mildewed wood, and rotten flesh emanated from the box in an invisible cloud. The forensic pathologists in the room couldn't ignore it; the civilians pulled back and covered their noses.

The casket's interior was a mess. The inch-thick wooden sides were water-stained and spongy. Some of the moldy fabric lining had fallen loose from the lid, covering the corpse underneath. We gingerly removed the fabric remnants and there he was, lying on a rotten straw mat.

We were finally face-to-face with what was left of the man buried in Lee Harvey Oswald's grave, or at least what appeared to be a man-shaped blob of black cream cheese in a cheap brown suit.

He wore no shoes and his feet had partially skeletonized. The muscles in his legs were long gone and a flimsy parchment of skin had shriveled around his dry bones.

His hands, also skeletal, were crossed politely over his belly in a classic funereal pose. On his left pinkie, two rings stood out amid the grim, fetid decay: a gold wedding band and a smaller ring with a red gem, which Marina confirmed she had asked the funeral home to put on her late husband's hand back in 1963.

Oswald's original embalmer, mortician Paul Groody, was admitted to the exhumation as a crucial link to the original burial. Now he peeked into the casket and studied the man in full, although the corpse's face was unidentifiable. After a few seconds, the now-sixtysomething Groody declared it to be the man he'd carefully embalmed and dressed eighteen years before, then left after being in the room less than a minute.*

---

* A few days later, mortician Paul Groody would suddenly recall that he hadn't seen a craniotomy incision on the corpse's skull, adding a colorful new chapter to the JFK conspiracy saga. Since Groody knew that Oswald's brain had been removed, he suddenly decided that he must not have embalmed Oswald but somebody else. He told reporters that shadowy figures must have dug up the body in Oswald's grave and switched the unknown corpse's head with Oswald's real head so the teeth would match if he was ever exhumed. But as our examination showed, Groody was wrong. Our report noted the corpse's neck column was intact, which made any beheading impossible, and that the skullcap had clearly been sawed off, although it had been camouflaged by "mummified soft tissue." Nevertheless, Groody continued to insist until he died in 2010 that the man he embalmed was not Lee Harvey Oswald.

Now the dirty work began.

First, we removed the rings on the corpse's finger and gave them to Marina, who stood nearby. Her presence was unusual—most widows don't attend their husbands' exhumations and autopsies—but she didn't seem to be shaken by the macabre nature of the moment. While we worked, she floated among the onlookers, talking softly, and she never broke down in any way. Maybe the degradations of her upbringing in postwar Russia steeled her against death's grotesquerie, or maybe she'd simply gotten hard in the fierce personal storms after the assassination, I don't know. But I saw her as a true survivor.

We four medical examiners encircled the casket as I gently opened the flap of the suit coat and exposed the flesh beneath—or what was left of it. The skin was mostly gone, replaced by grave wax. The ribs had become so brittle that they crumbled at the slightest touch. There was almost no way we'd be able to identify the fatal bullet wound.

Almost all of the abdominal flesh had disintegrated, exposing a wad of embalmer's stuffing that created the illusion of a healthy torso for the funeral, and the beige organ bag, which now held only a small amount of a congealed, tannish paste that had once been his vital organs.

The body and clothing showed no signs of mutilation, although they were blotchy with areas of multicolored mold. We found no maggots or crawling insects, and the body itself was held together mostly by a tissue of dry and decomposed flesh.

At his 1963 autopsy, Lee Harvey Oswald was measured at five-foot-nine, although the Marines had twice listed him as five-foot-eleven (more evidence to conspiracy author Eddowes that Oswald was in fact two different men). So we rolled up the corpse's trouser leg and measured his right tibia, a bone in the lower leg that correlates closely to a human's living height. It was about 38 centimeters, or 15 inches long, suggesting this man had been about 174 centimeters tall, or just under five-foot-nine. That didn't prove we had the right man, but it didn't prove we had the wrong man either.

In the end, we didn't remove the body from the casket, nor did we even turn it over. It was simply too far gone to withstand any handling, and Marina had asked that we not do any more damage to the body than absolutely necessary to identify it. But it wouldn't tell us what we came to find out anyway.

We needed only the head.

Our plan was to X-ray, photograph, and create plaster molds of the corpse's teeth for comparison to two sets of dental X-rays taken during Oswald's Marine Corps days. The first was reportedly taken when Oswald reported to the USMC Recruit Depot in San Diego on October 25, 1956; the second came from a routine military checkup on March 27, 1958.

Those two sets matched, so if our X-rays lined up with them, we'd know we had Lee Harvey Oswald, right?

Not necessarily. First, we had to determine if the dental records from the Marine Corps were authentic and if a handful of obvious inconsistencies in Oswald's charts could be explained. For example, military dentists had reported Oswald was missing a right molar, but in fact it simply had never grown in and it still lay hidden in his jaw, out of the normal X-ray's view. In another case, the dentist's notes simply listed a filling in the wrong tooth. Unfortunately, such charting errors are common in the military, where a soldier might see any number of different doctors and never build a history with any of them.

Our team—including accomplished forensic odontologists Irvin Sopher and James Cottone—studied Oswald's Marine Corps records and was comfortable that the relatively minor blips could be easily explained and that the X-rays were authentic.

Now the messy part.

We could see the teeth and jaw, but Dr. Linda Norton had already determined that we couldn't take our X-rays without removing the head, which was covered with patches of both mummified flesh and grave wax. The forehead ridges were definitely male. The calvarium—that domelike cranium bone sometimes called the brainpan—was mostly free of any soft tissues, but a topknot of brownish-black scalp hair, maybe four inches long, still clung stubbornly to the right front hairline.

With a scalpel, I severed several rotted muscles and dried tendons in the shriveled neck and detached the skull from the spine at the second cervical interspace, the upper neck. With very little force, I pulled the head away from the backbone.

We snipped an embalmer's wire that had held the corpse's mouth closed for the funeral, and the jaw came off in my hand. While Sopher and Cottone stripped away old tissue with hot water and a scrub brush, I examined the skull more closely.

We could clearly see where Dr. Rose had sawed the skull open, but mummified tissue held the skullcap firmly in place, like glue. We decided not to cut or force open the skull and look inside, especially with Marina standing nearby. It would prove nothing. It was empty.

But this disembodied skull contained the keys to other mysteries.

In February 1946, when Lee Harvey Oswald was six years old, his mother took him to Fort Worth's Harris Hospital with a painful, persistent earache. There a doctor diagnosed him with acute mastoiditis, a bad ear infection that had spread to the mastoid process, a bony protrusion just behind his left ear. A new, wartime antibiotic called penicillin still wasn't commonly used in civilian hospitals, so the only other cure was for a doctor to slit the skin behind a child's ear, then scrape or drill an eraser-sized hole in the bone to remove the pus.

Treatments for ear infections in that day make us cringe now. As a child in the 1940s myself, I had a bad middle-ear infection that slowly and excruciatingly accumulated pus. My parents didn't take me to the hospital. Instead, my uncle sat on me while my doctor-father pierced my eardrum with a needle. It hurt like hell for a few seconds but not as bad as a throbbing ear full of pus.

Oswald's surgery went much more smoothly, and he left the hospital four days later with a three-inch scar behind his left ear. In high school, he claimed to have an abnormal eardrum, but when he joined the Marines in 1956 at age seventeen, his physical exam listed the scar but no other physical defects. The scar was noted again when Oswald left the Marines in 1959.

But the scar wasn't noted in Oswald's 1963 autopsy. Dr. Earl Rose listed several smaller scars, but none behind his ear. Years later, British journalist Michael Eddowes took what might have been an ordinary, even understandable, oversight in a run-of-the-mill autopsy and turned it into the smoking gun in the murder of the millennium. In the most analyzed homicide of human history, that little scar was transformed into a big question mark: If a veteran medical examiner didn't see a three-inch scar in Lee Harvey Oswald's autopsy, is it possible a scar-less impostor had killed JFK and been liquidated by Jack Ruby in a plot of Machiavellian proportions?

Well, conspiracy theories always seem more credible in books and movies than in real life.

As we examined the skull, the small hole in the left mastoid process leapt out. Its man-made edges were rounded and smooth, healed but not natural. It was an old lesion that couldn't be faked. Our dead man and Lee Harvey Oswald had both undergone a mastoidectomy in the distant past.

So we had another strong point of identification, although many World War II–era kids bore the same scar. Again, the evidence didn't rule out the possibility we were holding Lee Harvey Oswald's head in our hands.

The final proof would come from his own mouth.

America's first forensic dentist was Paul Revere.

Yes, the quintessential patriot was not only a master silversmith but also an amateur dentist who crafted special working dentures from animal teeth, then wired them into the toothless mouths of fellow Bostonians. When the Revolutionary War broke out in 1776, Revere's friend Dr. Joseph Warren was shot in the face at the Battle of Bunker Hill by a musket ball and couldn't be identified. Months after Warren was buried in a mass grave with many of the other 114 dead rebels, his brothers searched for him. But which of the decaying corpses was he?

Revere was able to identify his friend's body from a set of unique ivory dentures he'd made for Warren from a hippopotamus tusk just a year before. Warren got a hero's funeral and American forensic odontology was born.

Two hundred years later, in 1981, forensic dentistry had blossomed into an indispensable science. Because teeth are more resistant to destruction and decay than bones or flesh, and because they can exhibit unique features, they can help us identify people reliably in difficult conditions. Simply put, forensic odontologists identify the dead by their teeth and, in the case of bite marks, they can sometimes tell who (or what) did the biting.

Forensic dentistry played a key role in confirming that rumors of Adolf Hitler's survival were greatly exaggerated, in proving that serial killer Ted Bundy had bitten one of his victims, and in identifying victims of mass disasters such as the 9/11 World Trade Center bombing, the Branch Davidian fire in Waco, and the 1975 crash of Eastern Flight 66 at New York's JFK airport, which killed 113 people—the biggest catastrophe in my father's career as Chief Medical Examiner for New York City.

Now we were using it to determine if the man buried in reputed assassin Lee Harvey Oswald's grave was in fact Lee Harvey Oswald.

But this wouldn't be the first time forensic dentistry helped to identify the remains of a presidential assassin.

After shooting President Lincoln on April 14, 1865, John Wilkes Booth was run to ground on a Virginia farm, where he was killed by US soldiers—although, as with Oswald, nineteenth-century conspiracy theorists claimed it wasn't Booth but a look-alike who died that night. Nevertheless, Booth's own dentist positively identified the remains by prying open his mouth to find a distinctive jaw formation and two gold fillings he'd recently inserted.

In 1869, Booth's reputed corpse was disinterred from an unmarked grave on a Washington military post and returned to his family. At that time, Booth's brother examined the body closely—including "a peculiarly plugged tooth"—and told reporters that it was undoubtedly John Wilkes Booth.

Booth was laid to rest in his family's Baltimore plot, but the conspiracy theories weren't. To this day, many people believe Booth escaped justice only to die penniless in an Oklahoma hotel and to become a famous sideshow mummy. We knew that no matter who we found buried in Lee Harvey Oswald's grave, the conspiracy theories would never die. They'd just mutate.

Luckily, we had two topflight "tooth men" on our team. My old Baltimore colleague Dr. Irvin Sopher, now the Chief Medical Examiner for West Virginia, was actually a dentist as well as a medical doctor, and he had written a highly regarded textbook on forensic dentistry. Dr. James Cottone was a retired Navy dentist who headed the forensic odontology section of the University of Texas Health Science Center in San Antonio (and would later work for nine years identifying unknown soldiers' remains at the Joint POW/MIA Accounting Command's forensic labs in Hawaii).

The normal human mouth is full of unique traits. Each of our normal complement of thirty-two teeth has five distinct surfaces, all with well-defined natural traits like pits, crevices, bumps, and facades. Our teeth can grow at angles or slightly rotate in their sockets. Life adds its own damage, and dentists leave obvious traces when they pull, drill, fill, and straighten teeth. Forensic dentists can see telltale similarities in fragments of teeth as well as whole jaws.

We'd outfitted our Baylor lab with everything we'd need to make molds of the corpse's upper and lower jaws, photograph them, then shoot and develop X-ray films to compare against the Marine Corps' images.

Sopher and Cottone dove into the work. They immediately saw several unusual and distinctive dental traits in the corpse's mouth.

First, almost none of Oswald's teeth lined up. He had a bilateral crossbite, a relatively rare misalignment of his front and back teeth typically seen in fewer than three of every hundred people.

Second, his top two front teeth were slightly rotated away from each other, rather than growing truly side by side, like planks in a fence.

Third, his upper right canine, or eyetooth, displayed a prominent cusp known as a tubercle, not ordinarily seen on the front of a normal tooth.

The two tooth sleuths carefully charted each of the dead man's thirty-one teeth (one had been pulled). When they compared the corpse's X-rays to Oswald's military films, they found at least three identical teeth and fillings, four more very similar.

This man was no substitute Soviet, not even a long-lost evil twin.

"Based upon the consistency of the dental charting, the dental radiographs, the dental records, and lack of any unexplainable, inconsistent items," the forensic dentists ruled that the decaying human before them was undeniably and reliably Lee Harvey Oswald.

The entire examination had taken less than five hours, but it had been more than six years in the making. Dr. Linda Norton delivered a brief, emphatic press statement to a kettle of reporters who'd gathered.

"We, independently and as a team, have concluded beyond any doubt, and I mean beyond *any* doubt, that the individual buried under the name of Lee Harvey Oswald in Rose Hill Cemetery is in fact Lee Harvey Oswald," she said.

At that moment, Oswald's remains were being recombobulated in a new, 20-gauge steel coffin worth $800—more than his entire 1963 funeral had cost. Author Eddowes picked up the $1,500 tab for the reburial, plus the considerable expenses of the exhumation, as he should have.

Marina hovered. A great weight had been lifted from her little shoulders. The next day she told a newspaper reporter that the confirmation of her late husband's remains had been a "cleansing medicine."

"I'm walking around here with a smile on my face," she said. "It's like getting rid of a disease."

It also signaled the start of a new life.

"Now I have my answers," Marina, who had since remarried a Texan named Kenneth Porter, told another reporter, "and from now on I only want to be Mrs. Porter."

At first Eddowes admitted publicly he'd been entirely wrong, but then he quickly contrived a new explanation: The KGB had helped Oswald's dentist swap Lee's and Alec's dental records, enlarging the conspiracy exponentially. But nobody was listening to Eddowes anymore. He was largely considered to be among the wackiest of the JFK wackos. He died in 1992, but whatever other marvelous things he'd done in his life had apparently died when we confirmed that Lee Harvey Oswald was exactly where he'd been planted.

Back in the autopsy room, before Oswald's new casket was closed and he went back into the damp earth of Rose Hill, a grateful Marina gave Dr. Norton an odd gift: the red gemstone ring we'd taken off the corpse's pinkie a few hours before. It was her way of saying thanks for the team's work.

But Linda was visibly uncomfortable with this morbid reward. As soon as Marina left the room, she inconspicuously slipped it into my hand. She didn't want it.

Neither did I. As well-meaning as her gesture might have been, it was a sordid souvenir of a grim task and an even grimmer history. I wished for it . . . for Oswald . . . for Kennedy . . . for the bad memory . . . for the whole wretched mess to just be buried once and for all.

So just before they sealed Lee Harvey Oswald's coffin for his next eternity, I dropped the ring into the box with him and then drove home to San Antonio in the dark.

‹ SIX ›

Monsters Among Us

People haven't changed in five thousand years. They are still driven by money, sex, and power. Some are purely and inexplicably evil, some are purely and inexplicably good. The rest float along like leaves on the stream, bumping into good and evil all the way to the sea.

I remain shocked by people who refuse to believe in monsters. Do they not realize there are people out there who would cut their throats just to see if the knife was sharp?

KERRVILLE, TEXAS. TUESDAY, AUGUST 24, 1982.

A lot of mothers in Kerrville were excited when the new pediatrics clinic opened on Water Street, just a block off Main Street, literally a stone's throw from the Guadalupe River. And, even better, the new doctor was a woman, Dr. Kathy Holland. And her nurse, Genene Jones, was a star, recruited from a San Antonio hospital's pediatric ICU. Until now, an appointment with Kerrville's lone local pediatrician was hard to get, and children's serious health scares required a one-hour trip to the big city.

For sure, the new clinic was a godsend for Petti McClellan, a mother of three who lived with her husband and three kids in a mobile home on a rural patch west of town.

Their youngest, fourteen-month-old Chelsea, had been born prematurely and immediately life-flighted from Kerrville to San Antonio, where she spent her first three weeks in the pediatric ICU with underdeveloped lungs. Months later, she was rushed to the San Antonio hospital again when she stopped breathing and turned blue. After five days of tests, no obvious breathing abnormalities were found and Chelsea was sent home, where she later experienced a few minor "spells" of erratic breathing and a toddler's usual sniffles. Nothing that required hospitalization, but because of the frightening days after Chelsea's birth, every uncertain breath, every hiccup, every silent night rattled Petti.

Petti was a secretary and her husband was a lineman for the local electric co-op, so they couldn't really afford the time off to visit doctors in San Antonio, much less the expense of even routine trips, which required most of a day. The new clinic was a blessing for them.

Early on the morning of the clinic's second day, Petti McClellan called to make an appointment for Chelsea, who had a cold. They arrived around one p.m. and Dr. Holland took them straight into her office to get Chelsea's medical history.

As they talked, blond, blue-eyed Chelsea wriggled on her mother's lap and grabbed any loose thing on Dr. Holland's desk. So Dr. Holland's genial nurse, Genene, offered to take Chelsea to the treatment room to play with a ball. Genene scooped the child up and left.

A few minutes later, Dr. Holland heard Genene's voice down the hall: *Don't go to sleep, baby. Chelsea, wake up!*

Then a moment later, the nurse called down the hallway. "Dr. Holland, would you come here?"

Chelsea lay flaccid on the examining table as Genene quickly snapped an oxygen mask on her little face. They'd been playing, the nurse said, when Chelsea just slumped over, unconscious. She wasn't breathing. She was starting to turn blue around her lips. As Dr. Holland inserted an IV into the toddler's scalp, her little body was suddenly racked with seizures. The doctor ordered an anticonvulsant drug, then ran to tell some carpenters in the building to call an ambulance.

Back in the office, Dr. Holland told Petti that Chelsea had had a seizure, and she ran to see her baby splayed across the table, utterly still. The ambulance arrived and Genene rode with the child to the Kerrville hospital's emergency room, two minutes away. By the time they arrived, Chelsea had begun breathing on her own again.

After ten days of tests in ICU, doctors could find nothing to explain Chelsea's breathing spell and seizures, but she quickly regained her spunk in the hospital. The grateful McClellans believed the new doctor and her nurse had saved their little girl's life, and they told every parent they knew to take their kids to the new pediatrician in town.

So when Chelsea's three-year-old brother Cameron got sick with the flu a few weeks later, Petti was delighted to take him to see the fabulous Dr. Holland, who urged her to bring Chelsea, too, for a routine checkup. She'd been chipper ever since her distressing episode the month before, but it wouldn't hurt for the doctor to look her over, Petti thought.

Petti and her two kids arrived for the first appointment on September 17, around ten thirty. While unwell Cameron sat quietly, the lively toddler Chelsea giggled and scurried up and down the hall, a happy little girl in her happy little gingham-and-lace dress. Dr. Holland gave her a quick once-over on the waiting-room floor, then suggested two routine inoculations, one for measles, mumps, and rubella, the other for diphtheria and tetanus—ordinary vaccinations for toddlers. The doctor suggested that Petti not watch, lest she get upset by the injection, but Petti had grown protective. She wanted to hold Chelsea, just to ward off some of the fear and pain.

Back in the crash room, the smiling nurse Genene had already filled the syringes.

As Petti held Chelsea on her lap, Genene pushed the first needle into Chelsea's plump left thigh. In a few seconds, Chelsea's breathing faltered. She tried to say something, but the words froze inside her.

"Stop!" Petti hollered. "Do something! She's having another seizure!"

Genene comforted Petti. Chelsea was just reacting to the prick of the needle, she said. Petti calmed down as Chelsea relaxed.

Genene injected the second needle in Chelsea's right thigh. This time Chelsea stopped breathing completely, panicked for breath, then suddenly slumped over. It was happening again.

An ambulance arrived quickly. Genene carried Chelsea in her arms, and before they arrived at the Kerrville hospital, she inserted a breathing tube in the baby's throat. But Holland wanted to get Chelsea to a bigger hospital where they could do neurological tests, so Genene and Chelsea got back in the ambulance and rushed toward San Antonio, with Dr. Holland following in her car and the McClellans in theirs.

Eight miles from Kerrville, Chelsea flat-lined. The ambulance jerked to the side of the freeway. Jones gave Chelsea several injections while Dr. Holland climbed inside and began cardiopulmonary resuscitation, trying valiantly to restart Chelsea's little heart.

But Chelsea never regained consciousness. By the time the ambulance driver pulled into a little clinic in the small town of Comfort, Chelsea McClellan was dead.

Genene swaddled the baby's body in a blanket and handed her to Petti, who had lapsed into a fog of denial. *Chelsea was just sleeping,* she said, *and she'll wake up soon. She's been through this before.*

But Chelsea never awoke.

They all returned to the Kerrville hospital, where Genene took the child's body down to the basement morgue, then went back to work while Dr. Holland arranged for an autopsy.

Chelsea was buried on a Monday afternoon, dressed in a pink dress and wearing a pink bow in her hair, with a blanket to keep her warm and her favorite doll to keep her company. She wore tiny star-shaped earrings in her ears and a heart pendant on a silver chain around her neck.

Petti was a mess. She refused to believe Chelsea was dead. She wandered around in a mournful haze. When she first saw the miniature white fiberglass casket containing her daughter's body, she shrieked, "You're killing my baby!" as she collapsed in a heap.

They buried Chelsea under a bronze marker—"Our Little Angel"—in the Babyland at the Kerrville cemetery. Weeks later, the autopsy would blame the death on SIDS, a wastebasket term applied to the death of any young child when the real cause isn't known. In short, the autopsist didn't have any idea what killed her.

The McClellans bought an ad in the Kerrville paper a couple of days after the funeral, thanking those who'd helped bury Chelsea, sent flowers, cards, or brought food. "Special thanks" were extended to Dr. Kathy Holland and Genene Jones—the only two people named in the entire ad—for keeping Chelsea alive as long as they did.

A week after the funeral, a grieving Petti somehow got herself to the Garden of Memories Cemetery to lay flowers on Chelsea's grave. To her surprise as she approached, she spied nurse Genene Jones kneeling on the fresh grave, rocking back and forth, weeping and repeating one name again and again: *Chelsea. Chelsea. Chelsea.*

"What are you doing here?" Petti asked softly, watching from a distance, but the nurse didn't seem to notice her.

Without answering, Jones rose from the grave and walked away in a kind of weird trance.

After Genene had driven out of the cemetery, Petti saw that she'd had left a small spray of flowers on Chelsea's marker, but she also noticed the bereaved nurse had taken something, a pretty little bow.

How odd, Petti thought.

Only eighteen months before Chelsea McClellan died, I'd taken the job of Chief Medical Examiner of Bexar County, Texas. Our headquarters in San Antonio were about an hour's drive from the small town of Kerrville, a couple of counties northwest of the city, although at the moment I knew nothing of Chelsea McClellan's death.

In the previous nine years, I'd risen to deputy chief medical examiner under the legendary Dr. Charles Petty in Dallas, but even when he hit retirement age, Petty couldn't let go. It simply wasn't in his nature to quit.

I was still in my thirties but I'd learned forensic science from the best—Dr. Russell Fisher in Baltimore, Petty, and my own father. I was eager to run my own operation, but it wasn't going to be in Dallas. In March 1981, I took over as chief in San Antonio, which had become Texas's first medical examiner's office twenty-five years before.

Before 1950, while many big cities and other states were converting their old coroner systems to medical examiners, Texas dithered. It wasn't until 1955 that the state legislature passed a law permitting any Texas county with more than 250,000 people to abandon its county coroner and open a countywide medical examiner's office. The public's reaction was an immediate . . . yawn. Nothing happened.

But the winds shifted when tragedy struck.

Late on an early December night in 1955, a motorist crashed his car just four blocks from the home of a Bexar County justice of the peace, one of several elected officials who performed the tasks of coroner in their precincts. Police rushed the man to the hospital, where he was pronounced dead on arrival.

Cops called the justice of the peace where the crash happened, but he refused to hold an inquest because he believed police shouldn't have removed the body from the scene. So cops then called the justice of the peace whose precinct covered the hospital; he refused because he hadn't been called first. A third justice of the peace finally called an inquest, but by that time, the dead man had lain in the hospital an unseemly long time.

The local newspapers covered the bickering among the egotistical justices of the peace, and citizens finally came awake. At its next meeting, the Bexar county commissioners established Texas's first medical examiner's office. For $14,000 a year, the commission hired Dr. Robert Hausman, a Dutch-born forensic pathologist who was then the lab director at an Atlanta hospital. Coincidentally, before he started the job, Hausman spent a month alongside my father, getting a quick forensic refresher under New York's Chief Medical Examiner, Dr. Milton

Helpern. I was only fourteen years old at the time and certainly couldn't have imagined that someday I'd lead the office Hausman founded in San Antonio.

Death didn't dawdle. Two hours after Texas's first ME was sworn in on July 2, 1956, his first case—a suicide—arrived. He had only one assistant and a secretary, but he inaugurated a new era in Texas forensics when he was called to a ninth-floor suite in a downtown San Antonio hotel where a forty-eight-year-old white male had shot himself through the heart with a Spanish-made, .32-caliber semiautomatic handgun.

Case No. 1 (as it was officially labeled) was simple enough from a forensic perspective—the room had been locked from the inside and the single gunshot was heard as a bellboy knocked on the door at eleven a.m. But from a human perspective, it was much more complex: The dead man was Joseph Cromwell, the only son of a pioneering Oklahoma oil wildcatter and heir to his late father's vast fortune. A ninth-generation descendant of English Lord Protector Oliver Cromwell, he lived on the sprawling family ranch in nearby San Marcos. As a young man, he had graduated from a prestigious military college and Hoover's secretary of war, a family friend, had personally commissioned him as a second lieutenant. Parties at the family's sprawling ranch were legendary, and the last ten years of Joe's hedonistic life were boozy, gluttonous, and aimless. By the end, the money was almost all gone.

Joe Cromwell checked into the hotel a week before with only a couple of changes of clothes and no valuables. Police found him lying on his bed in his undershirt, boxers, and blue-gray socks, his face unshaven for a few days. He'd left detailed instructions for the hotel manager, police, and his son in a series of suicide notes on the nightstand.

Was it merely a coincidence that the first casualty on Hausman's first day wasn't an ordinary death? Well, no death is ordinary if you're the one who's dying. And I've found that most "ordinary" people have a few extraordinary stories somewhere in the book of their lives.

A medical examiner's job is to determine cause and manner of death (in this case a single bullet through the heart in a suicide), but a sentient human wants to know what is sometimes unknowable, the deeper why. The real reason Joseph Cromwell took his own life was never discussed by his family and is now forgotten, if it was ever known at all, but I know Dr. Hausman kept the suicide notes on his desk for a couple of days. Nevertheless, with an endless parade of suspicious or unattended deaths starting on that historic first day, he had to let the husk of Joe Cromwell go.

We all do.

When I first came to San Antonio, nobody from the ME's office went to death scenes. I changed all that when I started sending my own investigators—who had taken all their reports by phone—to the actual places where people died. I worried at first that the cops might chafe, feeling as if I didn't trust them to do their jobs. That wasn't the case; forensic investigators are simply looking for different clues than policemen. Luckily, most of my investigators had police backgrounds and my chief investigator was a retired San Antonio detective known to reporters as Mr. Homicide. As I write this, his nephew, also a former homicide detective, is the Bexar County ME's chief investigator, too.

Being at the scene was important. The more information we can gather in the earliest moments after an unexplained death, the better chance we have to explain it. I wanted my investigators and forensic pathologists to examine as many deaths as possible, even when the cause seemed apparent. Why? Because what is apparent isn't always true.

In those days, as now, local police routinely reported suspicious deaths, but hospitals weren't always quick or eager to call the medical examiner. The law didn't require hospitals to report the deaths of patients directly under a doctor's care if the doctor could certify without doubt why his patient died, but a wide spectrum of questionable deaths fell in the law's gray area. Hospitals naturally want to avoid bad reputations, lawsuits, and even uncomfortable questions, so they too often pretend that any death in their hospital beds was completely natural. Attending doctors, not wanting any second-guessers, often sign death certificates without the certainty the law requires.

And that's not how we should treat death.

In my first year as the chief in San Antonio, my frustration grew with stubborn hospitals that refused to report all questionable deaths— especially at the Bexar County Hospital, a county facility used as a teaching center for the University of Texas Health Science Center at San Antonio. By the fall of 1982, I was not so quietly stewing. I knew some unexplainable deaths were not being reported to the ME, so I rattled as many cages as I could to force hospitals to be more responsible. I even resigned from the faculty at the Health Science Center in protest, but nobody listened. I totally alienated the University of Texas bosses, who did nothing. It was a fool's errand to bang on the gates of a fortified culture that was arrogant, greedy, and opaque.

And whether by providence or accident, that's when the tragic case of little Chelsea McClellan materialized for me, literally on a whisper.

In January 1983, after a speech to San Antonio pathologists, my assistant medical examiner Corrie May struck up a conversation with an old friend from the local medical school. The doctor, a neuropathologist, mentioned that the Kerrville DA was looking into the unexplained death of a little girl. The DA, she confided, suspected a doctor and a nurse who had both recently worked at the Bexar County Hospital.

And, she whispered, there had been some suspicious baby deaths at the medical center, too. The hospital had been quietly investigating on its own for a few years, she said.

When Corrie May told me, I was shocked and angry. I had been beating the drums about unreported deaths at the hospital for months, and now here was evidence that my suspicions were valid. But I had no idea the reality might be even worse than I imagined.

The next morning I walked into the DA's office to deliver the frightful rumor: Somebody might be killing babies at the county hospital.

Indeed, the Bexar County Hospital was worried. At least one nurse had come forward earlier with suspicions. At least one doctor expressed qualms about a baby death he couldn't explain. The death rate in the pediatric ICU was higher than it should be. And whether this was anomalous or deliberate, it would all be an enormous embarrassment if it got out.

Two internal inquiries yielded no firm conclusions, but a common thread surfaced: Nurse Genene Jones's name kept coming up. A dark portrait began to emerge.

Genene Jones was born in San Antonio on July 13, 1950, and was immediately given up for adoption. She grew up short and chubby, felt ugly, and had few friends because she was a drama queen who lied chronically, yelled a lot, and was unpleasant to be around. Throughout her life, she occasionally told stories of sexual and physical abuse as a child, although the stories were always a little fuzzy, and after an endless string of lies, nobody took her seriously anyway. She also began to feign sickness as a way to get attention.

At sixteen, her younger brother was killed when a homemade pipe bomb exploded in his face. A year later, her slightly shady father died of cancer. Acquaintances say she was devastated, even though Genene was fond of saying she grew up unwanted and unloved. Her adoptive mother became her sole supporter.

After high school, Genene reportedly pretended to be pregnant to force her slacker boyfriend to marry her. But within a few months, he joined the Navy, and between affairs with a string of married men, Genene took beauty school classes.

When her husband returned from the Navy, they had a child, but they divorced after only four years of marriage. Soon she was genuinely pregnant, so she began to look for a better job that would pay more than she was making as a beautician (and would salve her unnatural fear of getting cancer from hair chemicals).

She'd once worked in a hospital beauty salon, and she'd developed a special attraction to doctors. A lightbulb switched on. Genene dumped her son on her mother and enrolled in classes to become a licensed vocational nurse. Shortly after graduation in 1977, she had another child, who also was dumped in her mother's care, and Genene began her new career.

Surprisingly, Genene proved to be a pretty good nurse, although she hated being just one cut above a candy striper. She believed deeply she should be in charge. She became obsessed with diagnosing people, even though it wasn't her job.

Now twenty-seven, she lost her first job at San Antonio's Methodist Hospital after only eight months when she was fired for being too bossy, too rough, and too eager to make decisions that were well above her pay grade. Her next job, at the small, private Community Hospital in San Antonio, was also brief.

In 1978, she was hired to work in the pediatric intensive care unit at Bexar County Hospital, a fairly new facility that largely served the poorest citizens in America's fifteenth largest city at the time. But the job didn't start well. Genene's tendency to boss people around—even though she was the lowest on the totem pole in rank and experience—chafed. Besides being her abrasive self, she habitually second-guessed and overruled doctors' orders. She also liked to brag about her sexual conquests, which she'd often describe in lurid detail. To make matters worse, she was brassy and openly libidinous around male physicians.

Early on, she imploded over the first child who died in her care, perplexing other nurses with an excessive and bizarre kind of public grief. She dragged a stool into the dead baby's cubby and stared at the body for a long time. At other times, she'd insist on escorting the bodies of dead babies to the hospital morgue, singing to them on their way . . . but she also participated in a kind of "dead pool," in which she'd bet on the next child to go.

Although her job was normally to provide basic bedside care, Genene developed a talent for inserting needles. She also seemed extraordinarily interested in various drugs and their effects. It all seemed natural, even praiseworthy, for a caregiver to want to know these things.

Just after Christmas in 1981, four-week-old Rolando Santos arrived at the ICU with pneumonia and was immediately placed on a respirator.

Three days later, he started having unexplained seizures. Two days after that, his heart stopped as he bled from several needle punctures on his body. When the bleeding restarted a few days later, a test showed he'd been injected with heparin, an anticoagulant drug for heart patients.

When the bleeding started yet again, it was stanched with a drug designed to reverse heparin's effects, and Rolando's suspicious doctor immediately transferred Rolando out of the ICU, even though he was still too sick. The ICU was apparently just too dangerous for the child.

Within four days, Rolando Santos had recovered enough to go home.

Armed with solid evidence that somebody had administered an overdose of heparin to a child who didn't need the drug, a hospital official described the "purposeful nursing misadventure" in a memo to the dean of the medical school. He promised to keep an eye on the ICU's dark and disturbing trend in unexplained deaths and near-fatal episodes.

Genene Jones worried some people in the ICU, but she wasn't immediately suspected in Rolando Santos's case, or in any of the other questionable cases that were piling up. In her four years on the ICU floor, she proved to be a divisive figure but was never fired, even though some of her colleagues sent up several red flags about the number of inexplicable tragedies.

And those numbers didn't look good. During Jones's time in the hospital's pediatric ward, forty-two babies died. Thirty-four of them— four out of every five of the hospital's dead babies—died while Jones was on duty. Other nurses began calling Jones's three-to-eleven tour the "death shift." Jones herself worried out loud that she'd be known as the "death nurse." And maybe for good reason: Overall, the hospital's infant mortality rate almost tripled during her tenure there.

Yet despite the hospital's growing concern, nobody ever reported any questionable deaths to me, the county medical examiner whose job it was to determine how and why people die.

By 1982, unable to prove anything and unwilling to set off a public spectacle, the hospital literally cut its losses in a brilliant PR stroke. It announced a plan to "upgrade" its pediatric ICU staff with more experienced registered nurses and quietly let two nurses go: licensed vocational nurse Genene Jones and the nurse who voiced suspicions that Jones was killing babies.

Armed with good recommendations from her bosses, Genene was quickly recruited by Dr. Kathy Holland, who'd just finished her residency at Bexar County Hospital, to work at a new pediatrics clinic in Kerrville, Texas,

Thus it was that a few months later, one of the San Antonio hospital's former nurses (and, at the moment, one of the doctors it trained) was embroiled in a death investigation in Kerrville, the San Antonio DA was snooping around about other deaths, and I was bringing pressure on the hospital's administration to be more transparent. A destructive perfect storm was about to break.

But even after Chelsea McClellan died, children continued to have unexplained and frightening episodes of seizures, respiratory failure, and unconsciousness at Dr. Holland's Kerrville clinic. Incredibly, in the afternoon after Chelsea's death, another child lapsed into a similar spell after an injection by Jones, who was staffing the clinic alone while Dr. Holland was busy arranging for Chelsea's autopsy.

When the flaccid child was rushed to the Kerrville hospital, an anesthesiologist there recognized the telltale symptoms of succinylcholine, a fast-acting drug that paralyzes all the body's muscles. He reported his suspicions to the little hospital's administrator, who eventually shared them with Kerrville's DA, Ron Sutton.

Suddenly, suspicion focused on Dr. Kathy Holland, her nurse Genene Jones, and a drug called succinylcholine.

Used since the 1950s, succinylcholine—commonly called "sux" by medical personnel—is a synthetic paralytic drug often used to relax clenched throat muscles when inserting emergency breathing tubes. It takes effect within seconds but lasts only a few minutes, long enough to intubate a struggling patient.

The human body quickly breaks it down into natural by-products normally found inside us, even when we haven't been injected with the drug. A routine autopsy would miss it. Up to the early 1980s, the only slightly abnormal blood chemistry was easily overlooked, and even when its use was suspected, it left no clear evidence on which to base a murder charge. Thus, famous defense lawyer F. Lee Bailey once called sux "the perfect murder weapon" because it vanishes without much of a trace.

An overdose of succinylcholine is a bad way to die. The unlucky victim will be completely conscious as all the muscles in his body—including his heart and diaphragm—seize up. Breathing stops and he suffocates.

This perfect poison is found in emergency and operating rooms, and is used almost exclusively by anesthesiologists and ER docs, at least when it's not part of the three-drug cocktail used in lethal injections of condemned killers. Ordinary people don't have access to sux. There's almost no reason it'd be found on the shelf in a small-town pediatrics clinic unless a doctor expected a child to suddenly crash and need emergency intubation. Not a likelihood.

Early in the Kerrville investigation, suspicion shifted away from Dr. Holland, who was now helping prosecutors connect all the dots in a horrid line that pointed straight to her nurse, Genene Jones.

Dr. Holland's clinic had two vials of succinylcholine, and Genene Jones had the primary responsibility for ordering the office's pharmaceuticals. One of those vials was briefly missing after Chelsea's death, but when Genene Jones reported finding it, it had been opened and two needle punctures were visible in its rubber seal. However, both vials appeared full.

Dr. Holland fired Jones shortly after the succinylcholine incident. The doctor was shaken to see needle marks in the seal of one of the vials, even though she had never prescribed it for any of her patients. Later, a chemical analysis showed that the open vial had been diluted with saline solution.

At the same time, the Bexar County Hospital in San Antonio was

ramping up its third investigation into the higher-than-ordinary number of deaths in its pediatric ICU during nurse Genene Jones's time
there. And a San Antonio grand jury was separately examining the records of more than 120 child deaths in the ICU between 1978 to early
1982—the period of Jones's employment.

Ultimately, the grand jury focused on about a dozen of those questionable deaths, all patients of Genene Jones and only one ever reported
to my medical examiner's office. Autopsies were done by students in
the medical school and all were certified as attended deaths. Suffice it
to say, no suspicious evidence was found in any of them, much less
succinylcholine.

But by 1983, we had a new tool. Renowned Swedish toxicologist
Dr. Bo Holmstedt, who helped select Nobel Prize winners in the
Royal Academy of Sciences, had developed a new method to detect
succinylcholine in dead humans. Problem was, his method had not
yet been tested in any court anywhere.

As we suspected that Genene Jones was a killer nurse who might
be using succinylcholine to kill innocent children, we reached out to
Dr. Holmstedt, who was eager to help. But he had one condition: He
would not testify in court if the State of Texas sought the death penalty for the nurse.

Faced with letting a possible killer go free or seeking a lesser penalty, DA Sutton took the latter. He agreed to Holmstedt's deal. If Genene
Jones were eventually indicted, the death penalty was off the table.

But a big question remained before any charges could be filed: Could
a little girl speak to us from the grave?

On a still, clear Saturday morning, May 7, 1983, we exhumed Chelsea
McClellan.

Before the gravedigger disinterred her little casket, buried just
three feet down, we set up our makeshift morgue—a canvas tent—
around the grave itself to block the view of gawkers and media people
who had flocked just outside the cemetery gates. Her parents had per-
mitted the exhumation, but they wanted to know nothing about it.

The thought of it turned their stomachs, but they knew it might be our only chance of getting justice for Chelsea.

We shouldn't have been here at all. Her original autopsy, done in the back room of the Kerrville funeral home, hadn't been performed by a forensic pathologist, but by a private pathology lab and a doctor at the University of Texas at San Antonio medical school—that same neuropathologist who first told Corrie May about this case and who personally knew Genene Jones. They were all stumped. They found nothing and their tissue samples hadn't been preserved well enough to avoid digging up a child's grave. But here we were, digging up a child's grave.

I knew this: SIDS probably didn't kill Chelsea McClellan. She was too old and the circumstances didn't fit. Typically, SIDS described the unexplainable crib death of a child under a year old, and such a death usually happened during sleep times. Fifteen-month-old Chelsea died in a doctor's office during a period of vigorous activity. After an injection. By a nurse.

Now she lay inside her casket just as the world had last seen her eight months before, pretty in her pink dress, with her knitted blanket and toy close. Wearing a pink bow in her blond hair, she was well preserved, like a delicate porcelain doll, and it seemed a shame to disturb her with our grim business.

Just a husk, I reminded myself.

After the mortician from the funeral home positively ID'd Chelsea, I undressed her and examined her legs closely for needle marks, but not surprisingly, I found none. I cut a small sample of the muscle in each of her thighs where she might have been injected with the succinylcholine. After taking both of her kidneys and pieces of her liver, bladder, and gallbladder, I closed her up. The mortician redressed her and gently laid her back in her casket, where she was again swathed in her blanket and reunited with her doll while I said a little prayer for her soul.

Just a husk.

It had all taken less than an hour.

I froze the samples, and to maintain the chain of evidence, they were escorted by a toxicologist to Dr. Holmstedt in Stockholm, more than five thousand miles away. Eleven days after the exhumation, we received Holmstedt's report: His new tests had found traces of succinylcholine in Chelsea's tissues.

The linchpin in the case against Genene Jones had fallen into place. On May 25, she was indicted by a grand jury in Kerrville on one count of murder and seven counts of injuring children, including Chelsea, in various near-fatal incidents at the clinic. Each charge alleged Genene Jones had injected the children with succinylcholine or a similar drug— although her motive remained murky.

Jones was arrested in Odessa, where she and a new husband were visiting relatives. She pleaded not guilty, and a judge set her bond at $225,000 before assigning her a public defender. A couple of weeks later, she made bail and walked free until her trial began.

If convicted, she faced from five years to life in prison on each of the eight charges.

Now the hard part started.

On January 19, 1984, almost a year and a half after Chelsea McClellan died, seven women and five men somberly took their seats in a Georgetown, Texas, jury box. They would decide if nurse Genene Jones was a cold-blooded baby killer or a falsely accused patsy for inept doctors. Was Chelsea McClellan murdered or did she die of tragically natural causes?

Reporters from all over America, including the *New York Times*, had flocked to this historic Austin suburb for a trial that promised some graphic copy. For almost a year, Americans had stolen brief glimpses of this gut-wrenching, sensational story in the media as it inched closer to trial, and they had a lot of questions. It wasn't just the unsavory details of infanticide they wanted. They still didn't know how or why any human could kill one baby, let alone dozens.

Kerrville DA Ron Sutton's case was largely circumstantial, but as he told the jury in his unusually brief opening statement, "there are an awful lot of circumstances here." Without the customary summation of the witnesses they would hear, he promised only to deliver all the pieces in a "strange and complex" puzzle.

The first week's witnesses established the prosecution's sad narrative: The Kerrville hospital's ER nurse who'd seen Chelsea after both of her traumatic visits to Dr. Holland's office; the anesthesiologist who thought the baby's clumsy movements resembled succinylcholine recovery; the ambulance driver who thought everything was going well until Genene Jones gave the little girl a shot; and the original autopsy pathologist, who admitted openly that Chelsea didn't fit the profile of a SIDS death, but until she heard about the succinylcholine, she'd had no clue what killed the little girl.

As I took the stand that first day, I flashed back to Martha Woods. Twelve years had passed, yet here we were debating SIDS and another child's death at the hands of another woman who'd also witnessed an extraordinary number of babies dying. History was, in a way, repeating itself.

"The child was too old [for SIDS]," I told the jury, adding, "SIDS is a fancy way of saying we don't know why the kid died."

They sat stone-faced as I described, in sanitized terms, the exhumation. They seemed to see it as I did: a gruesome but necessary indignity.

Then came Petti McClellan, Chelsea's twenty-eight-year-old mother. Tense and weepy from the start, she described Chelsea's life from birth to death, just fifteen short months, sometimes so softly the judge asked her a few times to speak up.

The courtroom was deathly silent as she described Chelsea's first breathing spell at Dr. Holland's office. She told how Chelsea had weakly whimpered, her eyes filled with fear as Genene Jones said the baby was "just mad" about getting a shot.

"And what did Genene do after she said that?" Sutton asked Petti.

"Gave her another shot."

"And then?"

"She went limp like a rag doll," Petti wept. "She was just like a rag doll."

Sutton led her through the last, fatal visit to the clinic and the desperate ambulance ride that ended, unexpectedly for Petti, in the parking lot of a small-town clinic where her husband talked to the ambulance driver and tried to prepare her for the worst news she'd ever hear.

"I told him there was no way Chelsea could die," she recounted painfully. "There was no way. She wasn't sick. She wasn't sick!"

On cross-examination, the defense delicately emphasized that Chelsea had been born prematurely and had other health issues, but Petti was strong. Yes, Chelsea started life weaker, she said, but she was in perfect health the morning she died. She wasn't even supposed to be at the doctor's office that day.

Petti was the emotional heart of the prosecution's case, but everything turned on Dr. Holmstedt's science. The only problem was that his new test for a hard-to-detect drug had never been published, much less used in a life-or-death criminal case. In an acrimonious hearing away from the jury, both sides battled over the admissibility of Holmstedt's conclusions.

By the end of a long day, the judge allowed it. Thus, the grandfatherly Holmstedt, in his thick Swedish accent, delivered the most damning evidence against Genene Jones when he said that he had found traces of succinylcholine in Chelsea's tissues.

Throughout the prosecution's case, the accused nurse sat impassively—even bored—at the defense table. She wrote letters, doodled, chewed gum, and generally looked disengaged. She was convinced she'd be acquitted, a confidence her lawyers didn't share. At one point, she wanted to bring a copy of Stephen King's horror novel *Pet Sematary* into court to read, but her lawyers convinced her it wouldn't reflect well on her with the members of the jury, who often glanced at her as the days passed.

Among the last witnesses against Genene Jones was her former boss and friend, Dr. Kathy Holland. The pediatrician had gone from being a suspect to one of the prosecution's strongest witnesses . . . and her nurse's worst nightmare.

Over a few days, Holland described how she had hired Genene and how they worked together. She recounted the sudden episodes with Chelsea and the other children. She told the jury how she found needle marks on one of the vials of succinylcholine, which appeared full but later proved to be diluted. And she stunned the courtroom when she recalled how Genene Jones had left a note during a halfhearted suicide attempt, apologizing to "you and the seven people whose life I have altered." It seemed to be a clear admission.

Genene's demeanor changed. She grew angry and declared not so quietly that Holland was lying and betraying her. Under cross-examination, Holland admitted she had changed her opinion about Chelsea's death, but was it enough?

Once again, as in the Martha Woods case, the judge had to decide whether past "bad acts" were relevant to proving Genene Jones's "signature." In the end, he allowed several witnesses to talk about children who'd had frightening encounters with the nurse. As Sutton had promised, all the puzzle pieces were falling into place.

When it was over, the prosecution put up forty-four witnesses and sixty-four exhibits, all clearly pointing to Genene Jones's guilt.

The defense put on its own vigorous case, mostly with a stream of medical experts to rebut the DA's evidence. They also advised Genene not to testify, knowing she'd be exposed as an arrogant liar very quickly. After some tense moments when she appeared she would ignore their advice—just as she had so often ignored doctors' orders in the ICU—and testify anyway, she demurred.

A month after it began, the *State of Texas vs. Genene Jones* was nearing its end. All that remained were the closing arguments.

Nick Rothe, a San Antonio assistant DA who was helping Sutton because of a second pending case against Jones in the near death of little Rolando Santos, summarized the prosecution's case in an emotional two-hour presentation.

"What we need to do is get back to what this is all about," Rothe started. "It is about a dead little girl, this one."

He held up a photo of Chelsea McClellan.

He reminded them of the evidence they'd heard, of the visits to doctors that ended in death or frightful emergencies. He implored the jury to consider the patterns as he directed their attention to a large calendar on an easel. A little rag doll marked the date of every reported seizure in Dr. Holland's office.

"There are rag dolls all over that calendar," Rothe said.

Then he pointed out one week on the calendar when no seizures were reported. The days were blank. Why?

"That's the week Genene Jones was in the hospital," he said. "There are no rag dolls that week because the nurse wasn't there."

Silence.

The defense summed up its case: Chelsea died of natural causes. Genene Jones was an innocent scapegoat. And Dr. Holland was too suspicious to ignore.

"They have done everything in their power to direct your attention away from the facts of this case," Jones's lawyer said, "in an attempt to hide the truth from you, and confuse you, and panic you, and bully you into returning a verdict of guilty."

After a short rebuttal by DA Sutton, the judge handed the case to the jury a little after two p.m. on February 15, 1984.

"You might as well just settle down and get a good book to read," the judge told his court reporter, expecting a long, difficult deliberation.

But he was wrong. The jury took less than three hours to reach its verdict. I was surprised when the local TV station broke into a program with a bulletin the jury was back.

Guilty.

A small group of sign-carrying demonstrators outside erupted in cheers. Relatives of Jones's victims in the courtroom hugged and cried. The verdict was bittersweet for the McClellans; it wouldn't bring their daughter back, but her killer would spend the rest of her life behind bars.

"We can finally bury her," Chelsea's grandmother told a reporter, "and they can't dig her up no more."

A rattled Jones, so confident she'd go free, wept as bailiffs led her to a police cruiser and took her to jail.

A few days later, she was sentenced to ninety-nine years for the lethal injection of Chelsea McClellan. A few months later, she was also convicted of deliberately injuring Rolando Santos, and got sixty more years, to be served at the same time as her other prison sentence. Justice was done. (At the time, the San Antonio DA told a *Washington Post* reporter, "There will be no additional indictments of Genene Jones. No useful purpose will be served. I think [she] will spend the rest of her life in jail.")

But in the flush of the moment, nobody anticipated a hidden booby trap in the punishment that wouldn't rear its head for a few decades.

And when it did, it would feel like we were digging up that little girl all over again.

Why did she do it?

Nobody really knows. Like Martha Woods, some form of Munchausen syndrome by proxy is likely. Prosecutors say Genene Jones had a hero complex, a pathological need for the attention she received when she rescued a child (whose imminent death she had caused). It's possible, they said, that she never intended to kill them, but only wanted to draw them to the brink of dying so she could save them. Others say she relished the power she drew from playing the pivotal role in a life-and-death drama. Or maybe she just liked the excitement and the admiration she got from doctors, whom she revered as desirable demigods. Or maybe she was acting out her own alleged childhood abuses.

We simply don't know, and she isn't telling.

As was the case with Martha Woods, I believe Genene Jones's motives were complicated beyond rational understanding. No matter what they were, it falls to someone else, here on earth and beyond, to know. My first obligation is not to her, but to Chelsea McClellan and any other children whose paths might have ended in Genene Jones's arms.

Two villains emerged in this tragedy. One was Genene Jones, a psychopathic serial killer whose true death toll might never be known. The other was a political hospital culture that covered its own ass rather than face the truth.

Genene Jones might have murdered up to forty-six infants and children in her care, but the exact number will never be known because after her first conviction, the Bexar County Hospital (now University Medical Center) shredded nearly thirty tons of hospital records that covered the period of Jones's employment, destroying any potential documentary evidence against her. The hospital said the shredding was routine; prosecutors have surmised it was done to shield the hospital from any further legal liability and bad press.

Some good parents lost their kids. Some good people lost their careers. But the politicians, lawyers, and doctors walked away untouched, like they always do.

We learned nothing from Genene Jones's slaughter of innocents. Nothing.

In 2014, the Texas Parole Board denied Genene Jones freedom for a ninth time. In the early days, protesters always showed up to oppose her release; as the years passed, the protests grew smaller and quieter, until recently. Now at sixty-four, she begged for compassion, claiming to be dying of stage four kidney disease. Three decades had passed since she went to prison for murdering Chelsea McClellan. Her mug shot no longer pictures a cold-eyed thirtysomething but a dour, sagging frump, more lunch lady than serial killer.

Ah, but Genene Jones is still dangerous.

When she was sentenced to ninety-nine years in the 1980s, Texas had mandatory release laws designed to relieve prison overcrowding. No matter how evil or violent, every inmate was credited with three days of time served for every day of good behavior behind bars. More than a thousand criminals imprisoned in Texas between 1977 and 1987 are still in prison and eligible for mandatory release, and hundreds of those are killers. The law was later changed but still applies in Jones's case.

For more than thirty years, Genene Jones has kept her nose clean. So instead of dying in prison as she should, she is now scheduled to be released on March 1, 2018. A free woman.

The district attorney's office in San Antonio—where Jones might have killed dozens of children in at least one local hospital—has scrambled to find a new case against Jones among the many dead babies she left in her wake.

We have considered exhuming the little bodies of possible victims, but the likelihood of finding any solid forensic evidence at this point is slim. If Jones injected her victims with the extraordinarily hard-to-detect succinylcholine or merely smothered them, their remains likely wouldn't yield definitive clues.

More recently, old grand jury records from 1983 have surfaced. They might contain enough copies of old hospital documents to file new charges, but it could be the last gasp in the desperate mission to keep Genene Jones in prison where she belongs. Time will tell.

If something doesn't happen, and if Genene Jones survives long enough, she'll walk out of a Texas prison a free woman in 2018. And for the first time in the history of American crime and punishment, we will have knowingly and purposely released a captive serial killer back into society.

Her victims might be past caring, but the living deserve better.

<SEVEN >

Secrets and Puzzles

We're all tangled up in the puzzles of life. We accept there are mysteries we cannot answer, but we go looking for answers anyway. So we put the puzzle pieces together endlessly, then disassemble them endlessly. We always have, and always will. Death offers us a lot of puzzles, too, but I think death's mystery is in what we can see, not what is hidden. The clues are always there for us to find whatever answers we seek. It's not unnatural to look and wonder . . . it's unnatural to walk away.

WHEATLAND, WYOMING. THURSDAY, JULY 5, 1984.

Martin Frias spent the day after the Fourth completely alone, aching in body and spirit.

A running argument with his girlfriend had started a few days before, and it was still simmering. She didn't want to be around him, so she drove the kids to the park in town that afternoon, just so she wouldn't have to put up with his crap. He fell into a funk, half sorry, half pissed.

Martin had sneaked into America from Mexico in 1979, looking for work. He found his way to Wyoming, where there were plenty of jobs and a man could hide in plain sight. In 1981, he met Ernestine Jean Perea, freshly divorced and now raising her four-year-old daughter alone. They were both in their early twenties and were both desperately seeking a safe place to land.

They rented a green-and-white single-wide trailer on a dirt road, on the other side of the railroad tracks, in the badlands southwest of Wheatland, Wyoming, a prairie farm town. Martin found a good job at a local quarry. He was a hardworking guy, soft-spoken and serious. Although he was only about five-foot-nine, he was wiry and strong. He'd even been a promising baseball pitcher as a boy in Mexico.

Martin's boss liked him, and when he was working—when the money was coming in—life was good.

But things hadn't been right for a couple months, since Martin's right arm had nearly been torn off by a rock crusher. The first surgery on his arm had gone badly, and now he was drawing only worker's comp while his corrective surgery healed.

His right arm was useless in its sling, money was scarce, and he could do nothing but sit around the trailer, drink cheap beer, and watch TV all day while Ernestine took care of their three rambunctious preschool kids. He complained about her drinking. He complained about her cooking. He complained about her friends. He complained about everything. It drove her nuts and she threw it all back at him, with the same hostility. Her temper often flared, like the time long before Martin when she'd stabbed her ex-husband with a screwdriver. This time Ernestine told her mother she was planning to take the kids and move out. In fact, she'd already stored some of her possessions in her mother's Cheyenne garage.

So after the Fourth of July, still stewing, Ernestine trundled the kids to the town park, where she met some friends for a picnic. Somebody brought a lot of beer. Booze took the edge off Ernestine's furies, and pretty soon she was feeling no pain. She finally felt free as she wrestled playfully with some of the young men in the grass and forgot about Martin for a few hours. She liked it, but she joked to her friends that there'd be a big argument when she finally went home.

Ernestine didn't know Martin had followed her and watched from his truck. It enraged him to see her with those men, laughing and playing grab-ass. He drove away and got drunk.

That night around nine thirty, after the little town's sidewalks had rolled up for the night, Martin came home to a dark trailer. When Ernestine and the kids came in later, Martin helped put the children to bed in their separate rooms. Without a word, Ernestine went to her bedroom, where she'd been sleeping alone for the last couple of nights, and closed the door behind her.

Martin's long, sad day ended in silence. He turned off the light and curled up on the hide-a-bed where he'd been sleeping since Ernestine banished him from the bedroom. Restless after a turbulent day that had ended without resolution, he eventually fell asleep.

But he hadn't been asleep long when he was awakened by a thump, like somebody outside had kicked the side of the trailer. Maybe the wind blew something against the tin siding, or maybe a stray dog was nuzzling around. He got up and glanced in the kids' rooms and squinted into the dark outside. Nothing. He lay awake on the sofa for a while, listening, but he didn't hear it again and drifted back to sleep.

A couple of hours later, around one a.m., Martin awoke again to a baby's crying.

Groggy and still a little drunk, he shambled in the dark toward the sound of the cries, which seemed to be coming from Ernestine's room.

He opened the door and turned on the light, but it took a moment to comprehend what he saw: Ernestine was lying on her back on the floor, bleeding from a gaping belly wound. Her daughter sobbed uncontrollably as she tried to lift her mother's head. Blood and bits of flesh were sprayed on the wall beside the door. And Martin's .300 Weatherby Magnum hunting rifle lay between Ernestine's legs.

She didn't move. Or breathe.

Ernestine Perea was dead, just three weeks shy of her twenty-eighth birthday.

Horrified, Martin scooped up the child and ran to the kitchen to dial 911. His English wasn't good and he couldn't make them understand how to get to his trailer, so he arranged to meet the police at a café in town and lead them back.

The first responders—a town cop, a sheriff's deputy, and the little prairie town's mortician, who also served as the county coroner—found no signs of a struggle or intruder in the cramped little bedroom. Judging by the body's position, the rifle's location beside her left leg (immediately moved by a deputy, who checked its chamber for live rounds), her massive, ragged belly wound, and the splatter of blood, guts, and bone fragments on the wall and closed door behind Ernestine, they quickly concluded she'd killed herself in a messy, gut-shot suicide.

But as they looked closer, they started to wonder. Her jeans were ripped along the zipper, as if someone had tried to yank them off her. And when they rolled her body over, they also found a small bullet hole, no bigger around than a little finger, in Ernestine's back.

Their theory quickly changed. They knew entrance wounds are usually smaller than exit wounds. So because the wound in Ernestine's back was smaller than her belly wound, they reckoned she must have been shot from behind and the bullet exited her belly in a spectacular (and fatal) gust, spraying the wall just two or three feet away with gore.

This was the first murder in Platte County in five years, but Barney Fife himself could have solved this whodunit. Ernestine couldn't possibly have shot herself in the back with a high-powered hunting rifle, or any other gun for that matter. That seemed clear.

Less than twelve hours later, a clinical pathologist at the University of Wyoming examined Ernestine's barefoot, pudgy body, still wearing her blue-striped cotton tank top and jeans. She was five-foot-two, a hundred and forty pounds, with long black hair. He noted a name tattooed on her left hand—ARCENIO—with an X surrounded by stars, maybe an ex-boyfriend or ex-husband. He also found unexplained bruising on Ernestine's chest, and a staggering blood alcohol level of .26 percent, more than twice the legal limit for driving in Wyoming at the time.

And although Ernestine's innards were a bloody mess, he confirmed quickly what the cops told him: An inch-long oval entry wound in the middle of Ernestine's back that severed her spinal cord, and a jagged exit wound in her belly—more than four inches at its widest—from which pieces of her bowels now protruded. The bullet had passed back to front, according to his autopsy report.

So the pathologist who performed the autopsy and state crime lab technicians swiftly concluded that the bullet entered Ernestine's back and broke into two pieces when it smashed her spine. The fragments then passed perfectly horizontally through her abdomen, piercing her aorta, liver, kidneys, diaphragm, bowels, and spleen before exiting her belly. Two large chunks of the bullet's core and jacket lodged in the bedroom wall. The bullet's path was parallel to the floor, suggesting the rifle had been no more than twenty inches above the floor when it was fired.

Given the path of the bullet and the distance to the wall, state experts deduced Ernestine had been kneeling or squatting when she was shot, and her shooter had also been very low to the floor.

So Platte County's coroner—a quirky, gabby funeral director who campaigned for the job saying he was the only guy in town with a vehicle large enough to haul a dead body—ruled Ernestine's death a homicide.

Martin's fingerprints were found on his rifle's stock and the ammunition box, and Ernestine's prints were on the rifle scope and barrel, but neither of their fingerprints were found on the trigger, the bolt, or anywhere else on the big gun. Vegetable oil and graphite particles were found on Ernestine's left hand and the rifle barrel.

But no blood or human tissue showed up on the muzzle, and the state crime technicians found no gunshot residue anywhere on Ernestine's shirt, suggesting the shot had been fired from at least three feet away.

Martin swore he never heard a gunshot, even though he slept just down the hall in the little trailer. Impossible, the cops said. He must be lying. That .300 Weatherby Magnum—a small elephant gun, really—would awaken the dead.

Friends told the cops that Martin and Ernestine had a stormy, booze-fueled relationship. Her mother told them how Ernestine was threatening to leave him. But for every circumstance that hinted at Martin's guilt, another contradicted it.

Yes, Ernestine had flirted with suicide maybe a dozen times before—several unnatural scars on her wrists were casually noted in her autopsy—but she had been in a happy mood just hours before, partying that day with male friends. After all, Martin had seen her playfully wrestling with one of them in the park hours before the shooting. She didn't seem suicidal to friends who saw her that day.

Yes, Martin had been sleeping on the couch after an argument a few days before, but his newly broken arm in a sling made loading, cocking, and firing a high-powered rifle unlikely.

Yes, cops had been called to domestic disputes at the trailer a half dozen times before, and Ernestine had even begged them to seize Martin's hunting rifle, but time and again in brutal interrogations after the shooting, Martin had steadfastly insisted he didn't kill her. He'd been as helpful as he could the whole time, and the usual liars' tells were missing.

So it didn't add up perfectly, but investigators and prosecutors believed they had enough to prove Ernestine died in a homicide, not a suicide.

Their theory, completely circumstantial: A jealous Martin and a drunken Ernestine had quarreled in their bedroom. He'd grabbed her violently enough to rip the zipper and pop the button off her jeans, then thrown her to the floor. As she rose with her back to him, he grabbed his rifle from beneath their bed and shot her in the back from his kneeling position, spraying blood and gore onto the wall. Ernestine then twisted as she fell onto her back, they contended. Martin then placed the rifle between her legs to make it look like a suicide and called police.

Five days after a single, fatal shot in the dark, Martin Frias was arrested for the first-degree murder of his common-law wife Ernestine Perea, and the State of Wyoming seized his children. He was jailed on an impossible half-million-dollar bond.

Court dockets in Wyoming aren't long. Martin Frias went to trial five months later, barely understanding what everybody was saying about him.

His court-appointed lawyer, Robert Moxley, had just passed his bar exam a few years before and was assigned to the sleepy little public defender's office in Wheatland, where murder cases were rare. When his own investigator bought into the prosecution's theory that Martin had shot Ernestine in the back, things looked grim. Moxley threw his entire effort into a reasonable-doubt defense: Without witnesses or solid forensic evidence that Martin premeditated Ernestine's murder and pulled the trigger, the tiniest shred of doubt existed. Moxley crossed his fingers and hoped the jury would acquit.

Moxley miscalculated.

The prosecution put on a convincing case, even though it was entirely circumstantial. Witness after witness painted stroke after stroke on the emerging portrait of Martin Frias as an angry, jealous boyfriend who was capable of a rage killing. The only other people in the trailer that night were three preschoolers. And Frias's undocumented status only made him look more guilty.

Prosecution witnesses also described how a test-firing of the big rifle inside the trailer sounded like a car horn or a jackhammer, casting serious doubt on Frias's claim that he never heard a shot.

Moxley could only parry. He had no reason to dispute the state's autopsy, and he didn't have much of a budget, so he had no medical experts to refute it. About the best he could offer was a vain attempt to cast blame elsewhere.

A therapist who met with Ernestine's four-year-old daughter reported that the child first claimed she shot her mother.

"I shot her in the back. I shot her in the back. I shot her in the back," the child reportedly told the therapist.

"Did you talk to your grandma about what we talked about?" the therapist asked later.

"Uh-huh."

"What did Grandma say about that?"

The child just said, "Shhhhh!" then left the office to buy a soda from a machine in the hallway, chanting, "I can't tell you, I can't tell you, I can't tell you, I can't tell you, I can't tell you. . . ."

Chillingly, a psychiatrist who also examined the child described her as very aggressive with symptoms of deprivation and split personality. At one point in the examination, the child took a notepad and ran it across the psychiatrist's neck several times. "I cut your neck off," she said each time.

A crime technician testified that Martin's hands had been swabbed for gunshot residue, but inexplicably the swabs that could have helped prove his guilt or innocence were never tested.

Other defense witnesses testified that it would have been nearly impossible for Martin to have fired the big rifle, especially from a kneeling position, because his wrecked arm was in a sling and nearly useless. A crime technician admitted that he'd tried to cock and shoot the big rifle with one arm, but couldn't. The prosecution quickly countered with a doctor who said Martin could have fired the gun.

Finally, the former director of the state crime lab testified that, based on his evaluation of the state's forensic evidence, no substantial inculpatory or exculpatory evidence had been found. He found nothing that would prove (nor disprove) what happened that terrible night.

In the end, nothing stuck for Moxley.

After seven days of testimony, the seven-man, five-woman jury took less than five hours to convict Martin Frias on the lesser charge of second-degree murder. Just before Christmas 1985, the judge sen-

tenced him to twenty-five to thirty-five years in the Wyoming State
Penitentiary.

His children and his freedom were taken away, his lover was dead,
and Martin Frias would be an old man when he got out. He couldn't
understand most of what happened.

America hadn't turned out to be what he expected.

As Moxley prepared for his appeal in the dead of Wyoming's winter,
he got an unexpected break. A crime lab tech happened to mention
over coffee with Moxley's investigator that infrared photos of Ernestine's bloody tank top might show something they'd missed. Surprising everyone on the defense team, the subsequent images showed what
nobody had seen with their naked eyes: a huge flare of powder residue from the contact gunshot . . . on the blouse's front.

All at once, new evidence suggested Martin Frias might have been
telling the truth.

The dogged Moxley didn't stop there. He sought out the experts he
now knew he should have called before the trial. He asked prominent
blood-spatter expert Judith Bunker to take a look at the evidence, and
she in turn suggested Moxley call me, too. He did.

It was the sort of call I got routinely as the Chief Medical Examiner in Bexar County: A despairing but earnest young defense lawyer
with a futile case, grasping at forensic straws that didn't exist. The
way he described his case, it sounded like a desperately slim chance.

I discouraged him about his chances of finding a forensic absolution for his client, but I mentioned that, as luck would have it, I was
scheduled to speak to a law enforcement convention in Cheyenne,
Wyoming, in just a couple of weeks. Maybe I'd take a look but I was
busy and I didn't have much time to waste. . . . In his Wyoming way,
Moxley left all the details loose, and hung up.

I never expected to hear from the poor guy again.

January in Wyoming is beastly. I flew from San Antonio to Denver
and rented a car for a wind-blown, icy, two-hour drive to Cheyenne

to talk to a bunch of cops about gunshot wounds. I was cold the whole way.

The workshop planners put me up in the same hotel where I spoke. After a day of convention food, I craved something more substantial, so I went down to the hotel's Old West–themed restaurant, where I expected they'd know how to cook a nice, big steak. I sat alone in a booth and a waitress took my order. I ate my salad, and after a few minutes, she delivered a thick, sizzling steak. I was just about to cut into it when I sensed somebody standing at my table, and it wasn't the waitress.

"Dr. Di Maio?"

I looked up to see a young guy, prematurely balding, wire-rimmed glasses, more rumpled than he should have been for his age. He held a manila folder.

"Yes." Maybe my reply was more question than answer.

"I'm Robert Moxley. Martin Frias's attorney. We talked on the phone. . . ."

It took a bit but I remembered him. The desperate lawyer who'd lost his case. He'd found me. I admired his persistence, but I was more focused on my steak at the moment.

Still, he flopped his manila folder on the table.

"These are the crime scene photos. I just want you to look at them and tell me if you see anything. Anything at all."

Over dinner?

"I'm not sure if I can help you. . . ." I told him. Again.

"If you'd just take a look, Doctor, I'd really be obliged."

I picked up the folder and thumbed through the full-color photographs. In my career I'd seen thousands, maybe millions, just like them. A bloodied corpse on a floor. A gun nearby. Closeup photos—intimately close—of wounds, torn clothing, dead fingers. All the violent colors of death.

I paused a little longer over one image of a large, tattered wound in a young woman's belly.

"She was shot with a hunting rifle. That's the exit wound," Moxley informed me.

I looked closer, just a few seconds. But I'd seen more bullet holes than a battalion of M*A*S*H surgeons. I'd written the premier textbook on gunshot wounds. I knew exactly what I was looking at.

"No," I said. "That's not an exit wound."

He looked at me funny, as if I'd just told him he was adopted.

"Sorry, but that's not your exit wound," I repeated. "That's an *entrance* wound."

It's one of the great myths of forensics that bullets always make smaller holes when they go in and bigger holes when they go out. It's perpetuated by our media, which almost never portrays gunshot wounds authentically.

For example, when a human is shot in Hollywood, he is almost always blown backward sensationally, sometimes several feet, sometimes through a plate-glass window, sometimes through walls. In real life, though, a streamlined bullet focuses its awesome kinetic energy into a very tiny area at its tip, so it doesn't have the power to drive a human body backward. It penetrates, it doesn't punch. The bullet is going so fast when it hits a reasonably inert mass of flesh that it simply zips through and the body crumples on the spot. The victim drops straight down.

Then there's the myth of small entrance wounds and big exits. Fact is, it's generally true that a bullet often makes a smaller hole when it enters a body; then it tumbles and fragments inside, making a large hole when it exits in a surge of metal, blood, and tissue. But it's certainly not true in every case.

And in Ernestine Perea's case, it wasn't true at all. And the clues were all hidden in plain sight in Moxley's photographs.

When you fire a gun, it's not just a bullet that comes out of the barrel. There's a flame that burns up to 1,500 degrees, followed by hot gases, soot, burning gunpowder, and the bullet, of course.

If you press the muzzle of a gun against the skin, then that flame burns the skin, the soot is deposited around the rim of the wound, and the gases have their own effects.

There in Moxley's photos of what he believed was an *exit* wound, I saw it all. Burns and soot on the edges of her abdominal wound. That meant the muzzle was against her skin when the gun was fired. Those small but unmistakable signs told me this was an entrance wound, not an exit.

By the same token, the little wound in her back showed none of the searing or soot. It was clearly the exit path of a bullet (or piece of bullet).

And there was another thing. The torn zipper and missing button on Ernestine's jeans had been presumed by investigators to be the sign of a struggle. But they weren't.

Remember all that hot gas from the muzzle? With the barrel against her skin, it all blew into her, temporarily inflating her abdomen with enough force to rip her jeans and tear open the entrance wound. The muzzle gases had briefly expanded her abdominal cavity with a force of three thousand pounds per square inch, so forceful her jeans were torn open and the waistband was imprinted on her skin.

Poor police work and a bad original autopsy by a doctor with little or no forensic training had led to the wrong conclusion. Their erroneous leap to the conclusion that the entrance wound was always smaller than the exit supported a flawed prosecution theory that sent a man to prison.

Did it mean that Martin Frias didn't put the gun against Ernestine's belly and pull the trigger? By itself, no. But Moxley's other experts were examining other pieces of evidence and quickly coming to the conclusion that Ernestine had committed suicide—just as it had appeared at first glance to investigators, and consistent with Martin's account.

The prosecution claimed Ernestine had been shot from behind, then twisted around to fall onto her back. But blood-spatter expert Judy Bunker saw no way Ernestine could have twisted around with a smashed spine. And even if she had, she would have slung blood in a semicircle as she fell. There was no sign of that.

Using a scanning electron microscope, forensic chemist Dr. Robert

Lantz determined that gunshot residue had traveled from Ernestine's front, through her abdomen, and out her back . . . not the reverse. The prosecution argued that the residue on the front of the shirt might have been deposited there after blowing through Ernestine's body from the back.

And prosecutors thought it preposterous that if Ernestine had shot herself, Martin would not have heard the hunting rifle's blast. But Dr. Harry Hollein, an acoustics expert, showed how Martin might have missed the Weatherby's thunderous boom. A similar rifle fired into the body of a dead horse from several feet away emitted up to 120 decibels, equal to a live rock concert or standing within three feet of a power saw. But when the muzzle was placed against the skin and fired, there was only a muffled thump, akin to somebody kicking the side of a trailer house. All the sound was absorbed by the body, which acted like a silencer.

A thump.

Exactly what Martin Frias said he heard in the dark that night.

It all made more sense now, at least to Moxley. The forensic facts were consistent with Martin's story, and Ernestine most likely killed herself by sitting or kneeling on the floor of her bedroom, pulling the muzzle of the upside-down Weatherby against her tummy, and pushing its trigger with her thumb.

Four months after interrupting my steak dinner in Cheyenne, Robert Moxley was convinced he'd found the truth that would set Martin Frias free. He asked the trial court for a new trial, based on his discovery of new evidence, supported by a string of forensic scientists who'd examined the evidence.

The judge rejected his appeal.

So he took his case to the Wyoming Supreme Court with a unique, gutsy argument. Martin Frias, he said, should get a new trial because new evidence proved Ernestine's shooting didn't happen the way the prosecution said, and because Frias clearly had a bad lawyer.

The state's Supreme Court justices refused to grant Moxley's motion on new evidence. Why? He'd had every chance to gather it before

Frias's trial. It's not "new" evidence if he merely failed to look for it at all.

But ironically, his failure to look for that evidence in the first place proved that Martin Frias's lawyer—Robert Moxley—had been ineffective. Because of that, they said, Frias should get a new trial.

With a new trial granted, Moxley had one last chance to save Frias and he didn't want to screw it up again. This time he'd collect all the medical evidence that he'd missed the first time.

The first order of business: exhume Ernestine. I wanted to attend the second autopsy myself, but my schedule wouldn't allow it, so in my place, the defense hired my friend, the renowned forensic pathologist Dr. William Eckert, to observe the new autopsy instead. Eckert already agreed with me that Ernestine's bullet wounds had been misinterpreted.

Dr. Eckert was a New Jersey–born forensic pathologist who'd made his bones as a deputy coroner in New Orleans and Kansas before becoming a much-sought-after consultant in retirement. When Bobby Kennedy was assassinated in 1968, Los Angeles county coroner Thomas Noguchi sought advice from Eckert, who knew the jurisdictional issues that plagued JFK's death investigation five years before. He told Noguchi not to let Washington steal the case, and he didn't.

At the time the Frias case was revived in 1985, Eckert was fresh from a Brazilian expedition to identify the remains of Josef Mengele, the chief doctor at the Nazis' Auschwitz concentration camp who vanished after the war and secretly continued medical experiments in South America. The team concluded the corpse in Wolfgang Gerhard's grave in a small coastal town was indeed Mengele (and DNA confirmed it in 1992).

Later, Eckert was part of an eight-person team of pathologists—all fascinated by the new "science" of criminal profiling—who reopened the coldest case in modern history: Jack the Ripper's slayings of seven prostitutes in London in the late 1800s. They concluded the faceless killer had probably been a butcher by trade.

Although nobody had ever heard of or even cared about Martin Frias, this invisible immigrant laborer who lived on the margin of a small town in an alien place called Wyoming, his case was more important than finding Jack the Ripper or Josef Mengele. They were dead, and no amount of forensic skill would bring justice to them or their victims. But we had a chance to right this wrong and let an innocent man live the rest of his life, free.

Aside from the gross error on the bullet wound, Eckert was also perturbed that the scars on Ernestine's wrists—artifacts of prior suicide attempts—had been ignored, and how the original pathologist had overstated his qualifications to do forensic work. In the hearing for a new trial, Eckert had spoken eloquently about how good forensic pathologists work tirelessly to find the right answer.

Now he joined the prosecution's doctors at the graveside of a troubled young woman whose violent death had sent a man to prison. A year after she was buried in a Cheyenne grave, could she tell us anything new?

On a frosty autumn morning in 1986, a small army of doctors and lawyers—the defense lawyers, the hospital pathologist who performed the original autopsy, the state's hired experts, and my old colleagues Drs. Charles Petty and Irving Stone from the Dallas Medical Examiner's Office, Dr. Eckert, and some state investigators—converged on Ernestine's grave in Cheyenne's Olivet Cemetery, where her father had buried her four days after she died. Her obituary had asked that in lieu of flowers, mourners contribute to crime prevention programs, a subtle but deliberate accusation of murder.

Around dawn, more than two years after her funeral, they lifted Ernestine's coffin from the high plains earth and drove it an hour west to a basement morgue at the university in Laramie. Because of a ripe odor emanating from the box, the pathologists opened the casket in the ambulance garage.

Inside lay Ernestine, wearing her glasses. Although she'd been embalmed, her remains had naturally flattened out somewhat. She looked as if she'd been left out in the rain; her body was covered in large beads of condensation, formed by the change of temperatures between her cold grave and the warm hearse.

In the morgue, new X-rays were taken of Ernestine's remains from every angle, and Eckert observed that Ernestine's liver was shredded by the blast. The state's pathologists used a reciprocating saw to remove her spine where it had been hit by the bullet, then sent it to Dr. Petty's state-of-the-art crime lab in Dallas for analysis.

When science had finished with her, most of Ernestine was returned to the frigid earth in the Cheyenne cemetery, where she could lie unmolested for the rest of eternity.

After the second autopsy, the state's doctors stuck to their opinion, but Moxley was more firmly convinced she had died in a tragic suicide, not a homicide.

Both sides were utterly convinced their theories were correct.

And Martin Frias's freedom hung in the balance.

In December 1986, almost exactly two years after he was convicted of murdering Ernestine Perea, Martin Frias's new trial began. But this time, his defense team came loaded for bear.

For seven days, the prosecution pushed its same old theory: Ernestine had been shot from behind during a struggle with someone in her bedroom, fell onto her back, and died as her assailant staged the room to look like a suicide. Lack of gunshot residue and char on Ernestine's cotton-knit, blue-striped tank-top suggested to state crime technicians that the shot had come from at least three feet away, from an assailant lying on or crouching near the floor. That assailant was an enraged, jealous Martin Frias, they said.

This time they put the eminent Drs. Petty and Stone on the stand to say the physical evidence pointed to homicide.

Then all of Moxley's forensic experts took the stand—blood-spatter expert Judy Bunker, forensic pathologist Dr. Bill Eckert, acoustics expert Dr. Harry Hollein, electron microscopist Dr. Robert Lantz, and others—to connect the dots that ended in Ernestine's suicide.

The blood spatters were consistent with a contact wound in the belly as Ernestine sat on the floor, and gunshot residue was present but nearly invisible to the prosecution's outdated technology, they said. The sights and sounds were consistent with Martin's account, they said. And Ernestine's past flirtations with suicide suddenly weighed heavier.

I testified again how the telltale clues around the young mother's belly wound told us everything we needed to know about the shot that killed her, from the seared edges of her wound to her torn jeans.

And this time around, the investigators' failings loomed larger. They had made no diagrams of the crime scene, taken no measurements. Some crucial tests were never done. The jury was left with reconstructions based largely on crime scene photos.

Bottom line: Moxley's experts—who all worked for free—agreed that Ernestine almost certainly shot herself. And in the end, even the small-town coroner admitted that he now believed our suicide theory, too.

This time the jury deliberated for less than three hours. At one point in the jury room, they even requested Martin's rifle and reenacted how Ernestine might have shot herself while sitting on her floor. It was possible and now it all made sense to them.

As they announced their "not guilty" verdict, Martin Frias wept and hugged Moxley. His two years and ten days in prison had been hard on him, but now he was free.

In coming days and weeks, he was granted citizenship under new federal amnesty legislation, and he petitioned the court for custody of his children. Ultimately, he moved away from Wyoming, remarried, and had another child, although, tragically, he never won back custody of his kids with Ernestine. And even today, his prosecutors, investigators, and many locals in the town of Wheatland continue to believe he's a murderer.

But he's free.

Martin Frias's case had to be recognized as a puzzle before it could be solved. Sometimes these mysteries are never recognized and justice isn't done. Murders sometimes present as suicides, accidents as murders, or suicides as accidents. It's not just the stuff of Hollywood drama. Humans are imperfect and they sometimes see only what their subconscious is secretly whispering for them to see. Real-life mysteries often unfold into unexpected conclusions.

I've seen more than my share of cases where the *first* conclusion isn't always the *best* conclusion. Sorting them out is one of the few real rewards of the grim work I've chosen.

Forty-two percent of Americans die from natural causes, and 38 percent in accidents. Nine percent are suicides, and 6 percent are homicides (not always murder, but always deaths caused by other humans). That leaves 5 percent of deaths that we simply can't explain.

So in America today, almost one of every five Americans dies in a suspicious way. Something is out of time or place, and we must go deeper to find answers.

Frias's puzzling case wasn't the first time nor the last that poor police work, shoddy forensics, and rushed conclusions clouded the real cause or manner of a death. It is the bane of medical examiners everywhere. A gut reaction isn't always correct. Sometimes, as Martin Frias's experience proved, the most significant clues aren't always obvious, but they're there. We must only be willing to see them and open-minded enough to interpret them honestly—and even then, as we've seen so often in the relatively recent shooting deaths of Trayvon Martin and Michael Brown, the world might prefer its own conclusions, in spite of the facts.

Like I said before: The forensic pathologist's only mission is finding the truth. It's not supposed to be for the police or against the police or for a family or against a family. I'm supposed to be impartial and tell the truth. Now, sometimes what I told them they didn't want to hear, and sometimes they did. But I didn't care, because I was telling them the truth.

The truth isn't always satisfying.

SAN ANTONIO. WEDNESDAY, JANUARY 11, 1984.

Something wasn't right.

A cold wind blew out of the north, plunging the normally balmy

South Texas temperatures well below freezing. A low, sepulchral sky made this morning feel like death.

Ann Ownby didn't sleep well the night before. Her husband Bob hadn't come home. He hadn't even called to say he'd be late. So before dawn, she drove to the Army base where he'd gone that night, Fort Sam Houston, to see if he was still there.

She entered the two-story building where he kept an office, but it was locked. She drove around a while, then returned, but he still wasn't there, so she left.

Then there was a sudden commotion in the building. At 0640, the duty day hadn't even really started, but a base employee coming to work early had used a vaulted stairwell toward the rear of the building and found Bob.

He'd been hanged, dangling in the cold open space between floors. The noose around his neck was tied to the stairway's handrail on the floor above. There was a little blood on his face and his hands were tied behind his back with a military-style web belt.

Pinned to Ownby's sweater was a chilling typewritten message, in all capital letters:

CAPTURED. TRIED. CONVICTED OF CRIMES BY
THE UNITED STATES ARMY AGAINST THE PEOPLE
OF THE WORLD. SENTENCED. EXECUTED.

In the next hour, investigators found another foreboding note on Ownby's office desk, hastily scrawled in the general's own handwriting:

10 Jan 84. I started out of the building and caught a glimpse of some people inside who quickly moved toward the back. I don't know who they are or what they are doing. They were apparently startled. I came back here to call the MPs, however I cannot get any of the telephones to work. Just as a precaution, I am placing my office keys in my shoe. I will call the MPs as soon as I can get to a working phone.

Reserve major general Robert G. Ownby—a two-star general in charge of the 90th Army Reserve Command, and at forty-eight, the youngest general in the Reserves' history—had been murdered.

And his killers might be terrorists who'd infiltrated an Army base on US soil.

Anti-American terrorism didn't start on September 11, 2001, not by a long shot. We've been in revolutionaries' and anarchists' cross hairs for at least a century, and our military provides the easiest target. A steady stream of menacing attacks made headlines in the early 1980s.

In 1981, US brigadier general James Dozier was kidnapped in Italy by the radical Marxist terror group known as the Red Brigades, who threatened to kill him. After forty-two days in captivity, he was rescued by an Italian counterterrorist team, but the terror was just beginning.

Nine months before General Ownby's body was found, a suicide car bomber crashed a stolen van full of explosives into the American embassy in Beirut, Lebanon, killing sixty-three people. Eighteen were Americans.

Less than three months before he died, another suicide car bomber crashed through the gates of the US Marine barracks in Beirut, killing two hundred and forty-one American servicemen and wounding eighty-one. And only two months before, a time bomb exploded in the US Senate as a protest against the invasion of Grenada, hurting nobody but sending a shock wave through the government, especially the Pentagon.

It wasn't terribly far-fetched to think evildoers might steal across the porous US-Mexican border and in a mere two hours be in the heart of one of America's biggest military cities.

So on this unseasonably cold day in January, when they found a dead US Army general with a chilling death message pinned to his chest, the possibility of a terrorist hit against the military wasn't unthinkable. In fact, it might even have been some investigators' first fear.

General Ownby commanded sixty-three reserve combat units in Texas and Louisiana, more than four thousand reservists who were ready to deploy to any trouble spot in the world. He wasn't the chairman of the Joint Chiefs of Staff, but he was an easier target at Fort Sam Houston, an unfenced, ungated post in the middle of sprawling San Antonio. What self-respecting terrorist wouldn't leap at the opportunity to kill a two-star general if his front door were left open, literally and figuratively?

The Army issued an immediate alert, asking border authorities to watch for terrorists fleeing into Mexico. It issued bulletproof vests to two other generals at Fort Sam Houston, and warned high-ranking reservists to be especially vigilant.

But federal agents and Army investigators weren't ready to call it an act of terror. Despite the sinister message left on Ownby's body and his hastily scrawled note about mysterious intruders, the evidence didn't add up to the violent invasion of a military post.

For one, other than a small smear of blood on Ownby's face, we found no bruises or other marks on him suggesting a beating or struggle. There was no sign of forced entry. In fact, his jacket was found neatly folded on the second-floor landing, with his wallet lying tidily on top. His eyeglasses, folded closed, had been laid beside it.

Also, no group claimed responsibility for the assassination, as commonly happened in such crimes.

And the building's telephone system had been working properly all day and all night before, despite Ownby's note about phones not working.

Our only evidence suggesting a terrorist slaying was the note pinned to Ownby's sweater.

Good investigators keep open minds. For several days, they pursued other leads, looked at evidence from all angles, and considered alternative explanations. Yes, it might have been a terrorist execution, they knew . . . but it might also have been a murder staged to divert attention away from the real killer, or maybe an elaborate ruse to camouflage a suicide.

We began to look closer at General Ownby. Who might have wanted him dead? Might we find clues to his killer in his life story and his final days?

Robert Ownby was born on September 9, 1935, in Durant, Oklahoma. He was steeped in public service: His father, then Durant's postmaster, had risen through the ranks from a buck private in World War I to colonel in World War II. His mother was a public school teacher.

He grew up on Main Street, a quiet, studious kid who was well liked by his neighbors and classmates. He had a paper route and joined the Boy Scouts. A member of the high school honor society, student council, speech club, and Future Farmers of America, he was the epitome of small-town America in the 1950s, a golden boy full of wholesome promise.

In 1957, with a degree in animal husbandry and a commission from the Reserve Officer Training Corps at Oklahoma State University in Stillwater, Ownby started two years of active duty in the infantry. He attended basic infantry and parachute schools at Fort Benning, Georgia, before becoming a platoon leader in Washington's prestigious Old Guard unit that, among other solemn duties, escorts dead soldiers to their final resting places in Arlington National Cemetery and elsewhere.

After three years in the inactive reserve, Ownby joined the Texas National Guard and switched to the Army Reserve in 1972. In the 90th Army Reserve Command at Fort Sam Houston, he quickly rose through the ranks. In 1981, the youngest major general in Army Reserve history took command of the entire unit.

Ownby seemed equally successful in civilian life. He and his wife Ann had three children, and they lived in a big house in an upscale neighborhood. He could afford it: He was president and CEO of the Bristow Company, which made metal doors and frames for commercial buildings, and director of the Liberty Frost Bank.

His life was full of other strategic moves, some better than others. In 1982, he had left an executive job at a soft-drink maker to become an executive vice president at an independent oil company in San Antonio, but left after a few months, as drilling started to bust.

So why had this deeply religious community leader and exemplary father of three died? His autopsy quickly showed the *cause* to be asphyxiation by hanging, but was it murder or suicide?

Bureaucratic and jurisdictional confusion had delayed the Bexar County Medical Examiner Office's first examination of Ownby's body for nine hours after he was found, so it was impossible for me to determine the precise moment of death.

That's another Hollywood myth, that time of death is a simple, quick, infallible calculation.

When I was young, when you watched TV or went to the movies, the medical examiner or coroner was always this cadaverous guy who showed up at the murder scene carrying this small physician's bag— let's just call him Doc. Since a real forensic pathologist is not supposed to manipulate the body at the scene, I assume Doc carried his lunch in his little valise.

A cop always asked Doc the time of death, and Doc always had an answer. "Oh," he'd say gravely, "between one and one thirty this morning."

In real life, detectives might have arrested him immediately because the only person who could give the time that exactly was the murderer himself. Estimation of the time of death is usually an educated guess. Many factors affect a corpse after death, slowing or speeding natural processes, and they can occur in myriad combinations. Time of death might be a good investigative tool, but it is not exact science.

When I was in training, I was instructed to determine when the individual was last seen alive and when he was found dead, then to say he died some time in between. In court, my answer is usually something like "He was dead about twelve hours—give or take six hours."

So we couldn't precisely peg the general's moment of death, but we could safely say what killed him: asphyxia by hanging.

Ownby's neck wasn't broken; he died by strangling. Another Hollywood myth is that hanging always breaks a neck. Yes, sometimes it happens, but usually only in judicial executions. The only times I've seen broken necks in suicidal hangings is when an elderly victim has severe cervical osteoporosis that makes his neck bones brittle.

Death in these "nonjudicial" hangings is usually caused not by compressing the trachea (windpipe), but by choking the arteries in the neck that carry blood to the head and brain. The hanged person will lose consciousness in about ten to twelve seconds, convulse briefly, then be brain-dead within three minutes of passing out.

How do we know? Sadly, we know a lot more about hanging deaths in the digital age because many people now record their suicides with smartphones, webcams, and high-resolution video cameras. Forensic pathologists now can see all the grim details, captured forever in high definition.

We found no drugs or alcohol in the general's system; no injuries consistent with a physical assault; and no unexplained fingerprints, hairs, or fibers in the area. The handwriting on the note in Ownby's office was definitely his (although the typewritten note didn't come from typewriters in Ownby's Army office or home). The blood on his face wasn't conclusive of a fight; a small amount of blood from the nose and mouth is common in hangings.

Ownby struggled dreadfully to save himself. I noted numerous gouges and scuffs from black-soled military shoes high on the stairwell wall and metal handrail nearest the hanging body. General Ownby might have flailed frantically for several seconds, desperately seeking scant purchase on the slick, steeply slanted rail, trying to relieve the weight on his noose by perching there. But he kept slipping. Or he might have convulsed violently after blacking out. The damage was so prolific that after the crime scene was released, the wall needed two coats of paint to cover the scars.

Bigger questions troubled us. How could he have lashed his own wrists behind his back? If not hanged by his unknown assailants, how could he have hanged himself while awkwardly bound? Where had the purported terrorist note been typed?

We reenacted several possible scenarios at the death scene, seeking answers, while the pieces of our puzzle slowly fell into place.

Three days after his death, some three thousand mourners attended Ownby's funeral at Trinity Baptist Church, a stone's throw from the military building where he died.

The Reverend Buckner Fanning, a prominent Texas evangelist and Ownby family friend, delivered a poignant eulogy, aimed partly at defusing media speculation that was now front-page news across the country.

"We are not here today because Bob Ownby died, but because he lived," Fanning told the somber overflow crowd. "Today, the world is swirling frantically with questions about his death, but we're standing firmly on the unquestionable facts of his life, his faith, his love of family. . . .

"It is always important to ask the right question. [But] mankind has a propensity for asking questions that don't matter."

Under corpse-cold, gray skies, Ownby's flag-draped casket was carried to his grave in the Fort Sam Houston National Cemetery, in a section reserved for heroes and generals. A howitzer fired a thirteen-round salute, each thunderous clap precisely eight seconds after the last—proper military protocol for a major general.

All the while, Ownby's family and friends believed passionately he'd been murdered and chafed at any suggestion that he killed himself. He wasn't depressed or teetering on a financial brink, they said. Nobody who saw him in his last days saw changes in his usually upbeat mood. His life seemed perfect to them. The general's disbelieving brother, himself a doctor, told the press he planned to hire an independent legal advocate to review everything the medical examiner, the FBI, and the US Army Criminal Investigation Command (CID) found. For them, our questions were intrusive, insulting, and immaterial.

But our questions *did* matter. While my team of forensic sleuths continued to work feverishly on this case that had drawn international media attention, the FBI and CID agents probed deeper. In the few days after he was discovered dangling in the stairwell, they found signs that Ownby's life might not have been as idyllic as it appeared.

At the time of his death, his comfortable home was mortgaged to the hilt, and several bank loans were coming due. To make matters worse, his former oil-field employer was being sued by several creditors—including Liberty Frost Bank's parent—for unpaid loans. In all, he owed an estimated $2 million, bigger money than most of us will earn in a lifetime.

Ownby's safety net was two life insurance policies for a total of $750,000. Both contained "suicide clauses" that would have prohibited any payments if the general killed himself, but not if he was murdered. In fact, if he had died in any way other than suicide, his family would have received all the money and have avoided the oncoming financial catastrophe.

This bizarre case was coming into focus, but all the dots hadn't yet been connected. We suspected but couldn't say with certainty that there had been no terrorists or conniving murderers.

In our re-creations with the FBI, we discovered Ownby could have easily bound his own hands behind his back with a canvas belt, as some of Ownby's own military colleagues demonstrated for us.

First, he tied his hangman's rope to the top railing of the stairwell and looped the noose around his neck. Then he likely slipped his hands through a loosely knotted belt behind his back and tightened it by pinning the loose end against the railing and tugging.

Then he simply straddled the second-floor railing and slipped off, falling six feet. Not far enough to break his neck or to let him escape his predicament . . . just far enough to strangle him as he thrashed, maybe having ghastly second thoughts. But it was too late.

So we could prove that it was *possible* he bound his own hands and killed himself, but we needed more.

Then we found the typewriter that had created the reputed "execution" note.

In the general's civilian work office. Not his home or military office, but a place where only he and a few others had access.

It was an IBM Selectric, a popular electric model that employed a typeball and a pre-inked plastic ribbon in a disposable cartridge. When the typist touched a key, the machine instantly rotated the ball and banged it against the carbon-film ribbon, transferring the corresponding letter, numeral, or symbol to the paper. In less than the blink of an eye, the ribbon moved a fraction of an inch to expose fresh carbon "ink" for the next keystroke.

What General Ownby might not have known is that the carbonized plastic ribbon essentially recorded everything he typed. Investigators were able to actually read the terrorist note in letters left directly on the ribbon when he'd typed it in his private office at Bristow.

With no unidentifiable fingerprints on the keys, and the unlikelihood that the killers would have typed their note here and killed the general elsewhere, it was the last proof we needed.

Nine days after Ownby died, I officially ruled his death a suicide. I announced my decision and explained all the evidence to a swarm of reporters who'd been impatiently awaiting an ending to this strange tale. Ownby's family remained militantly unconvinced, but federal and Army investigators concurred. There was simply no evidence to support that the general had been killed by someone else—a terrorist, a serial killer, a jealous lover, a hit man.

Reserve major general Robert G. Ownby killed himself.

If he had given his family a choice between his life or a check for $750,000, it's safe to assume his family wouldn't have hesitated to choose his life. But he didn't give them that choice, and in the end, they got neither.

People fake murder. They do it for many reasons. In Ownby's case, maybe only because a big life-insurance policy wouldn't pay for a suicide. But he might also have considered the act of suicide a disgrace, the ultimate admission of failure. Maybe he had religious reasons for his ruse. Or maybe he just felt it was his only chance to appear a hero in death.

I'd seen such fatal subterfuge before and since. It wasn't even the last faked murder of a San Antonio military officer I'd see. General Ownby's suicide bore an eerie resemblance to the peculiar 2003 death of Air Force colonel Philip Michael Shue, a military psychiatrist who crashed his car into a tree one April morning on the outskirts of San Antonio.

When rescuers got to Shue, they found his undershirt had been ripped open from the chest to the navel and there was a six-inch vertical gash in his chest. Even more bizarre, both of his nipples had been removed (and were never found). His earlobe and part of a finger had been amputated. Both wrists and ankles had been wrapped in torn duct tape, which now dangled from his cuffs.

Dr. Jan Garavaglia, then one of my medical examiners in the Bexar County ME's office and now one of the most recognizable faces in forensics as TV's "Dr. G," autopsied the fifty-four-year-old Shue while investigators dug into the case. They found a history of psychiatric problems, and he had been seeing some of his professional colleagues for depression and panic attacks.

She also found superficial hesitation wounds around the colonel's deeper cuts, shallower incisions or abrasions commonly caused by tentative attempts to build up courage before the final, fatal wound is inflicted.

He had no alcohol in his system, but Dr. Garavaglia found the anesthetic lidocaine—self-prescribed by Colonel Shue ten days earlier—in his blood. It had likely been smeared or injected around each nipple and in the middle of the chest. If his torturers had intended to cause pain with such cruel mutilation, would they have given him a drug to ease the pain?

In the end, there was no evidence that anyone but Shue himself had inflicted his weird wounds, and he died of massive head trauma caused by the crash. The death was ruled a suicide by both my medical examiner's office and a grand jury.

Colonel Shue's widow continues to believe he'd been abducted and sadistically tortured before escaping his captors and dying in a car accident during his urgent flight. She argues that no cutting tools, no body parts, and no injection sites were ever found. The lidocaine, she says, was to relieve itchiness on Shue's shaved chest before a routine medical procedure. And she points to the fact that Shue's fingerprints were not on the duct tape, and no rubber gloves turned up.

Motive? The colonel's widow points to a life insurance policy that paid $500,000 to his ex-wife and ominous, threatening letters in weeks before his death. No charges have ever been filed, although a Texas court ruled Colonel Shue's death a homicide in a 2008 civil suit over insurance payments—but didn't suggest any suspects.

The physical evidence simply didn't support his widow's scenario at the time, and no new evidence has come to light since. Ask yourself: If you had been perversely tortured and had broken free, where would you go? Probably the police or a hospital, or maybe a public place where someone could help. But Shue was driving *away* from the city and its many hospitals. He passed three of the exits into his own suburban town. He even had a working cellphone in the car. Does that sound like someone fleeing a vicious, pitiless assailant?

Shue's widow's reaction is normal, even reasonable, but her view of the case is distorted by her love. I feel genuinely sorry for her and for thousands of other relatives who have simply refused to accept my forensic conclusion that their loved ones committed suicide. Even in a modern society where we know more about mental illness, many relatives feel embarrassment or guilt, so it's common for families to doubt or reject such a conclusion.

But my first priority is to establish the cause and manner of a death as precisely as I can, using all the tools at my disposal. In this case, we simply found no hard evidence of homicide and plenty to suggest suicide.

Around this same time, death touched me, too.

My mother died on a Monday in the lull between holidays in 2003. She was ninety-one. My parents had been married for sixty-three years, shared a good life, and had likely forgotten a time when they weren't together.

Violet Di Maio died of the natural causes one might expect at ninety-one, but it was the one death my father couldn't set aside. Six days later, a Sunday, he died, too. Maybe he died of a broken heart, because he loved my mother with all of it, but I couldn't see into his heart either.

Their funeral brought my sisters and me home to Brooklyn, where we gathered to say good-bye and lay them together in Green-Wood

Cemetery, among many of the people—mobsters and mechanics, mothers and teachers, some famous and most unknown—my father had examined in his long career.

I didn't cry. It wasn't that I didn't grieve for them. I did. It's just that my mother would have been horrified at the undignified display of public tears, and I loved her too much to break her rule.

I cannot know the real why in these deaths. It's beyond knowing. Fantastic tools allow us to analyze microscopic remnants of what actually happened, but we have no science to detect traces of the fears, nightmares, and inner demons that caused it. The human heart isn't a hard drive that I can open up to discern every secret single keystroke of a life. I'm sure the families of General Ownby and Colonel Shue would like to know even more than I do.

Broken hearts happen, even if they leave no trace evidence.

Dying is sometimes easier than living with dying.

SPARKS, NEVADA. FRIDAY, FEBRUARY 5, 2010.

Malakai Dean was an ordinary two-year-old, with the gift of boundless curiosity and the energy of a whirlwind. His heart was as big as his smile and he showed both when he picked all the neighbors' pretty flowers and delivered tiny bouquets to their porches. In some ways, he belonged to his whole neighborhood. A child of the village.

They all knew his story. His young mother Kanesia, only sixteen when she got pregnant with him, still lived at home with her own mother, and her baby daddy was in prison. Grandma's busy suburban duplex was crowded with her other kids, some just a few years older than her first grandson, little Malakai. Kanesia and her son lived in the garage of the crowded little house. Ends were met, but life was in constant motion and upheaval.

So the kid didn't have the best start in life, but things were looking up. Now nineteen, Kanesia had met somebody. Kevin Hunt was a responsible guy with a future. A handsome active-duty US Marine who'd even gone to college to become a cop. A friend had introduced them while Kevin was on a weekend leave from his base in California. Now Kevin spent all his free time in the Reno area, with Kanesia and Malakai.

He and Kanesia had already talked seriously about getting married. Kevin treated Malakai like a son and planned to adopt him after the wedding. He changed his diapers, read him bedtime stories, and took him to the movies. Malakai had begun calling him "Dad." He'd already bought Malakai his first bike and spent almost as much time with the child as he did with Kanesia. Oh, there was some friction with Grandma, but Kanesia just reckoned it was her mother's protective streak rearing up. Grandma was protective and wanted only the best for all her kids. Yeah, Kanesia had made some bad choices before, but this time, to her, it felt so right.

And now Kanesia was pregnant again. Five months along. Stuff was getting real.

But today their world was in more upheaval than usual. The pregnant Kanesia (and others in the house) had some kind of stomach bug. Because Malakai had been born six weeks premature and had required three weeks of constant, expensive medical care, she was nervous about anything that could disrupt this pregnancy. When her stomach cramps began, not wanting to risk damaging her unborn child, Kanesia needed some medical reassurance. So Kevin took her to the hospital—where they hooked her up to an IV drip as a precaution—and Grandma took Malakai to her Sparks beauty salon, where everybody was getting ready for a big family portrait that weekend.

But Malakai being Malakai, he was soon bouncing off the salon's wall like a turbine in a bottle. He scribbled in the magazines, flirted with the hairdressers, jumped on the chairs, and ran amok. When Grandma couldn't control him any longer, she called Kevin to fetch the toddler.

Kevin arrived at the salon within minutes and left with Malakai at 4:21 p.m. He didn't want Malakai to see his mom in a hospital bed, connected to strange wires and tubes, and it was an unusually warm winter day in the Sierra foothills, so he drove to a small park nearby where Malakai could blow off some energy while he waited for Kanesia's all-clear call.

Unleashed on an empty playground, the rambunctious Malakai was in heaven. He clambered over the enormous play structure, exploring its tunnels, climbing up ladders, dangling on swings, skittering across its elevated bridges, leaping onto its slides.

Then Malakai fell.

While scrambling up a slide, the little boy lost his footing and tumbled over the edge, dropping four or five feet into the sand below. He started to cry, but Kevin brushed the sand from his face and calmed him. There were some superficial scrapes on the right side of his face, but nothing worse than a thousand kids on a thousand playgrounds suffered a thousand times a day. It didn't take long for Malakai to return to his old self, happy and ready to play.

But this ten-minute playdate was done. Around 4:30 p.m., Kanesia called Kevin to pick her up.

On the sidewalk outside the hospital a few minutes later, a security camera caught Malakai reaching up to hold Kevin's hand, smiling and nearly running along beside as they went inside.

Kevin Anthony Hunt had been part of Malakai's life for more than six months. In a house full of women and children, he'd been instantly cast as the father figure in the boy's life. But who was he really?

Kevin, then twenty-four, was the oldest of seven kids. His father was a federal worker and his mom worked in child protective services. His parents ran a tight ship, but they trusted Kevin implicitly, often leaving him in charge of the other kids. There'd never been any problems.

He grew up mostly in a Boston suburb, where he was a track and football star in high school and kept a 3.4 grade average. He learned to play the piano at music camp, and also became fluent in Spanish and Portuguese. He attended church regularly with his family. After graduation, he enrolled in John Jay College of Criminal Justice in New York City, with a dream of becoming a US marshal or a detective.

There he met a young woman, who was soon pregnant. To support his new family, he dropped out of college in 2006 and worked a year as a prison guard before separating from his wife and two young sons. He joined the Marines in 2007, still hoping to become a cop.

After his basic training and schooling, he was stationed at the Marine Corps' Mountain Warfare Training Center in Bridgeport, California, a small town two and a half hours south of Reno. When he had liberty, he'd always drive toward the bright lights of Reno, where a friend introduced him to nineteen-year-old Kanesia Dean. This single, young mother captivated him, but he also fell immediately in love with her two-year-old son named Malakai.

And very quickly after they started dating, Kanesia got pregnant again. Kevin didn't just want to do the right thing. He genuinely loved Kanesia and her little boy, and he wanted a family, too. He asked her to marry him not out of obligation, but out of genuine hope for the future.

They checked Kanesia out of the hospital and drove to a favorite Mexican diner for supper. But they had barely settled into their chairs when Malakai turned lethargic and quiet. Then he vomited. And vomited again. Kevin and Kanesia scooped up the sick child and rushed home.

At home, it only got worse. Kanesia was sure that Malakai had caught the stomach bug that had wreaked havoc in the house that week, so she put him in her bed, hoping his little body could fight it off. But he continued to vomit through the evening. It was so bad Kevin changed the bedsheets and Malakai's pajamas more than once.

At bedtime, Kevin and Kanesia crawled into bed beside Malakai

Around 11:20 p.m., Kanesia instinctively reached out and touched Malakai. He wasn't breathing.

She screamed in the dark. Kevin leapt up and began CPR on the little boy right on the bed while Kanesia frantically dialed 911.

Soon Grandma rushed in from the other room and took charge. She roughly shoved Kevin out of the way. She straddled Malakai's unbreathing body on the soft bed and began a manic, forceful attempt to save her beloved grandson, pushing, thumping, and puffing with every fiber of her being, hoping to revive him.

Paramedics arrived within minutes, but it was too late.

Malakai was dead.

The next day, Malakai's little body, still in his soiled pajamas, was autopsied while the medical examiner's investigators tried to piece together what happened.

Grandma pointed a finger directly at Kevin Hunt. She said Malakai was always subdued around Kevin, who thought the child was babied by the women in the house. The day before, she said, the usually effervescent boy didn't want to go with Kevin at the salon. And she now suspected the child's injuries were not from an accidental fall, but from a beating by Kevin.

In the morgue, Dr. Piotr Kubiczek autopsied the child under the watchful gaze of two Sparks detectives and a deputy DA, who feared this might be murder.

Dr. Kubiczek saw the bruising and scrapes on Malakai's right temple and cheek. He noted a patterned bruise—including two parallel marks about the width of fingers that were emerging postmortem—that looked like it might have been created by an adult's hand slap. The child's diaper was stained with pink urine, suggesting blood in his bladder. He found other bruising on the boy's chest and back.

Inside, Dr. Kubiczek found more damage. Malakai's pancreas, spleen, and the tissues of his abdominal wall, all of which had seeped almost a pint of blood into the child's belly. His kidneys, bladder, and intestines were bruised. He also found a purplish-gray embolus—in this case, a large blood clot thicker than a wine cork—bulging in the arteries leading to Malakai's lungs, but didn't believe it was involved in the child's death. No effort was made to determine where it came from.

Dr. Kubiczek would later describe Malakai's internal wounds as similar to injuries from a multistory fall or a high-speed car crash. They happened within minutes or a few hours before death, he said, and would have been immediately painful, almost crippling.

Finding no other troubling evidence—all other organs were normal, he said—Dr. Kubiczek ruled that Malakai Dean died because his vital organs had been violently ruptured and leaked blood until the child died.

"It is my opinion," Dr. Kubiczek wrote in his autopsy report, "that the death of Malakai Dean is due to multiple blunt force injuries of the abdomen. The manner of death is homicide."

Three weeks later, Kevin Anthony Hunt was arrested for child abuse resulting in murder. If convicted, he could serve the rest of his life in prison.

In two lengthy interviews by police, Kevin—who had never been in any trouble before—told the same story: He'd spent less than forty minutes alone with Malakai, who'd fallen from a playground slide but didn't seem to have been hurt seriously. Defense lawyer David Houston, who'd known a few liars in his time, felt Kevin was either one of the best liars he'd ever seen, or he was telling the truth.

But cops and prosecutors had a different theory: During those forty minutes with Malakai, Kevin had beaten him, mortally damaging his internal organs and causing some superficial bruising on his face. He was lying about the playground fall, they said. And the abuse had probably been going on for a while, they believed.

When a child dies, a family bears the unimaginable weight of the emotional suffering, but nobody escapes unharmed. Not the accused, not first responders, not cops, not medical examiners, not prosecutors, not defense lawyers, not judges. And not a community.

When race is introduced, the anger is often amplified. Races can be suspicious of each other in places where there's little mixing.

And Kevin Hunt was black in mostly white Reno.

The local reaction to Malakai's death was swift. Some wept, some cried for retribution. Most reader comments posted on local media stories and blogs ran a very short gauntlet from astonishing fury to naked racism. Some Internet trolls called for a lynching.

Houston, who'd grown up in Washington, DC, and was one of

Reno's celebrity litigators, stepped in to help. Something didn't add up, and he thought Kevin was unfairly accused. He represented some big Hollywood clients just so he could afford to take cases like this one.

After a local forensic pathologist found multiple errors in Dr. Kubiczek's autopsy, Houston called me. He soon sent a robust packet containing the complete autopsy, photos, investigative reports, and slides containing tissues samples collected from Malakai Dean— everything I'd need to evaluate the case.

America is a funny place sometimes. Our mantra is "innocent until proven guilty," but in child deaths, we often go through the looking glass: The accused is secretly presumed guilty and the defense must prove him innocent. In such cases, jurors often think with their hearts, not their brains. We all want justice for innocents, of course, but we must guard against being blinded by our zeal to get it.

Many of my greatest cases have been child deaths, but as a private consultant, I rarely take them. Every so often, though, I see a blatant injustice and I can't turn away. Some things just leap out. I quickly saw clues that had been missed.

That's why I took Kevin Hunt's case.

When the trial began two years later, the scene had been set for a forensic showdown. On one side was the original medical examiner, who had corrected many of his errors; on the other side were a couple of forensic pathologists, including me, who saw something he didn't. But the prosecution still wanted to punish a baby killer, and pursued Kevin with a special animosity, despite their largely circumstantial case.

In the meantime, while Kevin sat in the Washoe County Jail, Kanesia gave birth to their son, Jaiden.

When the trial began in early May of 2012, Malakai's relatives, including Kanesia, stood firm in their conviction that he'd been beaten to death by Kevin. They recounted the sad series of events leading up to the boy's death. Kevin's father sat in the courtroom every day, and some days, some of Kevin's uniformed Marine comrades attended the proceedings.

Dr. Kubiczek took the stand to explain his conclusions that Kevin Hunt had murdered Malakai. The bruises and scrapes on the boy's face and head. The split-open organs. The blood pooled in his abdomen. It must have all sounded grimly logical to the jury.

But there was a different story to be told when I took the stand.

For one, the scrapes and bruises on Malakai's face and head were ordinary classic playground injuries, common in falls. A big-city ME's office sees them regularly. The most specific thing that can be said about such injuries is that they are caused by impacts (falls, blows, etc.), but where some investigators saw evidence of a slap, I saw only marks left by paramedic's tape that might have been holding a mask or tube on the boy's face.

In short, I saw nothing that I could say was caused by a beating.

The wounds to Malakai's internal organs were serious, but they didn't cause him to bleed to death. At most, Malakai lost only about 28 or 29 percent of his total blood volume, and he could have tolerated almost twice as much.

More important, though, they weren't inflicted during the brief time the child was alone with Kevin Hunt seven hours before.

How do I know? Such injuries would have been extremely painful and caused almost immediate shock, but in the hours immediately following the park visit, Malakai showed none of the signs of shock (profuse sweating, dizziness, weakness, thirst, shallow breathing, blue lips or fingernails, clammy skin, among them). Even if shock were somehow delayed, he would have exhibited unmistakable symptoms before eight p.m. that night. He didn't.

Here's another point: Dr. Kubiczek's autopsy found nothing unusual about two-year-old Malakai's heart weighing 115 grams. In fact, his heart was grossly enlarged, about the size of a normal nine-year-old's heart. Malakai's heart should have been about half as large.

So what? If he had lived, Malakai would have suffered severe medical problems in the future. Even at his young age, it's likely that his enlarged heart wasn't able to adequately pump blood throughout his body, especially to his legs. That, in turn, probably led to the formation of blood clots in his lower extremities.

I believe one of those clots—so large that it must have formed over a period of days or weeks, not hours—broke loose from a vein and traveled to Malakai's heart. There it plugged the pulmonary artery, which carries blood from the heart to the lungs, and he died when his blood-starved lungs ceased to function.

The clot could not have been created by any alleged beating seven hours before. It was too big and couldn't have formed that quickly. It also could not have originated in Malakai's abdomen, where only one blood vessel is large enough to carry it, and no such evidence was found.

But here was the clincher for me: The lacerated organs showed no inflammation.

Inflammation is the body's attempt to defend itself from trauma, whether mechanical, chemical, or infectious. When tissue is injured in any way, its cells release two groups of chemical compounds. One of them causes local blood vessels to dilate, allowing damaging fluid to escape. The other attracts white blood cells to the area of the injury to break up and consume injured cells and begin the repair process.

In the abdomen, this happens almost immediately. Within two or three hours, abdominal injuries are inflamed as the body rushes to fix its problems.

In Malakai Dean's case, there was no inflammation. Even seven hours after the alleged fatal trauma to his internal organs, no inflammation.

How is that possible? It means only one thing: The trauma that caused those injuries was done around the time of death, probably after the child had died.

The damage to Malakai's organs was not caused by a beating by Kevin Hunt or anyone else. It wasn't caused by foul play of any kind.

In my opinion, two-year-old Malakai Dean died of natural causes when a blood clot, probably caused by poor circulation from his enlarged heart, caused his lungs to stop breathing.

The organ damage that cops and prosecutors attributed to a beating by an abusive boyfriend were, in fact, caused by his grandmother's desperate but inept CPR attempts upon a soft bed (instead of the firm floor, where professionals are taught to position patients). Malakai was already dead when Kanesia discovered he wasn't breathing. Thankfully never felt the intense pain his would-be rescue would have inflicted. He was already gone.

But these cases are never quite as easy as all that.

The jury eventually deadlocked 6–6, unable to reach a verdict. Given the highly charged nature of the case, and the natural prejudice against accused child abusers, it was a victory for Kevin Hunt.

Now the prosecution was in a pickle. It knew the conflicting medical evidence—including dozens of admitted errors by the medical examiner—made a second trial just as treacherous, so the state offered Kevin a deal: Plead guilty to voluntary manslaughter in return for four to ten years in prison, with credit for nearly four years he'd already served in county jail.

But the defense's pickle was no less tricky. Public opinion, lingering anger, and barely concealed racism made an acquittal dicey. If the choice was between a black kid with an imperfect story and a big city's investigative, forensic, and legal system, the jury might fracture. Winning outright seemed unlikely; losing sent Kevin Anthony Hunt to prison for life.

His choice was excruciating: Continue to insist on his innocence, as he'd done since suspicious cops first talked to him . . . or "confess" to killing the child who once called him "Dad," avoid the risk of a life in prison, end four years of angry litigation and recrimination in the papers, maybe even walk free within months to start a new life.

Kevin took the deal. On November 4, 2013, he was sent to Nevada's Warm Springs Correctional Center, a medium-security prison in Carson City.

At this writing, he was still there.

His dream of being a cop is gone. No dream has yet replaced it.

Kevin has never seen his son Jaiden, much less held him. And as it stands now, he will probably never see him until the boy is a man who can make his own decisions. If there is ever a relationship between them, it will start too late.

"My plan is to be the best dad I can ever be to my kids," Kevin wrote from prison in 2015. "I forever-long have been wishing for that day."

At those times when I think forensic science might not yet be perfect, I am always reminded that neither is justice.

‹ EIGHT ›

Death, Justice, and Celebrity

In a civilized society, we tend to idealize or build up myths about people and their behavior . . . and what constitutes civilization. We like to think that famous people have exceeded the ordinary in some important way, that they have achieved some higher plane of civilization and are somehow pulling us forward with them. But civilization is an extremely thin veneer. There's no difference between us and the people two thousand or four thousand years ago. We just make more laws, have keener tools, and conceal our violence with more class and finesse.

ALHAMBRA, CALIFORNIA. MONDAY, FEBRUARY 3, 2003.

Some time after sunset, Phil Spector—the music mogul, the puny genius, the onetime wunderkind who now wore wigs to conceal his baldness and high-heeled shoes to conceal his shortness—walked out of his lonely Jazz Age mansion to find someone, anyone, in the hollow light of another indifferent Los Angeles Sunday night.

Spector hated being alone, not just in his empty castle on the hill. In his life, too. He sometimes raged at being left alone, and he'd go to profound lengths to keep people in his orbit. In his sixty-five years,

he'd amassed a fortune by producing a soundtrack for two generations, from the Righteous Brothers to the Beatles to the Ramones. His
"Wall of Sound" made him famous and kept many people close. He
was a Rock & Roll Hall of Famer. He partied with Jagger, Dylan, Bono,
Springsteen, Lennon, Cher, and all the rest. His power and his money
attracted many more, although he had no friends, no confidants. Oh,
there'd been a couple of wives and many lovers, even a few children.
But none ever stayed.

His chauffeured black Mercedes, with a little red devil air fresh-
ener hanging from the rearview mirror and vanity plates that purred
"I ♥ PHIL," waited at the foot of his splendid back terrace, on the
piazza by the fountain. Adriano, a computer scientist in his native Bra-
zil but a limo driver in LA, opened a rear door for his boss, who wore
a cool rock-star mane and a white ladies' dinner jacket over white
slacks and a white shirt, part Gatsby, part Gollum.

Adriano drove Spector to Studio City to pick up an old friend for a
long dinner, nothing romantic, at The Grill on the Alley in Beverly
Hills. It worried his date when he ordered a couple of daiquiris before
dinner, partly because he'd been on the wagon for most of the past
ten years, and partly because she knew he took a complex cocktail of
mood-altering prescription drugs to regulate his bipolar disorder, seizures, and insomnia, but she didn't say anything. She didn't say anything either as he flirted with their waitress. That was Phil, always
seeking new satellites to draw into his orbit.

After a few hours, Adriano and Spector dropped his friend back at
her house, then sped back to The Grill around eleven p.m. to pick up
the waitress for a night on the town. They went to a nightclub called
Trader Vic's, where Spector drank 150-proof tequila and more daiquiris, then on to Dan Tana's for more drinking at his usual table near
the back. After one-thirty a.m., Spector left a five-hundred-dollar tip
on a fifty-five-dollar tab, and they decamped in Spector's limo to another nearby club, the House of Blues on Sunset Boulevard.

A drunken Spector and his star-struck waitress headed right up to
the Foundation Room, where all the Hollywood celebrities partied,

away from the little people. But hostess Lana Clarkson, a tall, strikingly beautiful blonde who'd been working at the House of Blues only a month, stopped him at the door.

"Excuse me, ma'am, you can't come in here," she said before her supervisor pulled her aside and whispered that was no woman, but the multimillionaire, multi-platinum music producer Phil Spector, who was a big tipper. *Treat him like gold,* the bouncer said, *like he was fucking Dan Aykroyd.*

Red-faced, Clarkson immediately escorted Spector and his date to the best open table.

Despite the embarrassing moment at the door, Spector was smitten again. At closing time, around two a.m., when his waitress-date ordered only water, he called for his driver to take her home. He ordered a Bacardi 151, straight up, while he flirted with another cocktail waitress and kept an eye on Clarkson, who cruised through the room, tidying things, pulling out chairs for customers, snatching empty glasses off tables, making small talk.

"She won't stay still," he observed to his new waitress about Clarkson. "She's like fucking Charlie Chaplin."

Maybe because she needed this job. At forty, Clarkson was an actress who hadn't had any good roles in too long. Six feet tall and still gorgeous, she stood out in this Hollywood crowd, especially after last call. She'd been somebody once, at least in B-movie cult circles, for her starring role in Roger Corman's *Barbarian Queen,* but that was nearly twenty years ago. She'd broken both wrists in an accident a few years before, the roles mostly dried up, and she grew depressed. She contented herself with the occasional commercial and the fawning fans at little comic-cons. At the moment, she worked for nine bucks an hour just to pay the $1,200-a-month rent on her 454-square-foot bungalow in Venice Beach and for a few expensive personal habits like fashionable clothes and prescription painkillers. If she lived on the edge, it was the far edge.

Spector invited his waitress to come home with him, and she made up a story about an early appointment the next morning. He needed somebody else to go back to his empty castle with him, so he invited Clarkson over to his table for a drink. She cleared it with her boss—conversation was allowed, but no drinking—and sat down with the odd little man after her shift ended.

Spector asked her if she wanted to see his castle. She did, of course, but she couldn't risk losing her job by getting too cozy with a customer. Instead, she asked him for a ride to her car. So he left another extravagant tip, $450 on a $13.50 tab, and called his driver.

At the employee parking garage, standing outside his limo, Spector continued to beg Clarkson, like a child. *Just one drink! Let's go to the castle!* Finally she relented and climbed back into the Mercedes. A little abashed, she told Adriano she was just going for one drink, but Spector barked at her, "Don't talk to the driver! Don't talk to the driver!"

On the half-hour drive back to Spector's opulent mansion, called Pyrenees Castle—literally a thirty-three-room turreted castle and wooded estate built in the 1920s amid the winding streets of Alhambra, an otherwise humdrum LA suburb—they petted, giggled, and watched an old Jimmy Cagney movie, *Kiss Tomorrow Goodbye,* in the back of the limo.

Around three a.m., Spector and Clarkson went inside while Adriano parked near the fountain and settled in until he had to take Clarkson home. It might be a while.

Two hours later, about five a.m., Adriano heard a pop. Not an explosion or loud bang. Just a muffled pop. He got out of the car and looked around. Seeing nothing, he got back in the car.

In a moment, Spector opened the mansion's back door, and Adriano got out, ready to take Miss Clarkson home. He saw his boss wore the same clothes but had a stunned look on his face—and a revolver in his hand.

"I think I killed somebody," Spector said.

Behind Spector, Adriano could see a woman's legs splayed out. When he looked closer, he saw Clarkson slumped in a chair, her long legs stretched out in front of her. Blood spattered her face and ran down her front.

"What happened?" Adriano asked, stupefied.

Spector shrugged and said nothing.

Adriano freaked. He ran back to the car and drove to the main gate, where he fumbled with his cellphone in the glow of the dashboard. He didn't know the address or Spector's number or anything. His fingers trembled as he punched buttons. His first call was to Spector's secretary, whose number was programmed into the phone. When she didn't answer, he left a message and dialed 911.

At 5:02 a.m., the police dispatcher picked up and asked why he was calling.

"I think my boss killed somebody."

Why did he think there'd been a killing? the dispatcher asked.

"Because he have a lady on the . . . on the floor," Adriano explained in his agitated, halting English, "and he have a gun in . . . in his hand."

Police found Clarkson's corpse slouched in a fake Louis XIV chair near the back door. Her legs were sprawled out in front of her, with her left arm at her side and her right draped over the chair's arm. Her leopard-print handbag was still slung on her right shoulder, its straps twisted around the chair's arm. Blood and other matter had spilled from her mouth and nose and cascaded down the front of her little black dress.

On the floor under her left calf was a bloody .38-caliber, six-shot Colt Cobra revolver, with five live rounds and one spent cartridge under the hammer. Blood had congealed on its wooden grips, trigger guard, barrel—in fact all over . . . but it appeared to have been wiped clean. A bit of Clarkson's front tooth—actually a cap—had lodged in the gun's front sight, and other tooth fragments were scattered on the floor.

Within arm's reach beside her was an ornate bureau, its top drawer open. Inside was a holster that fit the Colt Cobra.

On a matching chair nearby was Spector's leather briefcase, which contained, among other things, a three-pack of Viagra in which only one pill remained.

Soft, romantic music was still playing in the background. The adjoining living room was lit only by candles on the fireplace mantel. A Picasso hung on one wall, a drawing by John Lennon on the other. An almost-empty bottle of tequila and a brandy snifter with some kind of liquor in it sat on the coffee table.

In a nearby bathroom, cops found another brandy snifter and a pair of false eyelashes atop the toilet tank. On the floor, they found a cotton diaper soaked with blood and water.

In the master bedroom upstairs, a detective found Spector's white jacket, with a couple of small bloodstains and flecked with almost invisible blood specks, crumpled on the closet floor.

A deputy coroner from Los Angeles County arrived around five-thirty p.m., more than twelve hours after the shooting. Flies had already laid eggs in one of the dead woman's ears and in the clotted mess on her chest.

A dead actress. Shot in the mouth. In the wee hours. At a super-celebrity's mansion.

Lawyers and reporters would be crawling all over this one, so there was no room for error at autopsy. But the coroner's office had plenty of experience with these kinds of high-profile cases and knew the drill.

The next morning, Deputy Coroner Dr. Louis Pena performed the autopsy. Lana Clarkson died from a single gunshot wound to her head and neck. A copper-jacketed .38-caliber bullet entered through her mouth, gouged the top of her tongue, ripped through the back of her throat, completely tore her spinal cord from her brain stem, and lodged in the base of her skull.

The instantaneous disconnection of her spinal cord from her brain meant Clarkson could do nothing at the moment of impact except die. Her heart stopped beating, she stopped breathing, every nerve went dead, every muscle went limp. Her brain lived long enough to consume whatever oxygen it contained, but she wasn't likely conscious.

The bullet traveled straight back and slightly upward. The revolver's recoil shattered her two front incisor teeth, both recently capped. Dr. Pena found a bruise on the left side of Clarkson's tongue not caused by the bullet but possibly by the barrel being forced into her mouth.

He found other bruises on her hands, wrist, and forearm consistent with a struggle.

She had enough alcohol in her system to make her drunk, plus traces of the powerful painkiller hydrocodone and antihistamines. Her purse contained a number of prescription and nonprescription drugs, including cold medicine and medication for herpes.

The crime scene yielded more evidence, although it was as confounding as it was lurid.

On the floor, police found a cracked acrylic nail from her right thumb.

Criminalists found a mixture of Spector's and Clarkson's DNA all over the place: on the pair of false eyelashes in the bathroom, on the brandy snifters, on the mansion's back doorknob and latch, and in the blood they swabbed from both of Clarkson's wrists.

Clarkson's blood was on the stairway banister and the diaper found in the second-floor bathroom, although it had been diluted with water in some spots. The mist-like spatter and bloodstains on the jacket's left cuff, left elbow, pocket, outside right-front panel, and inside the left-front panel were Clarkson's, too, but they weren't massive.

Criminalists found Spector's DNA on Clarkson's left nipple but not in her vagina. They also found Clarkson's DNA on Spector's scrotum, suggesting she had performed oral sex on him. They found none of Spector's DNA under her fingernails.

Most fascinating—and befuddling: Only Clarkson's DNA was found on the gun, and only her hands had gunshot residue, a lot of it. Spector's hands and clothes were utterly free of any GSR, and except for the bloody specks and stains on the jacket, Spector had no foreign biological matter on his skin, hair, or clothes. Nobody's fingerprints were found on the gun.

That morning, cops recorded Spector calling Clarkson a "piece of shit."

"And I don't know what her fucking problem was," he said on tape, "but she certainly had no right to come to my fucking castle, blow her fucking head open."

Unconvinced investigators told Dr. Pena that Spector had fired the gun. They found no evidence Clarkson had ever been suicidal, and no suicide note was found. They believed Phil Spector shot Lana Clarkson while she sat on the faux antique chair, just as they had found her. Given the physical evidence Pena saw at autopsy, his opinion leaned toward homicide.

Two weeks after the shooting, Lana Clarkson's ashes were interred in Los Angeles' Hollywood Forever Cemetery, among so many of the great stars she had admired. Some had more in common with her than she ever dreamed. Beyond the stars, by the lake, was Virginia Rappe, the ambitious starlet who died in 1921 after a drunken party with the highest paid actor of his day, comedian Fatty Arbuckle. Across the lawn was William Desmond Taylor, a famous film director who was murdered in his home in 1922 and launched a million headlines but never a single arrest. And in another crypt was mobster Bugsy Siegel, who died when he was shot in the face at a Beverly Hills mansion in 1947. Nobody was ever charged.

Phil Spector was arrested the morning of Lana Clarkson's death but released on a one-million-dollar bond as police and coroner continued their investigation. Spector immediately began building an expensive dream team of topflight lawyers like Robert Shapiro and forensic experts, while plotting his end run around the suspicious media to prove his innocence, even before he was formally charged. Privately, he railed against "friends" who weren't publicly flocking to his defense. In strange videos from his castle, he claimed Clarkson had accidentally shot herself ("She kissed the gun," he told *Esquire*) for reasons he didn't know or care about.

But investigators had been hearing a lot of stories about Spector and guns. He'd reportedly brandished pistols in the studio at various times with John Lennon, Debbie Harry, and other rock icons. But there were darker stories, from women he dated or employed, about a crazy-drunk Spector pulling a gun when they prepared to go. He'd just freak out and try to prevent them from leaving. This famous music magnate seemed to have a profound fear of being alone or abandoned.

Homicide or suicide? It wasn't an easy call for the Los Angeles County coroner's office. The scientific evidence of murder was nonexistent; the final ruling rested more on the suggestion of sheriff's investigators than forensic proof.

Seven months after the shooting, LA county coroner Dr. Lakshmanan Sathyavagiswaran—just the latest in a long line of "coroners to the stars"—approved Dr. Pena's conclusion that Clarkson's death was officially a homicide (although he allowed for the possibility that she had shot herself). He later admitted that "intraoral" (in the mouth) gunshot wounds are almost always suicides. Or put another way, almost nobody shoots somebody else in the mouth.

Two months later, the Los Angeles district attorney charged Phillip Harvey Spector with murder and promised to seek either a first- or second-degree murder conviction. (First-degree murder requires evidence of premeditation, while second-degree murder does not, but both carried a maximum sentence of life in prison.) Spector pleaded not guilty.

In Los Angeles, however, celebrities seemed to have the magic Get Out of Jail Free card. The acquittals of O.J., Robert Blake, Michael Jackson, and so many other stars left a bad taste. Money, influence, and powerful friends had redefined justice in a city where entitlement, delusion, and egomania are celebrated virtues, not ugly quirks.

A cynical public saw Phil Spector as a weird little man whose excesses and demons had turned him into a rich, raving, trembling troll who lived in a hilltop castle, surrounded by ostentation and paid companions, drunkenly looking down upon the peasants and prowling in the dark for fresh meat to feed his ego and obsessions. But he was rich and famous—and it was LA, after all—so the case against him wouldn't be a slam dunk.

From a thousand miles away, that's what I thought, too.

One day my friend Linda Kenney Baden called. She was the wife of my old colleague Dr. Michael Baden, my father's former chief deputy in the New York Medical Examiner's Office and now one of America's most familiar forensic pathologists. But this wasn't a social call. Linda was a blue-chip defense lawyer, and she had joined the ever-changing team representing Phil Spector. He had fired Shapiro and hired the feisty Leslie Abramson, who had defended the Menendez brothers, but when Abramson abruptly resigned, Spector hired Bruce Cutler, the burly, bald Brooklyn brawler who defended mobster John Gotti.

Linda needed a gunshot wound expert.

Would I be interested in looking at some of the evidence against him? she asked. *Just to see if there was anything that might help?*

To be honest, I didn't have a good feeling about Spector. To me, he was peculiar, pompous, and perfectly capable of deadly gunplay. The case against him sounded plausible. I'd heard the strange stories about him, but I hadn't seen the evidence. So I agreed to take a look.

I wasn't alone. Spector had already begun building one of the most powerful teams of forensic experts ever amassed for a criminal trial. I knew most of them: Baden; my old boss in Baltimore, Dr. Werner Spitz; blood spatter expert Dr. Henry Lee; forensic toxicologist Dr. Robert Middleberg; and several others. My rate is only four hundred dollars an hour, but a quick glance at Spector's list of expert witnesses told me he'd probably spend half a million dollars before he ever got to trial.

Spector was desperate to avoid a conviction, and the prosecution was equally desperate to nail him. The district attorney's office had a long string of failures in high-profile celebrity prosecutions and wanted to break the streak. They would bring the entire weight of the state's own experts against him, sparing no expense.

I wasn't sure I wanted to be involved. Celebrity cases are a pain. Such trials are too often about the celebrity—whether he or she is the defendant or a victim—instead of the physical evidence. Where once newspapermen and broadcasters were the only media watching, now bloggers, Tweeters, and all manner of self-appointed "citizen journalists" join the throng of "reporters," all fighting for attention amid the clangor of our modern information wars. Court TV carries trials wall-to-wall. The Internet live-streams every minute. Every armchair criminalist posts an opinion based on little more training than binge-watching episodes of *CSI*. The end result is more carnival than court of law.

But I had agreed to take a look, and in a few days, a fat package arrived in the mail. It contained all the coroner's reports and autopsy; crime scene photos; the results of various forensic tests, such as toxicology and ballistics; and police accounts. There was also part of Lana Clarkson's rambling sixty-page memoir, detailing her childhood with an itinerant, single hippie mom, rock festivals and acid parties, and her years as a jet-setting, cocaine-snorting, B-movie hottie, but it stopped well short of her dismal final years. She was a sad, sympathetic figure. Hollywood is hard on women of a certain age, and in the eyes of casting agents, Lana Clarkson was past her expiration date.

As I waded through hundreds of pages, questions bubbled up.

I found no hard evidence that absolutely proved Spector innocent of the crime (or guilty, for that matter), but I could see a few cracks in an imperfect case against him. A lot of good forensic evidence was well collected, but it remained a largely circumstantial case. Maybe he was guilty as hell, but it wasn't the sure thing prosecutors claimed it to be.

For one, in my thirty-eight years as a medical examiner, I had seen hundreds of people shot in the mouth. All but three—99 percent—were suicides.

Women don't shoot themselves, some argued. In fact, shooting is the most common method of suicide among American women.

But a beautiful actress, even if she was suicidal, never would have shot herself in the face. The largest forensic study of suicide ever undertaken found that about 15 percent of female suicides shot themselves in the mouth (although admittedly, the women's beauty was not considered as a factor).

She never attempted suicide before, never talked about it, and didn't leave a note. Only about 8 percent of suicides previously attempted it, and only one in four leaves a note. Lana Clarkson didn't expressly threaten suicide, that's true, but it's often an impulsive, desperate act that requires no warning, especially among those who use guns. Her medical and personal papers proved she had a history of depression that required powerful drug therapy. Booze and hydrocodone can actually contribute to depression. So her alcohol and drug use, coupled with a disappointing career and financial situation, could have complicated her despondency.

Does that all prove Lana Clarkson shot herself? No, but when considered with physical evidence, homicide might not be the only explanation.

Clarkson was a foot taller, thirty pounds heavier, and infinitely fitter than the sixty-five-year-old Spector. She could have easily overpowered him if she tried. There are two explanations for why she didn't: She was intimidated into submission by having a gun drawn on her, or she was never accosted.

There was no damage on Clarkson's lips, tongue, or teeth that suggested a gun was forced into her mouth. Is it natural to assume she would have voluntarily opened her mouth to an assailant with a gun?

The presence of gunshot residue on both of Clarkson's hands but not on Spector's suggests she was holding the gun when it fired, not Spector. Even if Spector had washed his hands, traces of GSR would still be present on his skin and clothing, but only two tiny particles were found on his clothing. They could have been transferred by the air, by his handcuffs, or in the police car.

The barrel of the snub-nosed Colt was about two inches into Clarkson's mouth. When it fired, a violent burst of 1,400-degree gases exited the muzzle with a force of about 5,000 pounds per square inch. In an instant, it filled her mouth, bubbled out the cheeks, and escaped along the paths of least resistance. Some went out through the nasal passages, doing damage along the way; the rest blew *backward,* out of the mouth, carrying a turbulent cloud of blood spray, gunshot residue, gases, pulverized flesh, teeth, and other biological material called back-spatter.

In this case, the blast blew Clarkson's blood and a piece of her front tooth more than ten feet onto a banister in front of her. The shoulder and sleeves of her jacket, plus the backs of her hands, were coated with back-spatter.

So it stands to reasons that anyone standing within four to six feet of the victim would be splashed with a giant grisly wave of bloody material. If Spector had been standing close enough to put the gun in her mouth—the edge of his sleeve would have been only a few inches away—he would have been coated in back-spatter, especially that sleeve.

There was none. A single droplet of blood on the sleeve and the tiny bits of spray on his clothing could be explained by simply being in the little foyer at the moment of the shot, and by contact with her blood in the frantic aftermath. If he tried to administer first aid or touched her in any way, blood would have been transferred. He might have washed his hands, but he didn't wash his jacket or clothing.

So there was no physical evidence to prove that Spector was holding the gun when it fired.

But there was evidence that Clarkson was holding the revolver with both hands when it fired. The resulting cloud of GSR and back-spatter was all over her hands. It appeared that she pulled the trigger with her left thumb, and the recoil broke her acrylic nail.

Unbeknownst to me, my forensic colleagues Baden, Spitz, and Lee had all looked at the evidence and reached similar conclusions.

Those facts (and a lack of objective evidence to the contrary) led me to think that suicide was not just a distinct possibility, but the kind of reasonable alternative that should be argued before a jury.

A tortured genius worth more than $100 million, Phil Spector had no real peers, for better or worse, but this was now a question for a jury to decide.

More than four years after Lana Clarkson died in Phil Spector's castle, his second-degree murder trial began.

On April 25, 2007, in Los Angeles Superior Court, deputy district attorney Alan Jackson got straight to the point in his opening statement to the jury: "The evidence is going to paint a picture of a man who on February 3, 2003, put a loaded pistol in Lana Clarkson's mouth—inside her mouth—and shot her to death."

He promised to paint a chilling portrait of Spector as a man "who, when he's confronted with the right circumstances, when he's confronted with the right situations, turns sinister and deadly."

The jury would hear from a parade of four women who had survived Spector's gun-waving rages. "Lana Clarkson," he said, "was simply the last in a very long line of women who have been victimized by Phil Spector."

And finally, they'd hear from the driver, Adriano DeSouza, who'd recount the horror of that night and Spector's own damning admission: *"I think I killed somebody."*

A frail-looking Spector watched from the defense table, placid, sometimes cupping his face in his hands. On the first day of the trial, he wore a blond pageboy wig, a beige suit, and a purple shirt open at the collar, but as the trial wore on, his fashion and wigs would grow wilder. He also had married (in the very foyer where Clarkson died) a twenty-six-year-old aspiring singer who worked as his personal assistant and who sat every day of the trial in the front row of the gallery behind him. When they arrived in court and left together every day, they were escorted by three very large black bodyguards.

Of course, Cutler addressed the jury with a different take.

"The evidence will show that before [police] even had a cause of death, let alone a manner of death, they had murder on their minds," Cutler said. "Fame and success come back to haunt you."

Lana Clarkson, he told jurors, died while using the Colt revolver as "a sexual prop."

Over the next seven months, the jury heard the evidence on both sides, including all the complicated forensic testimony about blood spray, toxicology, ballistics, depression, pharmaceuticals, gunshot residue, and anatomy. But witnesses also talked about more unscientific things such as fear, intimidation, entitlement, fame, insecurity, and the limits of dreams.

Coroner Dr. Sathyavagiswaran readily agreed that intraoral gunshot deaths are usually suicides and only rarely homicides.

"Would it be difficult to insert a gun forcefully into somebody's mouth without leaving evidence of blunt force trauma?" Cutler asked.

Sathyavagiswaran admitted it would "unless they're intimidated and they're afraid that somebody will shoot them, and [then] they will open their mouth."

Suicide expert Dr. Richard Seiden, a former psychology professor at the University of California at Berkeley, testified that spur-of-the-moment suicides, as opposed to long-planned suicides, make up about 40 percent of all suicides.

The fatal decision mightn't take more than five minutes, he said. Depression isn't the key factor, but feelings of hopelessness about one's future or money, loss of a loved one, career disappointments, and chronic pain—all present in Clarkson's profile—were strong contributors.

Clarkson's mother took the stand to tell how her daughter was making plans for an upcoming commercial gig and bought new shoes. As promised, four women—some reluctantly—told of frightening experiences at the muzzle of Phil Spector's guns. Witnesses debated whether a missing fingernail was lost or hidden by the defense. And in the trial's most dramatic testimony, the chauffeur described his moments of horror after Clarkson died, leaving those incriminating words hanging in the air: *I think I killed somebody.*

But Cutler argued Clarkson was depressed over a recent breakup, racked with financial problems, and helplessly watching her acting career dissolve as she hit forty. Impaired by booze and powerful pain-killers, she simply grabbed Spector's Colt and killed herself.

Clarkson's friends vigorously rejected the suicide theory. Lana was sometimes a drama queen, but she wasn't self-destructive. She was planning for the days and weeks ahead, they said. *Is that how a suicide behaves?*

In the end, a complex portrait of two very different men emerged, and both were inside Phil Spector: One was an old-fashioned, funny, chivalrous gentleman whose dates included long-stemmed roses, romantic evenings, and a farewell kiss on the cheek. The other was a profane, abusive drunk who sometimes shoved a gun in the faces of his dates when they wouldn't stay with him.

It was a real-life Jekyll-and-Hyde story, and it was all on live TV. Ratings went wild.

When the jury finally retired to its deliberations, they took a quick straw vote. Four leaned toward guilty, five not guilty, and three were undecided. The next fifteen days were gut-wrenching as they reviewed the evidence, ticked down through testimony witness by witness, and debated among themselves.

In the end, two jurors simply were not convinced beyond a reasonable doubt that Spector shot Clarkson. The jury deadlocked at ten to two in favor of conviction.

The judge declared a mistrial.

The prosecution was undeterred. A week later, Deputy DA Jackson announced his intention to retry Spector, and a year later a new trial got under way.

This time Cutler had quit the defense and a new lawyer—Spector's fourth—took the lead. Over the next five months, we did it all again: the same evidence, the same witnesses, the same arguments with very little new. This time, the media wasn't as interested, Spector had toned down his wardrobe and hair, and the courtroom tension was significantly reduced. But it all came down to the interpretation of the evidence and the man.

Again, when the jury finally retired for its deliberations, the straw vote was split. But over the next thirty hours of debate, reasonable doubts diminished and the twelve reached their verdict: Phil Spector was guilty of second-degree murder

On May 29, 2009—more than six years after Lana Clarkson died— the judge sentenced sixty-nine-year-old Spector to nineteen years to life in prison. He'll be eighty-eight before he's eligible for parole in 2028.

As part of his sentence, the judge ordered Spector to pay Clarkson's burial expenses, so his lawyer handed Clarkson's mother a check for

$17,000 before the diminutive music mogul and convicted murderer was taken to prison.

Spector's lawyers appealed the conviction. Among their many issues was the irrelevance and prejudicial nature of testimony from five women about gun-wielding experiences with Spector in the past. The defense argued those long-ago encounters proved nothing about what happened in the death of Lana Clarkson.

In one last strange twist in a twisted case, the California Supreme Court rejected the argument, citing a thirty-year-old federal case—*US vs. Martha Woods*. Prior bad acts and simple logic, the justices said, can help a jury determine the guilt (or innocence) of a defendant. Just as the children who died or got sick in Martha Woods's care over a twenty-five-year period were relevant to her prosecution for killing Paul Woods, those five women's stories were relevant to determining Spector's guilt.

Death and justice ripple across generations in strange ways.

Phil Spector wasn't the only one on trial in his nationally televised case.

So were expert witnesses.

Deputy DA Alan Jackson waved off all of Spector's experts, including me, as "pay to say" mercenaries who accepted more than $400,000 to spout whatever Spector told them to spout. (Oddly, he didn't mention how much the state paid its experts.)

"How does a homicide become a suicide?" Jackson asked the jurors at the second trial. "You write a big, fat check. If you can't change the science, you buy the scientist."

That's what happens in a trial: One side calls experts to explain something highly technical or hard to understand, and the other side calls them liars, charlatans, idiots, and hired guns. Both sides need expert witnesses, and both sides undermine them. During the Spector trial (and others), I was called innumerable names, none good, inside and outside of the courtroom. Why? Simply because my forensic opinion ran counter to the perceptions of onlookers who had already made up their minds.

This grumbling isn't new. As early as 1848, respected American jurist John Pitt Taylor wrote that juries should be skeptical about "skilled witnesses" (as well as slaves, women, and foreigners).

Expert witnesses exist on every subject known to man, from the proper width of stair treads to brain function on the molecular level, but they are both inevitable and necessary. In our increasingly complex and specialized world—made exponentially more complicated by the digital age—Renaissance men (and women) are as scarce as buggy-whip makers and honest politicians. It is likely impossible to conduct a trial of any complexity in this day and age without an expert. Juries and judges simply no longer possess the depth and breadth of knowledge to make life-or-death decisions without an expert's explanations.

The key in any trial is to convey information in a meaningful and useful way. An expert not only must possess the requisite knowledge on the subject, he must be able to explain it. Denzel Washington's lawyer character in the film *Philadelphia* comes to mind. "Explain this to me like I'm a six-year-old" is a very potent line.

This magical element of connection isn't common at all. The most knowledgeable expert in the world is utterly useless if he cannot convey his knowledge in a user-friendly, comprehensible way. The best experts are teachers, too. As with anything else, this ability is enhanced the more it is practiced. Thus, the best experts are those that testify often.

Expert witnesses seldom ride in with all the answers that everyone else was too stupid to glean. They aren't always right. Justice doesn't teeter on their knowledge. They are experts, not the final word on everything.

What an expert witness says must be evaluated by every juror for credibility and given its proper weight.

Many fine experts, medical and otherwise, will never testify because they're uncomfortable in an adversarial legal setting. Why submit themselves to the excessive scrutiny, the confusing legal lingo, the conflict with superiors or colleagues, or the name-calling from opposing lawyers, media, and (now) every armchair detective watching Court TV?

Justice loses when good experts avoid trials for these and other reasons.

Expert witnesses aren't liars. They are telling the truth as they see it, and we all know that the truth can be interpreted many ways. The Spector case proves nothing if not how a single set of facts can be construed in different ways.

Are there hired guns in forensic pathology (the only area I can confidently talk about)? Yes, but not many. They are usually inept, inexperienced, and quickly exposed in court. More common are the true believers, who see themselves as junior policemen who must nab all the bad guys. They identify more with cops and prosecutors and they tend, maybe unconsciously, to find clues suggesting guilt. This isn't about money, but it sure isn't blind justice.

If the expert always testifies for one side or the other, he or she is labeled a whore for that side. Some try to blunt this criticism by testifying for both sides, but that merely causes them to be labeled a whore for anybody who'll pay. It's a no-win situation.

The public never knows how many times an expert witness has turned down a lawyer's overtures or been rejected because his opinion doesn't help. Personally, I have walked away from many cases and been politely excused by many more when my forensic conclusions simply didn't support the lawyers' strategy.

As long as an expert can convince the judge and jury that he approaches the subject with an open mind, the number of times he testifies, or even how often he testifies for either side of a particular issue, really becomes irrelevant.

As a medical examiner and a forensic consultant all of my adult life, I've testified for the prosecution and defense, for plaintiffs and defendants, in criminal trials and civil trials, in big cases and small. My conclusions aren't swayed by money. *Not for the police or against the police, nor for a family or against a family. I must be impartial and tell the truth.*

Finally, if you're on trial for your life and you desperately must clarify an intricate bit of evidence to your jury, do you not seek the most credible, knowledgeable person you can afford to make it crystal clear? Maybe you can't afford the expert who wrote the book, but you are still entitled to bring someone who can explain what you cannot.

Ultimately, there is no way out. Experts are usually learned professionals who are willing to dive into the legal crucible and should be paid for their time. A jury must weigh whether they are qualified, whether their fees are unreasonable, and whether their conclusions are credible.

In the end, we simply cannot determine the facts "beyond a reasonable doubt" if we don't let capable, skilled professionals use their special knowledge to explain difficult, technical issues to juries. Juries can embrace it or ignore it, but they must hear it.

What happens if they never hear it?

The death of Ernestine Perea in Wheatland, Wyoming, was one example. Now let me tell you a about a little town called West Memphis.

‹ NINE ›

The Ghosts of West Memphis

Nothing moves us humans like unfairness, the sense that justice hasn't been done. We are quickest to rise up when we feel something grievously wrong has happened, whether an ordinary slight against one or a global neglect of millions. Good cops, judges, lawyers, and medical examiners feel it even more intensely because it's their job to right wrongs, even when everyone else shrugs it off and says, "That's just the way it is." However, wanting to make things right isn't the same as being right. Expect courage of us, not perfection. The best we can hope for is being right most of the time, plus the time and wisdom to repair what we did wrong. It's not just fixing what happened in the past, but it's also about fixing our future.

WEST MEMPHIS, ARKANSAS. WEDNESDAY, MAY 5, 1993.

On a warm springtime afternoon, with summer vacation barely a month away, in a small town where there were still a few wild places, boys will be boys.

Stevie Branch, Michael Moore, and Christopher Byers were best friends. They were in the same second-grade class at Weaver Elementary, joined the same Cub Scout troop, and like most eight-year-old boys lucky enough to find each other, they rode their bikes endlessly together, as far as their parents and the city limits allowed. Sometimes farther.

But it was all good. Nothing ever happened in West Memphis, Arkansas, a farming community where blues legends like B. B. King and Howlin' Wolf had once lived, worked, and made music. Folks here felt safely distant from the incessant violence and daily depravities of Memphis, one of America's most dangerous cities, just across the river in Tennessee. Just a small town like a thousand others, barely clinging to a river and the interstate as if they were life itself. And in some ways, they were.

Little boys don't waste daylight. As they often did after school, Stevie, Michael, and Chris found each other, as if some magnet drew these three friends together. They lit out—Stevie and Michael on their bicycles, and Chris on his skateboard—for a swampy, brush-clogged woodland known by locals as Robin Hood Hills, where they could catch turtles, race their bikes through the trees on narrow footpaths, or play in the soupy ditches. Across the drainage canal, accessible only by a sewage-pipe bridge or a rope that swung from one bank to the other, was a darker woodland known as Devil's Den, frequently haunted by transients, druggies, and teen partiers.

West Memphis parents always warned the kids to stay away from the woods, but that made them all the more enticing and adventurous.

Michael wasn't the oldest, but he was the leader of the pack. He loved being a Cub Scout so much that he wore the cap everywhere, and the uniform as much as he possibly could.

Chris earned the nickname Wormer by being in perpetual motion. He couldn't sit still. Just a few weeks shy of his ninth birthday, he'd been disciplined by his stepfather that afternoon for not obeying the house rules, and yet here he was again, breaking house rules by going out with his buddies without permission.

They knew Stevie as Bubba. He was heavily into the Ninja Turtles, already a little charmer with his shock of blond hair, blue eyes, and big smile.

Now they embarked on their next great adventure, as in the movie *Stand by Me,* as they plunged into the woods to discover whatever mysteries they concealed. They were on the move, crossing a neighbor's lawn a little before six p.m., passing Michael's house a few minutes later, then pushing their bikes into the woods a little after six thirty. Small-town people notice such things.

But small-town people don't see everything.

The boys never came out of the woods.

That night their parents called the local police, and a search was begun after midnight, but it was too dark to see anything.

The next day, around 1:45 p.m., a searcher spotted a tennis shoe floating in a filthy creek that flowed through the secluded thicket just fifty yards south of I-55.

A West Memphis detective walked along the root-choked ditch bank, cluttered with a thick carpet of leaves and twigs, to the spot where the tennis shoe was found. He noted that a patch had been cleared, maybe deliberately swept clean, down to the slick, moist dirt below.

The detective waded into the murky water, knee-deep. As he reached for the shoe he touched something unsettling just beneath the opaque surface. Something big and soft. Something that didn't belong.

A body.

It was Michael Moore.

The little boy was naked. He was splayed out in the water, hog-tied wrists-to-ankles with a black shoelace. Blood seeped from wounds on his head, face, and skinny chest.

Moments later, searchers found the corpses of Chris Byers and Stevie Branch submerged just a few feet downstream. They, too, were naked, hog-tied with shoelaces, and badly beaten. They all bore strange punctures all over their bodies. And Chris's penis had been cut off.

No murder weapon was found. Two pairs of underwear were missing. The boys' clothes and bikes had been dumped in the water, too, so any trace evidence left by the killer (or killers) was gone. And if there had been any semen in or on the boys' bodies, it was gone, too.

The small-town cops were shaken. They found a Cub Scout cap floating in the shallow creek, three tennis shoes, and one of the boy's shirts wrapped around the end of a thick stick that was jammed into the mud. They found another such stick when they fished Michael Moore's corpse from the water. Their bicycles had been thrown by someone into the canal near the sewage-pipe bridge.

The only signs of blood at the crime scene were in the murky water and where the bodies had lain on the bank after they were plucked from the creek. Luminol testing was done two weeks later and found extensive blood traces on the bank where it had been cleared.

But the crime scene had been compromised by the search and retrieval. The local coroner didn't arrive for a couple of hours. Some items, including sticks that might have been the murder weapons, were touched but never considered evidence until later.

Investigators collected the boys' bodies and feared the worst. Within hours, the whole town buzzed like a live electric wire with rumors of child rape, mutilation, and murder. What kind of evil people would do such a thing to three sweet little boys? Molesters who followed them? Drug dealers who'd been surprised? Satanists who hungered for innocent blood?

Within hours, police were developing a theory.

Dr. Frank Peretti, a veteran associate medical examiner in the Arkansas State Crime Lab, autopsied the boys. Under the intense glare of the morgue's lights, their wounds and mutilations were far worse than they had appeared out in the Robin Hood woods.

He estimated, very loosely, that the boys had been dead and submerged in the water for about seventeen hours. They all exhibited what's known as "washerwoman's skin," that wrinkled, white, soft, waterlogged skin condition that every swimmer and dishwasher knows well.

There on the autopsy table, old leaves and pond scum stuck to

them. Their wrists and ankles were still cinched together until someone could examine the shoelaces and knots for clues.

Michael Moore suffered wounds on his neck, chest, and belly that
appeared to have been caused by a serrated knife. Abrasions on his
scalp were likely caused by another weapon, likely a hefty stick. His
anus was dilated, and the soft, moist tissues inside were reddened—
evidence to Dr. Peretti that something had been forced into it. Bruising and open wounds inside his mouth suggested to Peretti that
Michael had been forced to perform oral sex. He'd still been alive when
he went into the water, because he had breathed water into his lungs.
He had drowned.

Stevie Branch's corpse also bore telltale injuries on his genitals and
anus; Peretti believed Stevie's penis, which was a reddish-purple color
halfway down, showed possible evidence of oral sex. The left side of
his face was grotesquely punctured and bloody; his teeth could be seen
through his lacerated cheek. His head, chest, arms, legs, and back displayed many irregular gouges that indicated he'd was moving when
he was stabbed. He, too, had drowned.

Chris Byers seemed to have suffered the worst of this hideous assault.

His corpse, too, bore signs to Peretti that he'd been forced to perform oral sex on a man. His penis had been skinned; his scrotum and
testicles were gone. Bloody cuts around his anus indicated he was still
alive when they were made.

His head was gashed and scraped horribly. One patch of skin had
been punched out, and one eye was bruised. The back of the skull had
been cracked with a heavy, broomstick-sized weapon. His inner thighs
were flayed with diagonal slices, and Peretti felt many of the cuts had
been inflicted with a serrated knife.

Unlike Stevie and Michael, Chris didn't drown. He bled to death
before he was thrown in the water.

When a reporter found Chris Byers's grief-stricken dad a few days
later, he expressed the horror of West Memphis.

"I can't understand why three innocent boys who still believed in

Santa Claus and the Easter Bunny should have to die such a terrible death," Byers said.

While the good folks of West Memphis raised money to bury the boys and turned their desks in a second-grade classroom into make-shift memorials, cops churned. A sado-sexual child killer was on the loose, maybe still among them.

The prevailing theory: The boys had been killed in a devil-worshipping ritual.

In the late eighties and early nineties, small-town police forces had three big bogeymen: an epidemic of cheap methamphetamine, urban gangs moving to the country, and devil worship. Meth was real, the gangs and occult fiends not as much. Satanic molestations and sacri-fices were fairy tales. But at that time, every small-town police chief made them all a priority.

The mutilation, torture, rape, and murder of three little boys didn't feel like the work of drug traffickers or gangbangers. The cops felt a twinge of "Satanic panic."

The day after the boys' bodies were discovered, a detective shared his theory of a Satanic link with the county's juvenile probation offi-cer. *Yeah*, he said, *there was a local kid who was involved in the occult and was probably capable of such horror.*

His name was Damien Echols.

He was eighteen, a high school dropout. His family was poor, and cops knew him because of a few busts for vandalism, shoplifting, and burglary. He was a strange, long-haired kid who enjoyed his reputa-tion as a fringe freak and a spiritual seeker who wrote dark poetry and described himself as a Wiccan. The rumor mill said he drank blood and participated in cult orgies.

Between 1991 and 1993 he attempted suicide a few times, but the hanging, a drug overdose, and a drowning didn't work. He'd spent a few months in a mental hospital with what a doctor called "grandiose and persecutory delusions, auditory and visual hallucinations, disor-dered thought processes, substantial lack of insight, and chronic, in-capacitating mood swings," but he was out now.

Damien had started to wear only black clothing, including a long overcoat that gave him a sinister air. Some said he occasionally carried a club or a walking staff, like some medieval wizard. He sometimes filed his fingernails into talon-like points. He'd told doctors at the asylum that he had conversations with demons, pondered suicide and murder a lot, and stole energy from people by casting spells. He even claimed the spirit of a murdered woman lived with him.

His real name wasn't even Damien but Michael; he had adopted the name of Father Damien, a Catholic priest who'd cared for lepers in the 1800s, but folks around West Memphis believed it was really after Damien, the little-boy Antichrist in the *Omen* movies, or maybe even Father Damien Karras in *The Exorcist*.

He liked his reputation as a freak. He cultivated it.

A detective first interviewed Damien in his bedroom at his mother's mobile home in a West Memphis trailer park, and later at the station. He snapped a Polaroid of Damien Echols, making note of a pentagram tattoo on Damien's chest and "EVIL" inked across his knuckles. As a local expert on the occult, the detective asked Damien, how did he think those three boys died?

Probably mutilation, Damien answered. A thrill killing just to hear the screaming, he speculated. He claimed he'd heard that "some guy" cut the bodies up, that they were in the water and probably drowned. He told the detective that one of the boys was probably "cut up" more than the others. The killer was a "sick" local guy, he said, and unlikely to flee. After all, he said, "the younger the victim . . . the more power the person would have gotten from the sacrifice."

At the time, the whole town was alive with rumors and half-truths about the killings, but the cops hadn't yet revealed that Chris Byers had been mutilated more than his friends.

Suddenly, cops had a break, but they didn't yet have enough to arrest Damien Echols.

For a month, cops looked for more evidence against Echols. In the process, they stumbled upon a local waitress who thought she could help by hooking them up with another teenager, Jessie Misskelley, Jr., a mildly retarded acquaintance of Damien's who might know something.

The waitress became an undercover informant for the West Memphis cops. She persuaded Jessie to introduce her to Damien, who reportedly took her to a field outside of town for a gathering of "witches" known as an *esbat*, where a dozen or more naked people chanted, painted their faces, and groped each other in the dark. She and Damien left early, but Jessie stayed, she said.

A month after the killings, West Memphis police visited seventeen-year-old dropout Jessie Misskelley. They told Jessie there was a $35,000 reward for anybody helping the cops arrest the killers, and the kid agreed to be interviewed at the police station, where he told a shocking tale over several hours.

It began early on May 5, he claimed, when a friend named Jason Baldwin, a sixteen-year-old friend from school, invited Misskelley to meet him and Damien Echols in the Robin Hood woods that morning. Baldwin was a wispy kid who looked much younger than sixteen. He was Damien's friend, wore black, and liked heavy metal, although he wasn't nearly the badass that Damien appeared to be. He didn't take part in the black magic stuff. He was still enrolled in school, where he did better in art than math, but he'd had a couple of run-ins with the law, starting at age eleven. If Damien was the leader, Jason was his admiring follower.

About nine a.m., the teenagers were jacking around in the creek when three kids rode up on their bikes, he said. Baldwin and Echols hollered to the kids and they came over. (Later in his statement, Misskelley estimated it had happened around noon, admitting that his times might be inaccurate. He explained the presence of the young boys by saying they had skipped school that day.)

As soon as they were close, Baldwin and Echols attacked them in a furious assault. Misskelley told cops that he watched as at least two of the boys were raped and forced to perform oral sex on Baldwin and Echols.

At one moment, one of the kids—Misskelley identified him as

Michael Moore—tried to escape by running out of the woods, but Misskelley chased him down and brought him back.

Using a folding knife, Baldwin cut the boys' faces and sliced one kid's penis, Misskelley said. Echols then whacked one of them with a big stick about the size of a baseball bat before they were forced to disrobe. Naked, wounded, and afraid, all three were tied up. That's when he ran away from the scene, he said.

"They started screwing them and stuff, cutting them and stuff," Misskelley told his interrogators, "and I saw it and I turned around and looked, and then I took off running. I went home, then they called me and asked me, how come I didn't stay, I told them, I just couldn't."

Misskelley's first polygraph exam and tape-recorded interview lasted about four hours, ending at 3:18 p.m. Around five p.m., he sat down for a second interview, and facts started to change.

This time, he said he got a phone call from Baldwin the night before the murders. He recalled Baldwin telling him they planned to get some boys and hurt them.

This time, Misskelley said he, Echols, and Baldwin had come to the Robin Hood woods between five and six p.m., but after prompting by the detective, he allowed that it might have been seven or eight p.m. In the end, he settled on six p.m.

This time, the three young victims arrived near dark, he said. (Official sunset would have been close to eight p.m.)

This time, Misskelley went into more excruciating details about the sexual assault. Both the Byers boy and the Branch boy had been raped, he said, and at least one of them had been held by the head and ears while being violated.

All of the boys, Misskelley said, were bound with pieces of a brown rope before he fled the scene, but he believed Chris Byers was already dead when he left.

"You said that they had their hands tied up, tied down," an interrogator said. "Were their hands tied in a fashion to where they couldn't have run?"

"They could run," Misskelley answered. "They just had them tied, when they knocked them down and stuff. They could hold their arms and stuff, and just hold them down like, where he couldn't raise up and the other one picked his legs up."

After he got home, Misskelley said Baldwin phoned, saying, "We done it!" and "What are we going to do if somebody saw us?" He heard Echols jabbering in the background.

Had he ever been involved in a cult? an interrogator asked.

Yeah, Misskelley admitted. For the past few months, he'd been meeting with other people in the woods, where they had sexual orgies and bloody initiation rites that included killing and eating stray dogs. At one such meeting, he said, he saw a picture that Echols had taken of the three boys. Echols had been watching them, he said.

What were Echols and Baldwin wearing that day? a cop asked.

Baldwin wore blue jeans, black lace-up boots, and a Metallica T-shirt with a skull on it, Misskelley recalled. As was his habit, Echols wore black pants, a black T-shirt, and boots.

Misskelley's story was a confusing mess. Times and events doubled back on themselves, and stark inconsistencies abounded. For one, Jason Baldwin had been in school all day. Had the crime happened at nine a.m. or noon, or closer to eight p.m.? Had Baldwin called that morning or the night before? Why was he certain the boys had skipped school when clearly they hadn't?

But some of Misskelley's weird confession was actually supported by evidence.

The boys had ridden their bikes to the Robin Hood woods. They had been severely beaten. Two of them had injuries consistent with bludgeoning by a heavy object like a baseball bat or tree limb. One had facial cuts. Chris Byers's genitals were grotesquely mutilated. All had injuries the medical examiner found consistent with forcible rape and oral sex. Michael and Stevie were alive when they went into the water, but not Chris, consistent with Misskelley's observation that Chris was already dead when Misskelley fled the woods. And the boys were in fact tied up, although with shoelaces, not a brown rope.

And a witness later told detectives that he'd seen Damien Echols near the crime scene that same night, wearing black pants and a black shirt—both muddy.

But during his interview, Misskelley was given a lie detector test and told he'd failed. Later, some would dispute whether he'd failed the polygraph. Some believe the alleged "failure" confused Misskelley, who grew frustrated and tried to please the cops even more by telling a wild story; others say it merely caused him to tell the truth.

Either way, the focus was now entirely on three social outcasts named Damien Echols, Jason Baldwin, and Jessie Misskelley. All three were arrested and charged with three counts of first-degree murder. Police had a few other leads on possible killers, but they were convinced they had the right guys.

In coming weeks and months, investigators collected evidence they felt was related to the murders. In Jason Baldwin's home they found a red robe that belonged to his mother, fifteen black T-shirts, and a white T-shirt. In Damien Echols's home they found two notebooks that to them appeared to have Satanic or occult writing, and more clothing. Divers searching the silty bottom of a lake behind Baldwin's house found a knife with a serrated edge.

Police seized a pendant from Damien's neck because it appeared to have blood spots on it. They later learned that Damien and Jason both wore the necklace occasionally.

And detectives also found several witnesses who claimed that Echols, Baldwin, and Misskelley had all confessed in some way to the murders.

A crime lab technician declared fibers on the victims' clothing to be similar to four fibers found in Jason's and Damien's homes. A green polyester fiber on Michael's Cub Scout cap was similar in structure to fibers found in Damien's home. And one red fiber from Baldwin's mom's robe was microscopically similar to fibers collected from Michael Moore's shirt. Not unequivocally the same, but similar.

The knife couldn't be positively included or excluded, although its serrated edge recalled medical examiner Dr. Peretti's conclusion that a knife with a serrated blade had been used in the slayings.

Very little useful testing material came from the necklace. Technicians could say only that the blood specks were two different blood types, one matching Damien Echols and one matching Jason Baldwin, victim Stevie Branch, and 11 percent of all humans.

The three accused teenagers all pleaded not guilty and were appointed two lawyers each. All would be tried as adults, and Misskelley's confession—although his lawyer argued it had been coerced—would be allowed. But because of Misskelley's confessions, which he allegedly recanted within days, he would be tried separately from Echols and Baldwin so he could testify against them (although he eventually refused to do it).

Less than ten months after the nude, broken bodies of those three little boys were pulled from a foul creek in West Memphis, their accused killers were going to trial. If convicted, they all faced the death penalty.

The case was purely circumstantial, but two juries would have a hard time overlooking the graphic confession of one of the accused killers, as muddled and inconsistent as it was.

On January 18, 1994, jury selection in the Jessie Misskelley trial began in the tiny farm village of Corning, Arkansas. A jury of seven women and five men was seated in a day, and the prosecutor opened with a warning: They'd see errors and wild inconsistencies in Misskelley's confession—the cornerstone of the state's case—but they could all be attributed to a frantic effort to minimize his own role in the murders.

But the defense quickly countered that Misskelley was a borderline retarded man who was a victim of public pressure on the cops to solve northeast Arkansas's most heinous murder in decades. Detectives fixated on Damien Echols early on and never truly considered other suspects or scenarios, then scared a kid with a pitifully low IQ into confessing.

The dead boys' mothers led off the grim parade of witnesses. They told the jury and the world about their last moments with their sons.

Then came graphic testimony from searchers and cops about the hunt for the missing boys and the discovery of their corpses, while jurors glanced at their bikes, propped up against a courtroom wall.

The hardest part of such trials is always when the crime scene and autopsy photos are introduced into evidence. In this case, prosecutors showed more than thirty images of these dead boys—bound, bloodless, slashed, frozen in distorted poses. Then came the medical examiner with more ghastly photos from his autopsy table, close-ups of little white corpses on bloodied sheets, necrotic gashes, disfigured parts nobody wanted to see. The jurors blanched.

Then the jury listened silently as prosecutors played thirty-four minutes of Misskelley's taped confession. They heard Jessie, in his own words, tell how the boys died.

The state's case wrapped up with wrangling over the fiber evidence, and some talk about Satanism and cult killings. The defense, as it had at every step, fought back.

Misskelley's team mounted a reasonable-doubt defense.

On the list of the defense witnesses was a well-known detective and polygraph examiner who believed Misskelley had actually been telling the truth when West Memphis police tested him with a lie detector—but when he heard he'd failed, he gave up and made a false confession. The same detective criticized investigators for not taking Misskelley to the crime scene.

But jurors never heard most of that testimony. It was ruled inadmissible by the judge.

A social psychologist testified that Misskelley had probably given police a false statement when he could "no longer stand the strain of the interrogation," but he was not allowed to express his opinion that the West Memphis investigators overwhelmed Misskelley's will and coerced a confession that was false.

In the end, Misskelley didn't take the stand in his own defense because his lawyers feared the poor kid would be slaughtered by prosecutors.

"If this defendant didn't chase down Michael Moore, he would have gotten to go home and be with his parents," the prosecution said in its closing argument. "Jessie Misskelley Jr. didn't let Michael Moore get away. He chased him down like an animal."

"The killing of one human being by another is only exceeded by the state killing an innocent man," the defense said in closing.

After more than a week of grisly photos, graphic testimony, and legal wrangling, the jury convicted Jessie Miskelley of one count of first-degree murder and two counts of second-degree murder. Asked if he had anything to say, Misskelley said, "No." He was quickly sentenced to life without parole plus forty years in prison and carted away.

A few days later, the jurors told a reporter that the vivid image of a frightened eight-year-old boy running for his life but being dragged to his eventual death by the teenager in front of them weighed heavily in their verdict.

Two weeks later, Damien Echols and Jason Baldwin faced their own jury in Jonesboro.

Misskelley refused to testify against them, leaving prosecutors with the same circumstantial case in which no single piece of evidence absolutely connected the three teenagers to the crime. But in Echols, they also had an unsympathetic defendant who would make jurors vaguely uncomfortable, and who had already made statements to investigators like "Everybody has demonic forces inside," and that the number three was "a sacred number in the Wicca religion"—when it also happened to be the number of eight-year-old boys he was accused of murdering. At other times, he'd threatened to eat his father, slit his own mother's throat, and kill his ex-girlfriend's parents. Everything about Damien Echols screamed bad seed.

In opening arguments, the prosecution promised to prove Echols's and Baldwin's guilt forensically and by their own statements; the defense claimed the state had twisted the facts to fit its own surreal puzzle. *No, they admitted, Damien Echols isn't an all-American boy, in fact, he's kind of weird, but no shred of physical evidence suggests he killed those boys.*

Again, the state's first witnesses were the mothers of the three victims. A police detective recounted Echols's interrogation, in which he made strange remarks about mysticism and demons. An ex-girlfriend told how Echols often carried knives in his overcoat. A cult expert talked about the "trappings of occultism" that marked the crime, from the shedding of "life force" blood to the full moon on the night of the killings to the potent "life energy" that can be stolen from young victims.

Medical examiner Dr. Peretti testified that the knife found in the lake behind Echols's house was consistent with the wounds he saw on Chris Byers's corpse, although he admitted on cross-examination that other knives might also have made the same marks. He also said Chris's penis was skinned and his scrotum sliced off while he was still alive; both Stevie and Michael were bludgeoned by a heavy object; and that Michael's lungs were filled with water, indicating that "when he was in the water, he was breathing." But on cross-examination, he admitted that the forensic evidence didn't completely match Misskelley's account, namely that he found no hard evidence that any of the boys were strangled, raped, or hog-tied with a brown rope.

A few prosecution witnesses testified that either Echols or Baldwin had confessed privately. One of them, Baldwin's teenage cellmate, claimed Baldwin admitted to "dismembering" the boys and that he had "sucked the blood from the penis and scrotum and put the balls in his mouth." Startling fact or self-serving fiction? A jury would have to decide.

In the end, the only physical evidence that the state offered to tie either Echols or Baldwin to the crime scene was literally scant: a trace of blue wax found on one of the boys' shirts and a polyester fiber on Michael's Cub Scout cap that were "microscopically similar" to items found in Echols's home.

The defense started strong. After Damien's mother testified that he'd been home with her on the night of the murder, and that he'd been talking to two girlfriends on the phone, the accused teenager took the stand for a few hours and coolly answered dozens of questions from both sides.

What interests you? his lawyer asked.

Skateboarding, books, movies, talking on the phone, Echols answered.

Who are your favorite authors?

"I will read about anything, but my favorites are Stephen King and Dean Koontz and Anne Rice."

What is a Wiccan?

"It's basically a close involvement with nature," he explained. "I'm not a Satanist. I don't believe in human sacrifices or anything like that."

Are you a manic depressive?

"Yes, I am.

What happens when you don't take your medication?

"I cry."

Why do you keep a dog skull in your room?

"I just thought it was kind of cool."

Why did you tattoo "EVIL" across your knuckles?

"I just kinda thought it was cool, so I did that."

Why do you always wear black?

"I was told that I look good in black. And I'm real self-conscious, uh, about the way I dress."

Did you know those little boys?

"I'd never even heard of them before 'til I saw it on the news."

Have you ever been to the Robin Hood woods?

"No, I have not."

How do you feel about being accused of killing them?

"Sometimes angry. Sometimes sad. Sometimes scared."

It was a valiant effort to rehabilitate an accused murderer who looked slightly menacing, had mental issues, and deliberately tried to shock his Bible Belt neighbors. But Echols's courtroom behavior didn't help: He sometimes blew kisses to the victims' families and licked his lips lewdly at the defense table. He occasionally glared at the gallery, snarled at photographers, or preened himself in a little mirror. As his lawyers tried to portray him as a kid going through an awkward stage, he sent strong signals that he was a manipulator and a creepy little narcissist who relished making people's skin crawl. And he reveled in all the attention.

The defense wrapped up its case with a cadre of more witnesses who rebutted some earlier claims about occultism, suggested other scenarios and other possible killers (including Chris Byers's father and a mysterious, blood-spattered man who stumbled into a West Memphis restaurant that night), and painted the police investigation as inept, overreaching, and desperate. Jason Baldwin never took the stand.

In closing, prosecutors invited the jurors to look into Damien, where they'd see "there's not a soul there." The defense lawyers for Echols and Baldwin begged them to see doubt.

The eight-woman, four-man jury deliberated for eleven hours: Both were guilty in all three murders.

Jason Baldwin was sentenced to life in prison without parole.

Damien Echols was sent to Death Row.

In 1996, the Arkansas Supreme Court upheld all three convictions, satisfied that justice had been done. Echols, Misskelley, and Baldwin—now known as the West Memphis Three—were submerged in prison, out of view, the last home they'd ever know.

But not everyone was so satisfied.

That same year, HBO aired a documentary called *Paradise Lost: The Child Murders at Robin Hood Hills*. It made a vivid case that the three oddball teenagers had been wrongly convicted by shoddy police work in a small town gripped by "Satanic panic," in farcical trials by country-bumpkin jurors. The film convinced many people, especially some vocal celebrities. Soon a website was launched, then sequels, and more celebrity voices. Some pointed at a different possible killer.

Then a 2003 book, *Devils Knot: The True Story of the West Memphis Three*, by Mara Leveritt, also argued that the 1994 trials were gravely flawed. (Later, a 2012 documentary financed by Oscar-winning director Peter Jackson and directed by Amy Berg, *West of Memphis*, added new fuel to the long-smoldering fire.)

Things got worse for the authorities when, in 2003, the waitress who claimed she'd attended an *esbat* with Misskelley and Echols admitted she lied.

What began as an indie-film exploration of a sensational murder case blossomed into a full-fledged movement to free the West Memphis Three. Celebrities such as actor Johnny Depp, Pearl Jam's Eddie Vedder, pop philosopher Henry Rollins, and the Dixie Chicks' Natalie Maines, among others, lent their voices, money, and moral support. High-dollar defense lawyers and legal experts galore also came to the party.

In time, even Chris Byers's father and Stevie Branch's mother were convinced the West Memphis Three had been wrongly accused.

Then in 2007, a bombshell revelation: Preliminary tests indicated DNA found at the crime scene didn't match Echols, Baldwin, or Misskelley—but a hair found in a knot that bound one of the boys was declared "not inconsistent with" hair from Terry Hobbs, Stevie Branch's stepfather.

A hair found tangled in a knot tied by the killer that didn't belong to one of the teenagers. At the very least, that single hair posed a huge obstacle for the prosecution.

While Damien Echols's lawyers awaited final results, they contacted me. They wanted me to examine the boys' wounds and Dr. Peretti's autopsy for any details the forensic pathologists, cops, lawyers, and judges might have missed. I agreed.

I was familiar with the case. As I've said before, the forensic community is small, and the news media is pervasive. I had recently retired after twenty-five years as the Bexar County medical examiner and now was consulting on a variety of forensic cases that needed a "second look." I knew what a lot of people knew about this particular grisly crime, and I'd had a few casual conversations with other medical examiners about it. I knew Dr. Peretti well and thought he was a good pathologist. In one of the most scrutinized cases in modern history, I doubted that I'd find anything new, much less evidence that would change everything.

Within days, a package arrived at my house. It contained hundreds of pages of autopsy reports, testimony, other experts' conclusions, and legal opinions. Most important, it contained a binder and compact disc with nearly two thousand high-resolution, full-color crime scene and autopsy photos.

Very quickly, just as in the Wyoming case, I saw a problem.

The horrific genital mutilation on Chris Byers was not in fact done by a human. It was caused by animals gnawing on the soft tissues after he died. Bruises and gashes in the boys' mouths—first interpreted as evidence of forced oral sex—were also caused by animals. Those strange punctures on the skin that looked like knife-inflicted torture? Animals nibbling and chewing. The huge bloodied patch on the left side of Stevie Branch's face? Also animal damage.

Similarly, the knife wounds and scrapes Dr. Peretti saw on the bodies were not inflicted by a blade but were the tooth and claw marks of feeding animals.

What animals? Snapping turtles, possums, feral cats, foxes, raccoons, squirrels, stray dogs, and the occasional coyote inhabited the Robin Hood woods. Any or all of these predators could have been attracted by the scent of fresh blood, found the bodies very quickly, and nibbled on the softest parts, which were most easily chewed off. To me, they looked like turtle bites.

The makers of the 2012 documentary, *West of Memphis,* tested the theory. They released several snapping turtles, like those found in the West Memphis area, near a pig carcass. The wounds they inflicted in a very short time looked nearly identical to the wounds I saw in the autopsy photos, wounds that investigators and prosecutors attributed to a serrated-blade knife and occult rituals.

It's an unsavory reality: At the moment of death, a human body becomes food. Bacteria, insects, and animals begin to recycle dead muscle, fat, fluids, and other tissues into their own life-sustaining nourishment. They don't allow a proper interval for grief, meditation, or cooling. The bacteria are already inside, mostly in the intestines, and they don't die when their host dies; insects and wild animals might take a little longer to find a dead body left in the open, but usually not more than a few minutes.

But there was more to suggest that the evidence jurors heard was not what it seemed.

The boys' dilated anuses were interpreted by the original medical examiner as possible evidence of forcible sodomy, either by a penis or another object. In fact, a dilated anus is a normal postmortem artifact. After death, the body's normal muscle tension relaxes. Sphincter muscles loosen, too, and if submerged in water for a time, can look misshapen and stretched. I saw no evidence of any anal trauma, and I don't believe any of the boys was sodomized.

And Stevie Branch's halfway discolored penis, which was interpreted as evidence of forcible oral sex, was simply caused by the positioning of his body after death, not by a sexual trauma.

These boys were obviously murdered, but the evidence didn't necessarily add up the way cops and prosecutors said.

At the time, I didn't know that a single hair found in one of the shoelace knots matched the DNA of Stevie Branch's stepfather, Terry Hobbs (plus about 1.5 percent of all humans). It generated an intriguing question: How could such a hair be tangled *inside* a knot that trussed up a little boy moments before he was murdered if his killer hadn't tied the knot?

Hobbs, who had a history of domestic violence, has steadfastly denied all implications and accusations—and there have been many— that he killed the boys. He claims Stevie could have transported the hair on his clothing and it was caught up in the vicious assault. No charges have ever been brought against him, although the angry debate rages among the West Memphis Three partisans to this day.

John Douglas, the famed former FBI profiler, examined the evidence and interviewed witnesses, too. He concluded the three boys died in a "personal-cause killing," motivated by emotional conflicts, not personal gain or sex. He thinks at least one of the victims knew their assailant—a lone killer who probably knew the boys and had a violent past.

Maybe more important for the West Memphis Three, Douglas saw nothing to suggest it was a ritualistic murder, the prosecution's primary theory.

Douglas also saw evidence that the murders were not planned and the killer lost control.

"There was another rational and logical criminal reason why the offender hid the victims, their clothing, and bicycles in the drainage ditch and bayou," Douglas has said. "The offender did not want the victims to be immediately found; he needed time in order to establish an alibi for himself."

So back in 2007, armed with new evidence and observations from me and my forensic friends such as the eminent Drs. Werner Spitz and Michael Baden, lawyers for the West Memphis Three asked for a new trial but were denied by the state court. They appealed.

In November 2010, amid a growing doubt that the West Memphis Three were guilty of murder, the Arkansas Supreme Court was convinced that the evidence, new and old, should be reviewed. It ordered a new evidentiary hearing.

Now, amid a swelling outcry that the West Memphis Three were innocent, the State of Arkansas was in a legal, financial, and public relations pickle. New trials would be expensive and potentially embarrassing. Prosecutors might also lose a new trial, given the widespread public outcry. Restitution for three wrongfully convicted kids could amount to tens of millions of dollars the state couldn't afford.

Ironically, the state dodged this speeding bullet when one of Damien Echols's lawyers offered a win-win compromise: *What if Echols, Misskelley, and Baldwin pleaded no contest under a so-called Alford plea, are declared guilty by a judge, and then are released with time served?* The three would go free and the state would keep its convictions with little expense, embarrassment, or restitution.

The Alford plea, a rare legal maneuver, has existed since 1970. It allows the defendant to admit prosecutors could likely convict him, but he needn't admit the crime. Under an Alford plea, a judge usually declares the defendant guilty, but the defendant maintains his innocence in case any further related charges or lawsuits arise.

If the deal sounded like a no-brainer, it wasn't. Jason Baldwin, who had been offered a reduced sentence to plead guilty and testify against Echols back in 1983 when he was only sixteen, didn't want to plead guilty to a crime he didn't commit. His former cellmate had publicly apologized for his graphic allegation about a confession, casting further doubt on whether it had happened at all. And Baldwin had grown strangely comfortable in prison. Instead, he wanted a new trial to prove his innocence. But if he didn't take the no-contest offer, then the deal was off, and his old friend Echols faced an impending execution.

On August 11, 2011, after eighteen years and seventy-eight days in prison, Damien Echols, Jessie Misskelley, and Jason Baldwin pleaded no contest to killing three young boys in 1983. A judge accepted their pleas, gave them ten-year suspended sentences, and freed them with time already served.

Convicted killer Jason Baldwin captured the legal bedlam succinctly: "When we told prosecutors we were innocent, they put us in prison for life. Now when we plead guilty, they set us free."

That day, three young ex-convicts walked out of the courthouse twice as old as when they went in. They were not exonerated. The boys were not magically resurrected. The case wasn't solved. No mistakes were admitted.

But the West Memphis Three were free.

Twenty years after the crime, a memorial stands in the playground of the boys' elementary school in West Memphis. Last I heard, two of their homes have been abandoned and boarded up. The Robin Hood woods were cleared and the land bulldozed, as if to erase an invisible stain. Now it's just an empty field beside a superhighway.

These three best friends who died together now lie in three different graves in three different states. Chris is buried in Memphis; Michael is in Marion, Arkansas; and Stevie in Steele, Missouri.

The convicted killers, now free, have resumed their lives. Echols married in prison, wrote a memoir after his release from death row, and now lives with his wife in New York City, where he teaches tarot reading. Baldwin went to Seattle, where he works in construction and hopes to someday study for a law degree. Misskelley moved back to West Memphis, got engaged, and is attending community college.

Trying to slog through the rest of the West Memphis Three case is like wading in the filthy ditch of the Robin Hood woods. It's murky and impossible to gain a secure foothold. Collecting facts is made especially treacherous by misinformation and disinformation, recantations, conjecture, bad journalism, Internet trolling, "new evidence" submitted by partisans, armchair sleuthing from a thousand mothers' basements, and the usual Internet noise. Every account is sliced and diced, parsed into oblivion by zealous fans and foes seeking only the pieces that fit a puzzle they've already solved. This case stands now as both an example of everything that's right and wrong with our system of crime and punishment. Confusion reigns.

I don't know who killed Chris Byers, Michael Moore, and Stevie Branch. It might very well have been Damien Echols, Jason Baldwin, and Jessie Misskelley. It might have been someone else whose name we know, or someone whose name we have never heard. It might have been Terry Hobbs. They were certainly slain by someone, and their killer(s) were sadistic, savage, and psychopathic. And maybe the killers are still among us. I just don't know, and no existing evidence provides a smoking gun against anyone.

The State of Arkansas, however, has no doubt. Prosecutors and cops are certain they got the right killers. The case is closed. Without an overlooked piece of irrefutable evidence and/or an unquestionable confession—unlikely after twenty years in one of America's most scrutinized murders—it will never be reconsidered.

Here's what I can say without doubt: After examining more than 25,000 deaths in my career and reading about many more, I haven't heard of, much less seen, a single ritual murder by a Satanic cult. They exist only in the movies, on the Internet, and in paranoid dreams.

"Beyond reasonable doubt" is the highest burden of proof in

American law. It doesn't necessarily mean that no doubt exists, but it means a reasonable person must look at all the evidence and see very little chance that the defendant is innocent.

All I know is that in those grim photos, I saw reasonable doubt. It isn't that I believe, as some do passionately, that Echols, Baldwin, and Misskelley *didn't* kill those children. They are good suspects. But when I look closely at the evidence with almost forty years of forensic experience, I believe the police and prosecutors didn't prove it beyond a reasonable doubt.

In matters of death and life, that's our only moral standard.

TEN

The Curious Death Of
Vincent van Gogh

Death is part of our lore.

It is the realm of mythmakers and poets as much as gravediggers and medical examiners. We humans invest death with a certain romance, a meaning that sometimes transcends its grim reality. Does life give death meaning, or vice versa? We've had it both ways since we began telling stories, whether it was Achilles, Cleopatra, Jesus Christ, the Spartans at Thermopylae, Czar Nicholas II, John F. Kennedy . . . or Trayvon Martin.

For me, death is more mundane. Nowadays, how many people truly die with style, with meaning, with purpose? Most of us die alone in a hospital bed in a tangle of IVs and dirty sheets. We might wish our deaths to be profound, but they typically are not. For a thousand selfish reasons, the living assign importance to death that speaks more to our own fears than to the reality.

It becomes our mythology.

And so it is with the troubled genius Vincent van Gogh.

The last Sunday of July 1890 dawned hot in Auvers.

For weeks, the strange Dutchman with a mangled ear and shabby clothes had kept to himself and to his usual routine of painting in the gardens and fields around the quiet French village, drinking alone in the café, dodging the teenagers who teased the *fou*—crazy—tramp in the street. They judged him to be mad because of his ragged appearance and his social clumsiness, for they couldn't possibly know anything of his demons, his spells, or his year in the asylum.

This sweltering morning started no differently than any other. All morning, he painted madly in the fields, then returned for his usual midday meal at the cheap inn where he lived in a suffocating upstairs room, No. 5, and was known only as Monsieur Vincent. He ate more quickly than usual, barely saying a word. Then he gathered his easel, brushes, knapsack, and an awkwardly large canvas to venture back out, as he did every day, rain or shine, to paint until sundown.

It was after dark when the innkeeper's family, eating supper on their veranda, spied the Dutchman staggering down the street, clutching his belly. He carried nothing and his jacket was buttoned tight, although the night was sultry. Without a word, he stumbled past them and climbed the stairs to his bedroom.

When the innkeeper heard moaning, he went to the dark little room where his boarder lay hunched on his bed, obviously in pain. The innkeeper asked what was wrong.

Aching, Monsieur Vincent rolled over and lifted his blouse to expose a tiny hole in his side. It oozed a little blood.

"Je me suis blessé," he said. "I hurt myself."

The feverish life and curious death of Vincent van Gogh have become a kind of myth, partly true and partly what we wish to be true. His disappointments, his genius, his demons, and even his birth have been inflated to metaphoric proportions. Legend colors his biography as vividly as any paint he ever applied to canvas.

Vincent was born in the Netherlands on March 30, 1853, the eldest son of an austere Dutch Reformed minister and a bookseller's daughter—precisely one year to the day after his mother gave birth to a stillborn child whom she also named Vincent. Having a dead brother with the same name and same birth date didn't seem to damage Vincent the way later armchair psychologists would speculate, but it nevertheless provides an ominous start to a tragic life.

In fact, Vincent's birth might have been physically difficult, damaging his head and brain in fateful ways.

As a child, the red-haired Vincent was bright and perpetually in motion, but also moody, unruly, and often cloying. He read obsessively and learned to sketch when very young. Still, visitors described him as "a strange boy" who was uneasy around people and unusually anxious.

Early schooling, both traditional and at home, failed the rebellious, defiant Vincent. At age eleven, his parents sent him to boarding school, where he was profoundly homesick and lonely. Two years later, they moved him to a new school, even farther from home, and the dispirited Vincent grew more resentful. At age fourteen, already a disappointment to his father, he literally walked away from the school and never returned.

After more than a year in the sanctuary and solitude of his parents' home, Vincent became an apprentice art salesman at sixteen. As he would do through his life, he threw himself into the job, reading every art book he could find and studying the great Dutch artists. But a new kind of art began trickling into the shop where he worked, loosely detailed, imaginative, impressionistic work that pleased a small but passionate clientele.

He was modestly successful at selling art and was posted to galleries in London and Paris over the next seven years. During this time, his younger brother Theo also became an art dealer, and Vincent experienced his first great disappointment in love.

In 1876, when Vincent was just twenty-three, he left his job. He returned to England, where he had immersed himself in London's galleries and museums and fell in love with the writing of George Eliot and Charles Dickens. He became a teacher at a church school and plunged again into Bible studies, which inspired him to become a clergyman like his father.

At first he only conducted simple prayer meetings, but he became obsessed about preaching from the pulpit. So in October 1876, Vincent delivered his first Sunday sermon, in which he quoted Psalm 119:19, "I am a stranger on the earth. . . ."

He also hinted at the relationship between God and the vibrant colors that swirled in his mind:

> *I once saw a very beautiful picture: it was a landscape at evening. In the distance on the right-hand side a row of hills appeared blue in the evening mist. Above those hills the splendor of the sunset, the grey clouds with their linings of silver and gold and purple. The landscape is a plain or heath covered with grass and its yellow leaves, for it was in autumn. Through the landscape a road leads to a high mountain far, far away, on the top of that mountain is a city wherein the setting sun casts a glory. On the road walks a pilgrim, staff in hand. He has been walking for a good long while already and he is very tired. And now he meets a woman . . . The pilgrim asks her: "Does the road go uphill then all the way?"*
>
> *And the answer is: "Yes, to the very end."*

Vincent briefly attended a Dutch university to study theology but left after his first year. When he failed to get into a mission school, he volunteered to preach to Belgian coal miners and their families in dreadful mining villages, where he tended to give away all his food, money, and clothing to the poverty-stricken families. While he didn't especially lift them spiritually—Vincent wasn't a very good preacher— he began to sketch them.

Suddenly, at age twenty-seven, he discovered his life's next path: art.

Vincent took some formal art education, but mostly, with his characteristic obsession, he was self-taught. At first he sketched, then later painted at a frenzied pace that never let up.

In 1882, Vincent began to experiment with oil paints. At the same time, he began a tumultuous love affair with a prostitute, with whom he lived for almost two impoverished years as he honed his drawing and painting skills.

When the relationship crumbled, Vincent hit the road. He became a nomadic artist, capturing the sights and people he encountered on the road.

In 1886, Vincent moved to Paris, where his palette was suddenly suffused with vivid reds, blues, yellows, greens, and oranges. More important, his technique evolved into the short, broken strokes favored by the impressionist painters he admired.

Vincent became more and more dependent upon the financial support of his younger brother Theo, with whom he kept up a prolific lifelong correspondence. But even Theo found his beloved brother to be increasingly unstable and quarrelsome.

In Paris, odd things started happening. Vincent began to suffer from minor seizures and panic attacks, often followed by periods when he was confused or couldn't remember what had happened. It was noted that Vincent had also begun drinking absinthe, a strong alcoholic beverage popular among French artists, even though a lot of it might cause convulsions.

In 1888, Vincent moved from Paris to Arles with fellow painter Paul Gauguin, producing bold, bright canvases and drawings at a prodigious clip, refining the unique brushwork for which he would eventually—but had not yet—become known. Here, Vincent's paintings turn slightly surreal and bizarre; his lines ripple, his colors intensify, and his paint is sometimes squeezed from the tube directly onto the canvas. His subjects become so dreamlike that Vincent himself wrote that "some of my pictures certainly show traces of having been painted by a sick man."

And here are painted some of his most transcendent masterpieces, including *Bedroom in Arles* and *Sunflowers*.

But Vincent's demons reared up at this time, too. He began suffering seizures, rages, dysphoria, and bouts of insanity, deeper and darker than the ordinary depression he'd known for so long.

Vincent and Gauguin painted together like brothers for months, but the two strong-willed artists were constantly at odds. Just before Christmas, they had a fight over, of all things, newspaper accounts of a condemned slasher's night terrors. Gauguin stormed out, once again leaving Vincent alone. Crushed and enraged, Vincent sliced off part of his left ear with a razor and carried it to a nearby brothel, where he gave his carefully packaged ear to a startled prostitute with a short note: *"Remember me."*

After his psychotic break, Vincent was hospitalized. A young doctor diagnosed him with epilepsy and prescribed potassium bromide. Within days, van Gogh recovered, and within three weeks, he had painted his *Self-Portrait with Bandaged Ear and Pipe*. He had no memory of the argument with Gauguin, his self-mutilation, or the circumstances of his hospitalization.

In letters to Theo, he reported his "intolerable hallucinations have ceased, in fact have diminished to a simple nightmare . . . I am rather well just now, except for a certain undercurrent of vague sadness difficult to explain."

In the coming weeks, Vincent was hospitalized three more times after suffering psychotic episodes—always after drinking absinthe. Worried that his demons were bigger than he, Vincent voluntarily entered the insane asylum at Saint-Rémy in May 1889. Doctors there didn't continue his treatments of potassium bromide, so more psychotic episodes of terrifying hallucinations and uncontrollable agitation followed, usually after he'd left the hospital grounds to drink with friends in town. The worst of these episodes lasted three months.

In the asylum, Vincent continued to paint. Even in the embrace of his demons, he sketched or painted some 300 works, including his masterpiece *The Starry Night,* which might have depicted the swirling darkness of Vincent's inner landscape at that moment. Some even said later the luminous stars resembled the explosive "nerve storms" that epileptics "see" during a seizure.

Nevertheless, in May 1890, the asylum's doctors pronounced Vincent cured. He gathered his few belongings and left for Auvers-sur-Oise, a tiny hamlet near Paris where Dr. Paul Gachet, a local physician and art lover, had promised Theo he'd care for Vincent.

There Vincent took a second-floor room at Gustave Ravoux's inn. He stopped drinking and painted furiously all day, every day. He kept a scrupulous schedule: breakfast at the inn, outside to paint at nine, a punctual appearance at noon for lunch, more painting until supper, and then usually writing letters into the night.

His scruffy clothes and eccentric habits soon became familiar to the locals, who immediately judged him to be odd. No matter, because he didn't care to get closer to them either. He was mad and he knew it, but he wanted to paint in spite of his madness.

In seventy days at Auvers, Vincent finished seventy paintings and thirty drawings.

But even if those days were productive, they were not necessarily blissful.

In early July, he visited Theo in Paris. Theo's wife had just given birth to their first son, whom they named Vincent. With a new child and the secretly ill Theo about to quit his job, money was suddenly tight. Vincent left Paris three days later, distraught that he'd become an anchor around his generous brother's neck, and dreading that his own support would soon dry up.

A few days later, Vincent painted the frenzied *Wheatfield with Crows,* which depicts swirling storm clouds over a churning field of amber grain and a flock of blackbirds fleeing the approaching squall.

Was it just a vibrant painting . . . or something else? I don't know. None of us does. Some have called it a glimpse into Vincent's surging torment; others say it was his suicide note. That seems an overly melodramatic conclusion, but the fact remains, we'll never know.

As a medical examiner, I learned it's important to limit speculation, step back from emotion, and focus on facts.

In Vincent's death, speculation is abundant, emotions run high, and facts are few . . . unless you know where to look.

. . .

What happened between Vincent's hasty noontime lunch and the moment he stumbled back home after dusk?

Nobody knows that either. Stories conflicted right from the start, and Vincent himself was reportedly confused about the details. But here's the customary account that's been told for the past century, much of it the sixty-year-old memory of the late Gustave Ravoux's then-elderly daughter Adeline, only thirteen when it happened. It was 1953 and Adeline was seventy-three when she first recounted what she learned from her father about Vincent's shooting. It went like this:

Vincent hauled his bulky painting gear and a large canvas up a steep, heavily wooded hill to a wheat field beyond the stately Château d'Auvers, more than a mile from Ravoux's inn. There he propped his easel against a haystack and wandered down a road in the shadow of the château wall.

Somewhere along that road Vincent drew a hidden revolver and shot himself in the side, then fainted. Some time after sundown, the night air revived him and he crawled about on all fours, searching for the gun so he could finish the suicide properly. When he couldn't find it in the dark, he staggered back down the slope, through the trees, to the inn.

Adeline said her father lent the gun to Vincent, who, she claimed, had wanted it to scare away crows while he painted in the fields.

No revolver was ever found, nor were Vincent's painting kit and canvas. Nobody saw him in the five or six hours he was gone. The only official investigation was brief and no report was ever written, leaving only inconsistent, foggy memories and local gossip.

And a lot of questions.

The first physician to see Vincent was Dr. Jean Mazery, a country obstetrician in the nearby village of Pontoise. He arrived at the Ravoux inn to find Vincent sitting up in his bed, calmly smoking a pipe.

Mazery described the bullet wound as just below the ribs, on the left side of the abdomen, about the size of a large pea, with a dark red margin and encircled by a purple-blue halo. A thin trickle of blood seeped from it. The doctor probed the wound with a long thin metal rod, an excruciating procedure, and believed the small-caliber bullet had lodged near the back of Vincent's abdominal cavity.

Mazery believed the bullet had traveled on a downward slant into the artist's belly, missing major organs and blood vessels. But without cutting Vincent open, he couldn't see what other damage might have been done.

Summoned from a Sunday fishing outing with his son, Dr. Gachet soon arrived, too. He carried his little black emergency bag and—being a believer in the therapeutic value of electroshock—a small electric coil. In Vincent's cramped little room, he examined the artist's wound by candlelight. Vincent had shot himself too low and too far to his left side to have hit his heart. Gachet, who considered himself a specialist in nervous disorders, was relieved.

The wound was in Vincent's left side, at the bottom of or below the ribs.

Even though Vincent begged the two doctors to cut him open and remove the bullet, they refused. Thoracic surgery was messy and difficult, even for experienced surgeons, which they were not. Although they didn't believe the bullet had pierced any vital organs, they surmised it had passed through Vincent's left lung cavity and lodged somewhere in his back, possibly close to his spine.

They saw neither hemorrhaging nor signs of shock. In fact, Vincent was lucid and calm. Yes, he spoke uncomfortably, but he showed no signs that blood was collecting unseen in his lungs or chest, slowly suffocating him. He'd even sat up in his bed and asked for the tobacco in the pocket of his bloodied blue blouse.

They concluded merely that the wound was caused by a small-caliber bullet that lodged dangerously close to Vincent's spine, and that it had been fired at an unusual angle, at some distance from Vincent.

The two doctors could have taken Vincent to the hospital, only six miles away, but they didn't. They merely dressed his wound and nothing more. That night they left him in his airless, sweltering cubby beneath the roof.

Dr. Gachet quietly pronounced Vincent's case hopeless and left. He never came back. The innkeeper Ravoux spent the rest of that restless night beside Vincent's bed as he alternately dozed and smoked his pipe.

The next morning, two gendarmes visited the inn to question Vincent about the shooting, but he was insolent. Where had Vincent gone to shoot himself? they asked. How did he, a former mental patient, get hold of a gun?

They asked Vincent if he had intended to kill himself.

"Yes, I believe so," he responded ambiguously. Didn't he know if he wanted to kill himself?

The gendarmes pressed further, but Vincent barked at them.

"What I have done is nobody else's business," he reportedly said. "My body is mine and I am free to do what I want with it. *Do not accuse anybody,* it is I that wished to commit suicide."

Was Vincent simply startled that police would suspect a crime, or was he deliberately deflecting suspicion away from someone else? The gendarmes left, satisfied there'd been no foul play.

But Vincent's vigor didn't last. A dreadful truth about gutshots in the 1800s is that they were almost always fatal.

That evening, a few hours after Theo arrived at his bedside, infection gripped him. Vincent went downhill fast. By midnight, his breath grew strained. He whispered to his beloved brother Theo, who'd rushed from Paris to be with Vincent, "I wish I could pass away like this . . . the sadness will last forever."

Ninety minutes later, about 1:30 a.m. on Tuesday, July 29, 1890, Vincent van Gogh was dead. There was no autopsy, no further investigation. The fatal bullet was never recovered, but it might have nicked a bowel, releasing fast-moving bacteria into the abdominal cavity. In the thirty or so hours since he'd been shot, the infection would have halted his normal intestinal activity, and his electrolytes would have been dangerously disrupted. Very quickly, his kidneys, liver, and lungs likely started to shut down as the peritonitis seeped through him.

The tragedy was complete. Vincent's unquiet mind was quiet at last. He died at only thirty-seven years old, never knowing he would become known as the greatest artist of his time.

As it was foretold by Vincent himself, his road had been uphill all the way.

They laid Vincent's corpse in a handmade coffin atop the inn's billiard table. His palette and brushes were arrayed on the floor. Yellow dahlias and sunflowers—because yellow was Vincent's favorite color—surrounded him. His newer, unframed paintings, some still wet, were tacked to the wall for the somber group of mourners to see. Ironically and sadly, Vincent van Gogh's funeral was also his first and only one-man show.

But because the village pastor believed Vincent had committed suicide, he refused him a church service and burial in consecrated ground. So Vincent's body was buried two days later in a tiny public graveyard less than half a mile from the sad, claustrophobic room where he died, beside the field where he'd painted the stormy skies and the fleeing crows several days before. Theo, the Ravoux family, some neighbors, and a handful of Vincent's artist friends attended the humid afternoon graveside rites.

After the burial, Theo returned to the inn to fulfill his brother's final wish: to donate all his recent canvases to neighbors in the village where he'd lived for nine weeks, then died. But while gathering his brother's belongings, Theo found a letter in Vincent's jacket pocket, written to Theo shortly before he'd been shot. It hinted at Vincent's fear that he'd become an unbearable burden to his brother. The last lines read:

Ah well, I risk my life for my own work and my reason has half foundered in it—very well—but you're not one of the dealers in men; as far as I know and can judge I think you really act with humanity, but what can you do

Did it mean anything that Vincent had not placed a question mark—or any other punctuation—after the note's last word, leaving

it dangling for eternity? No matter. The art world would come to embrace it as a sad suicide note, even though it contained no obvious
threats or good-byes.

It was just one of the many questions Vincent left hanging in the air.

Vincent van Gogh sold only one painting during his life, but in his
last ten years, he created more than 2,100 artworks, including 860 oil
paintings and more than 1,300 watercolors, sketches, and prints. Today
collectors have paid more for his works than for those of any other
artist in the history of mankind, and his life has been explored endlessly in books and films.

Vincent was a complex welter of his insanity, his upbringing, his
station, and his intensity. His paintings were not the paintings of a
madman, but merely paintings by a man who happened to be mad.
Somebody less intense might not have painted with such genius. But
we can look at his work and wonder if he would have been such a genius if he were not also mad.

So when authors Steven Naifeh and Gregory White Smith—winners
of the 1991 Pulitzer Prize for their biography of American abstract
expressionist painter Jackson Pollock and both Harvard-educated
lawyers—set out to write van Gogh's consummate life story, they
didn't expect to unearth too many surprises.

Naifeh and Smith delved deeper and further than any van Gogh
scholar ever had. They employed a brigade of translators, researchers,
and computer specialists over a ten-year period, and in the end, they
would deliver a 960-page book, plus 28,000 footnotes posted online.
They left no stone unturned as they searched for the mind and heart
behind the canvas.

They found a man far more complex than his legend. Vincent was
an indifferent student but spoke four languages fluently and was an
insatiable reader. He desperately sought to please his parents but
was an utter disappointment to his severe father and disliked by his
mother. He yearned for human connections but was so abrasive and
disagreeable that even his adoring brother Theo didn't like to spend

much time with him. And in the depths of his occasional depressions and breakdowns he often wished for death . . . but in various letters he also called suicide wicked, terrible, cowardly, immoral, and dishonest.

The true source of Vincent's madness is not known with certainty, but the most likely root cause according to many experts—including the doctors who treated him after he sliced his ear and in the asylum— was temporal-lobe epilepsy triggered in the last two years of his life by drinking absinthe, which at the time contained very small amounts of a convulsant in addition to its high alcohol content. His epilepsy was likely related to a strenuous birth that left Vincent with an asymmetrical face and head, and likely brain damage that went haywire with absinthe. Many accounts describe Vincent lapsing into delusional spells and seizures, followed by long periods of amnesia and confusion.

But apart from his presumed lifelong epilepsy, Vincent also had at least two clear major depressions and a series of manic-depressive episodes, often precipitated by losses of lovers, friends, and emotional equilibrium. "Van Gogh had earlier suffered two distinct episodes of reactive depression, and there are clearly bipolar aspects to his history," the *American Journal of Psychiatry* noted. "Both episodes of depression were followed by sustained periods of increasingly high energy and enthusiasm, first as an evangelist and then as an artist."

"I believe he has always been insane," his own mother once wrote about Vincent, "and that his suffering and ours was a result of it."

In short, his mind stormed violently for most of his life. As grim as it might be, nobody could be surprised that Vincent would commit suicide.

But the deeper Naifeh and Smith dug, the more questions arose about Vincent's botched suicide attempt. Most had no easy answers. For the two lawyers, much seemed illogical.

For example, Vincent claimed he'd tried to find the gun in the dark after shooting himself, but couldn't. How could it have fallen so far from his grasp, Naifeh and Smith asked, that Vincent couldn't find it?

More intriguingly, why could nobody find it the next day in daylight? In fact, why has no such gun ever been found?

What became of the easel, palette, brushes and canvas Vincent took to the fields? They have never been found. Had someone hidden the evidence?

How had this former mental patient gotten hold of a small-caliber revolver, which wasn't a common item in rural France at the time? Vincent had no experience with guns, and nobody would have entrusted him with a revolver if it were known he'd been institutionalized.

How did the dazed Vincent navigate the steep, wooded hill in the dark and totter as much as a mile home, mortally gutshot?

What had triggered his suicidal impulse?

Why didn't this obsessive writer write a suicide note, or at least leave some clear indication of his intent?

Why would a suicidal Vincent have chosen to shoot himself in the side at such an awkward angle? Why not the head or directly at the heart? And maybe more important, how and why did he miss so miserably?

Naifeh and Smith learned that almost immediately after the shooting, townsfolk in Auvers were whispering about how the *fou* artist had been shot accidentally by a couple of teenagers playing with a gun. That story was reported publicly for the first time in the 1930s by an art scholar, but the romantic notion of a brilliant, misunderstood artist committing suicide had taken root and the shooting "rumor" was dismissed.

Then in 1956, a tantalizing new piece of the puzzle hit French newspapers. An elderly Parisian banker named René Secrétan came forward to confess that he and his brother, then just teenagers, knew Vincent in Auvers. The two bullied and teased the artist by putting snakes in his paint kit, dousing his coffee with salt, sprinkling chili pepper on the brushes that he held in his mouth as he worked, and persuading some girls to pretend to seduce Vincent.

Sixteen-year-old René liked to dress in a buckskin outfit he bought when Buffalo Bill's Wild West show played in Paris the year before—

and likely posed for Vincent's sketch *Head of Boy with Broad-Brimmed Hat* some time in the weeks before Vincent's death.

But no Buffalo Bill poseur's garb would be complete without a gun, so René bought or borrowed a faulty old revolver from Gustave Ravoux. That ancient gun, René said in his 1956 interview, "went off when it felt like it."

Suddenly, a firsthand account lent a little credence to the old Auvers rumor that Vincent had been shot accidentally by two boys. Could it have been the inseparable brothers, René and Gaston Secrétan, and their balky pistol? Had René been playing cowboy when the gun went off? Had his teasing finally provoked Vincent into an ultimately fatal fight?

Nobody knows. René wasn't asked and never confessed to shooting Vincent, but rather, he suggested that the artist had stolen the gun from his rucksack and shot himself with it that same day.

René and Gaston disappeared from Auvers around the time of Vincent's death. In the 1956 interview, René claimed he learned of the shooting from an article in a Paris newspaper, but no such article has ever been found.

A follow-up interview never happened. René Secrétan died the next year.

In the 1960s, another piece fell into place when another former Auvers woman claimed her father had seen Vincent in a farmyard—in the opposite direction of the wheat field where he claimed to be—on that fateful afternoon. And soon after, another person came forward with a story about a gunshot that was heard in that same farmyard area, although no blood or gun was ever discovered.

If those recollections were accurate, Naifeh and Smith theorized, it's likely that Vincent was wounded in a farmyard closer to Ravoux's inn, and that the boys fled the scene with the gun and Vincent's painting supplies. The way back to the inn was also more navigable by a wounded man than the steep escarpment from the fields.

But why would the artist then claim to have shot himself? The sad answer, his biographers believe, is that Vincent welcomed death. He might have realized (or assumed) he was dying and made his peace with it. Maybe he thought dying was all for the best. The boys had done for him what he couldn't do for himself in good conscience. He returned the favor by lying to protect them from prosecution.

They found no smoking gun, either literally or figuratively. But this hypothesis made more sense to Naifeh and Smith than the accepted, overly romantic suicide theory. It answered so many previously un-answered questions: Why hadn't the gun ever been found? Why would Vincent choose to shoot himself in such a peculiar way? Why would he have lugged a large new canvas and all his painting gear a mile if he only intended to kill himself? Why were his deathbed "confessions" so tentative and hedged?

Some in the art world added one more question: "You're joking, right?"

Naifeh and Smith had blasphemed. They might as well have nailed a thesis about the impossibility of resurrection to the Vatican door.

Many van Gogh scholars have been quietly uncomfortable with the suicide story, but Naifeh and Smith's homicide theory didn't just feel like shameless book promotion; it threatened the romantic sym-bolism of an artist's struggle against an indifferent world.

"There's plenty of reason to look at the unclear circumstances again," said curator Leo Jansen of the Van Gogh Museum in Amster-dam. "We cannot yet agree with their conclusions because we do not think there is enough evidence yet. There's no proof."

Jansen admitted that Vincent's suicide confession couldn't be proven either. It's just what Vincent said, and he had no reason to lie about it.

While some art writers and Internet trolls were more caustic in their response to Naifeh and Smith, others argued that even a clumsy suicide was a far more logical conclusion, a last irrational act by a disturbed man who'd acted irrationally before. What's so incredible about a lunatic who had mutilated his own ear shooting himself in a highly unusual way?

And finally, there were the guardians of the sacred myth.

"If Vincent van Gogh would have died of old age at 80 in 1933, basking in glory and in possession of his two ears, he would never have become the myth he is today," the Dutch daily *De Volkskrant* editorialized after Naifeh and Smith's theory went public. "Van Gogh's psychoses, his depressions, his mistakes and their manifestations—an ear cut off, a suicide—are more pertinent to the painter narrative, mystique and inscrutability than his cypresses and corn fields."

In 2013, scholars Louis van Tilborgh and Teio Meedendorp of the Van Gogh Museum mounted a vigorous frontal assault on the homicide theory. Their far-reaching article in a prestigious British art magazine argued point by point that the only genuine inference was suicide.

As evidence, they prominently submitted the wound described by Dr. Gachet—a hole rimmed with brown and encircled by a purplish halo. The purple ring, they said, was a bruise caused by the bullet's impact and the brown edge was powder-burned skin, proving that Vincent held the gun against his side, possibly even under his shirt.

Van Tilborgh and Meedendorp argued that Vincent was highly agitated by turmoil in Theo's life and a little off-balance in Auvers. In Vincent's last paintings, Naifeh and Smith had seen brighter, more hopeful strokes, but the scholars saw ominous, darker emotions.

The scholars also disputed any interpretation of the Secrétan interview as a "confession" and dismissed the old, secondhand rumors about gunplay by teenagers.

"Truly nothing substantiates their argument for the train of events they construe," Tilborgh and Meedendorp summarized, "apart from a twentieth-century rumour arising from an authentic story of a trigger-happy brat in 1890, who merely claimed that van Gogh probably stole the gun from him. And we do not doubt that for a moment."

The *Burlington Magazine* article by two van Gogh experts offered more questions than answers, but they had unambiguously challenged the new theory

With their largely circumstantial argument under counter-attack, Naifeh and Smith needed solid scientific evidence. They needed an expert on gunshot wounds to examine all the evidence and reach a scientifically unassailable conclusion.

So one summer day, my phone rang.

It was easy to see what *didn't* happen. In all medical probability, Vincent van Gogh didn't shoot himself.

How did I know? I cannot know beyond a shadow of doubt, just as I cannot know what was in the mad genius's disturbed mind and heart on the day he was shot. Although it might have been dark and disordered, nothing suggests he was in a psychotic state.

Of course, I only knew what books and movies had said about van Gogh, his instability, his self-mutilation, his genius in art, his suicide. Like most people, I wasn't aware there had been any dispute about any of it.

Nevertheless, the new facts that lay before me 123 years later—and everything I know about gunshot wounds—spoke loud and clear: Vincent's mortal wound was almost certainly not self-inflicted.

There were several reasons for my opinion.

The first was the general location of his wound, although it was never recorded precisely. Drs. Mazery and Gachet described the wound's location differently. A 1928 book by Victor Doiteau and Edgar Leroy said it was "along the side of the left ribs, a little before the axillary line," an imaginary vertical demarcation from the armpit to the waist. In other words, the bullet entered Vincent's side about where his elbow would touch his chest if he stood with his arms at his sides.

But did it go through his rib cage or the soft tissue below the ribs?

If you accept Dr. Mazery's original observation, the wound was in Vincent's left abdomen, just under his ribs.

How odd would that location be for a suicide shot? When my colleague Dr. Kimberly Molina and I reviewed 747 suicides for a study of handgun wound locations, ranges, and manner of death, we found only 1.3 percent of self-inflicted gunshots were in the abdomen.

If you accept the 1928 account that the bullet pierced Vincent's left-side rib cage, we found that only 12.7 percent of suicides shot themselves in the chest. And overwhelmingly most of those were direct shots over the heart, not obliquely fired into the side.

Simply put, very few suicides, no matter how frightened or deluded, choose to shoot themselves in their sides.

But if Vincent did, that raises a whole different question.

Let's assume Vincent was the exception. Let's assume he consciously chose to shoot himself in his left side with a handgun. How would he do it?

It is widely accepted that Vincent was right-handed, so even if he'd decided to shoot himself in his side, why pick the side that would require the most awkward shot?

The easiest way for Vincent to have made this shot would have been to wrap his left hand's fingers around the back of the grip and pull the trigger with his thumb. He might even have steadied the pistol with his right hand, but he would have suffered powder burns on his right palm where he grasped the body of the gun, caused by flames, gas, and powder blowing out of the cylinder gap.

Using his right hand would have been even more absurd. He would have had to cross his right arm over his chest, wrap his fingers around the gun's grip and pull the trigger with his thumb. And again, if he'd used his left hand to steady the weapon, it would have suffered powder burns.

No such powder burns were reported by Theo, the two doctors, the two gendarmes, or any of the people who saw Vincent alive or dead after the shooting.

Even if you can accept the contortions it would have required in either case, the gun's muzzle would have been against Vincent's skin or, at most, a couple of inches away.

And that's the most important reason I believe his wound was not self-inflicted.

Vincent's wound was described by the attending doctors as pea-sized, with a reddish brown margin, and ringed by a purplish blue halo. The skin is otherwise clear and there's no sign of powder burns.

Some proponents of the suicide theory argue the purplish halo was a bruise caused by the bullet's impact. Not so. It is, in fact, internal bleeding from vessels severed by the bullet, and I've seen it many times in people who live a while after they've been shot. Its presence (or absence) means nothing significant.

The reddish brown rim around the entrance wound itself is not powder-burned skin, but an abrasion ring seen around virtually all entrance wounds. Again, not significant except that it signifies an entrance wound.

But the most important element of this entrance wound is what *isn't* there.

Handgun cartridges of the 1890s were loaded with black powder, which burns very dirty. Smokeless powder had been invented in 1884, but at the time of Vincent's shooting, it was only used in cartridges for a few military rifles.

Close-range wounds by bullets from black-powder cartridges are messy. When black powder ignites, some 56 percent of its mass is solid residue, which bursts forth in a scorching spray of carbon particles.

If Vincent shot himself, he would have held the gun point-blank against his skin, or maybe just a couple of inches away (because in 98.5 percent of all suicides the shot is fired against or close to the skin). So the skin around his wound would have been blistered by searing gases and spattered by hot soot and burning flecks of powder. The burns would have been serious and hundreds of flecks of burnt and partially burnt powder would still be embedded in his skin.

What if he shot himself through his clothing? If Vincent had pressed the gun's muzzle against his blouse, the edges of his wound would have been seared and blackened. There might or might not have been a wider area of tattooing, but his clothing would have been covered with soot.

None of this was described by the doctors or anyone else who looked at the wound or had contact with Vincent after the shooting.

Thus, the muzzle of the gun could not have been held against Vincent's side. The lack of powder tattooing or burns of any kind suggest the gun was at least twenty inches away when fired.

So Vincent van Gogh was mortally wounded in an atypical place for a suicide, by a gun that he couldn't possibly have held so far from his body.

We'll likely never know beyond any reasonable doubt what happened on that Sunday afternoon in France. Even if civil authorities could be convinced to exhume Vincent, there's very little to be learned about his death. Today he is probably just bones. A well-embalmed corpse in a lead coffin might have lasted more than one hundred years, but Vincent wasn't embalmed—typical in nineteenth-century Europe—and he was buried in a simple handmade wooden casket.

A forensic expert would likely find the small-caliber bullet that killed him, but without Ravoux's old revolver for comparison, even modern-day high-tech ballistics couldn't establish confidently that it fired the bullet. It might have come from any small pistol. And if all the soft tissues had decomposed, we couldn't determine the bullet's path or damage. We might end up with more questions than answers.

We all invest in things we believe to be true, often without any real evidence. Myth can be more magical than truth. Do you believe somebody other than Oswald killed Kennedy?

By and large, some in the art world resist the notion of a homicide, whether accidental or premeditated, because it's neither dramatic nor poetic enough. After all, painters, poets, and lonely lovers die so much more romantically if they drink from their own little poison vials, or cut their veins beneath a pale blue moon, or swim far out into the sea with no intention of swimming back.

Yes, the shooting—bathed in wishful conclusions, never fully investigated, and confused by conflicting accounts—is a puzzle. Nobody who was there is still alive, and we must glean forensic details from scant observations at the time. But these details don't support the mythology.

Nevertheless, the manner of Vincent's death has become part of his greater legend, and the mystery might endure forever. As with many of my cases, what you believe might depend more on what you *want* to believe than the forensic facts. It might be more about Vincent's tragic life than his actual dying.

Whether he embraced death is for poets and academics to argue, but the forensic facts point to a shooter who escaped our questions.

My personal verdict: Vincent van Gogh didn't shoot himself. I don't know who did or why. I don't know if Vincent wanted to die. I don't know if he feared the end or embraced it. It all comes down to something no medical examiner can determine with his scalpel, a computer, or sophisticated tests. Maybe he simply came to terms with his accidental dying. Even logic sometimes fails to provide answers.

I can't know what's in a human heart.

At the End of Things

Somebody once said that if you carry your childhood with you, you'll never grow old. Nice sentiment, but not really true.

I have been a forensic pathologist for more than forty-five years. All the lions I looked up to when I was young—Helpern, Fisher, Rose, among many others—are all gone. My father retired as Chief Medical Examiner of New York City at sixty-five and finally retired at about eighty-five. Even my contemporaries are mostly retired or "gone."

I've carried my childhood the whole time, and yet here I am, getting old. Go figure.

Then there's this: Some researcher recently concluded that an animal's perception of time is inversely correlated with the rate of its heartbeat. The slower the heart, the faster time seems to pass. At least for this researcher, that explained why, as we get older and our hearts slow down, it seems like the days aren't so long anymore. I don't know how that works or if the theory even has legs, but a lot of old folks certainly would agree.

We do stuff like that. We make up little homilies, post cheerful

Facebook memes, or contrive bits of pop science to make us feel better about dying. Too many of us end up believing it will be poetic.

In this book, I've told a few stories about endings, even as I was telling the story of my own beginning. I haven't really pondered my own ending. Maybe because in my world endings happen only to other people. So far, anyway.

Still, I don't romanticize death. I've seen too much of it to expect a dreamy Hollywood ending.

Since the 1600s, when cheaply printed pamphlets circulated graphic descriptions of local murder, humans have been fascinated by crime stories. Shakespeare's plays were full of homicide. Nothing sold better than intrigue . . . and the ultimate victory of morality and reasoning over disorder and depravity. And nothing was more mysterious than death.

We haven't changed much. Modern pop-culture depictions of forensic science, in all their glorious, computer-generated glory, tend to overglamorize the forensic pathologist and credit hypercool high tech with solving every crime and conquering evil. But as with all things Hollywood, it just ain't so. It's not about the gee-whiz technology.

Let me repeat: A good forensic pathologist's best tools are his hands and brain. With a day's training on new sciences like DNA, a smart medical examiner from the 1940s could be operating in a modern morgue quite capably. Why? Because reasoning is still our most powerful forensic tool.

I'm often asked, "How can you work in such a depressing field?" I would like to give a glib answer, but I cannot. If you get depressed in my work, then you do not belong. I will just say that it is interesting and challenging. I could never work with children dying of cancer, but I have had no difficulty handling disfigured corpses or explaining honestly (and gently) to their grieving families how they died. There is a value in that.

Yet, my profession is at a crossroads. As I write this, fewer than 500 board-certified forensic pathologists are at work in America. At full tilt, each one can do only about 250 autopsies a year. We need twice that number.

Sometimes I don't know if I chose medicine or it was just born inside me, a seed waiting to blossom. But I know I became a doctor because I wanted to help people.

Computers and various forensic sciences are booming, with more exciting developments to come, but the human factor is woefully lagging.

Future forensic pathologists must finish four years of undergraduate college, four years of medical school, three to four years of training in pathology, and a one-year fellowship at one of thirty-six approved medical examiners' offices, and pass an American Board of Pathology certification examination. Doing that, they accumulate a median debt of $170,000.

There's money in medicine—except for forensic pathology. Almost every other medical discipline earns far more. The average salary of a medical examiner is just under $185,000 a year; a deputy chief or chief ME are much better off at $190,000 and $220,000 a year. Their salaries are all much lower than those of their hospital-based pathology peers, who commonly earn an average $335,000 a year.

And then there are the irregular hours, weird smells, emotional traumas, unhelpful patients, images that will never be erased from their brains, exposure to disease, lawyers, cops, trial testimony, bureaucrats, and budgets drearier than a morgue cooler. Sure, it looks fascinating on TV and the prospect of solving a real-life mystery is captivating, but who really wants to wade through corpses every day for less money than most of their medical school classmates?

As a result, we train an average of twenty-seven board-certified forensic pathologists every year, but only twenty-one actually go to work as medical examiners.

We need more forensic pathologists. As our population grows and ages, as we trust technology more and more (and humans less and less), and as the number of new pathologists declines, forensic pathology will hit a disastrous wall. Fewer autopsists mean fewer autopsies.

Investigations suffer, evidence is lost or overlooked, crimes are unsolved.

If that happens, we don't just lose money or time . . . we lose justice. My patients no longer are suffering, but I know many of them would want justice. I can't give them their lives back, or even a few more minutes to say good-bye, but I can give them justice.

Acknowledgments

We are profoundly grateful to our many friends whose contributions, large and small, made this book possible. Some of them became more than mere sources during the two years that we worked on this book, and some were friends long before.

For their various contributions, we must thank many in the forensic and medical community, chiefly: Dr. Randall Frost of the Bexar County (Texas) Medical Examiner's Office; Dr. David R. Fowler, Bruce Goldfarb, and Shea Lawson in the Office of the Chief Medical Examiner of Maryland; Platte County (Wyoming) coroner Phil Martin; Dr. Irvin Sopher; Dr. Werner Spitz; Dr. Douglas Kerr; and Dr. James Cottone.

We could not have told these stories without some expert legal interpretation, either. We are grateful for the legal minds of Charles Bernstein, Don West, Robert Moxley, Bruce Moats, Mark Drury, David Houston, Washoe County (Nevada) alternate public defender Jennifer Lunt, and Laury Frieber.

And for their various contributions and courtesies, we also thank Steven Naifeh, Robin and Edward Cogan, Rudolph Purificato, Allen

Baumgardner, Leigh Hanlon, Jessica Bernstein, Mark Langford, Lee Miller of the Platte County (Wyoming) Public Library, Lisa Milliken of the Platte County (Wyoming) Sheriff's Office, Paul McCardell of the *Baltimore Sun News* Archives, and Maryland state trooper (Ret.) Rick Lastner.

Patrick Connelly of the National Archives in Philadelphia was the single bright note in our copious federal research. He found most of Martha Woods's 60,000-page federal trial transcript, and tried hard to find the rest, without success. Sadly, we are disappointed that five separate Freedom of Information Act (FOIA) requests filed in 2013–14 with the National Archives in Washington, DC, the Federal Bureau of Prisons, and the Federal Bureau of Investigation (FBI) remain unsatisfied to this day.

Creating a book requires like-minded company, too. Dr. Jan Garavaglia, a former colleague, has our deepest thanks for her beautiful foreword. Many thanks to editor Charles Spicer, April Osborn, and their team at St. Martin's Press for making the book you now hold. And literary agent Linda Konner has been an extraordinary adviser of infinite value.

Closer to home, we relied heavily on the memories and scrapbooks of three amazing Di Maio sisters—all of them medical doctors—Therese-Martin, Mary, and Ann. Without them, the autobiographical segments of this book would lack focus and poignancy.

And finally, to the two women who sustained us through this project, Theresa Di Maio and Mary Franscell. They were always in our corner. Without these two remarkable wives, these stories aren't worth telling.

Index